The Sea and the Marsh

The Medieval Cinque Port of New Romney

revealed through archaeological excavations

and historical research

Published by Pre-Construct Archaeology Limited

ISBN 978-0-9542938-9-5

Edited by Victoria Ridgeway

Typeset by Cate Davies

Printed by Henry Ling Limited, The Dorset Press

Front cover: The building and foreshore at New Romney, reconstruction by Jake Lunt-Davies

Back cover: Detail above doorway of the alien priory of Pontigny on Ashford Road; Detail from the Tithe Map of New Romney 1840; Naturally perforated flint pebble fishing weights

The Sea and the Marsh

The Medieval Cinque Port of New Romney

revealed through archaeological excavations and historical research

Gillian Draper and Frank Meddens,

with Philip Armitage, Geoff Egan, Damian Goodburn, Chris Jarrett and Ian Riddler

Pre-Construct Archaeology Limited, Monograph No. 10

PCA Monograph Series

1   Excavations at Hunt's House, Guy's Hospital, London Borough of Southwark
    By Robin Taylor-Wilson, 2002
    ISBN   0-9542938-0-0

2   Tatberht's Lundenwic: Archaeological Excavations in Middle Saxon London
    By Jim Leary with Gary Brown, James Rackham, Chris Pickard and Richard Hughes, 2004
    ISBN   0-9542938-1-9

3   Iwade: Occupation of a North Kent Village from the Mesolithic to the Medieval period
    By Barry Bishop and Mark Bagwell, 2005
    ISBN   0-9542938-2-7

4   Saxons, Templars & Lawyers in the Inner Temple, Archaeological Excavations in Church Court & Hare Court
    By Jonathan Butler, 2005
    ISBN   0-9542938-3-5

5   Unlocking the Landscape: Archaeological Excavations at Ashford Prison, Middlesex
    By Tim Carew, Barry Bishop, Frank Meddens and Victoria Ridgeway, 2006
    ISBN   0-9542938-4-3

6   Reclaiming the Marsh: Archaeological excavations at Moor House, City of London 1998-2004
    By Jonathan Butler, 2006
    ISBN   0-9542938-5-1

7   From Temples to Thames Street – 2000 Years of Riverside Development: Archaeological Excavations at the Salvation Army International Headquarters
    By Timothy Bradley and Jonathan Butler, 2008
    ISBN   978-0-9542938-6-4

8   A New Millennium at Southwark Cathedral: Investigations into the first two thousand years
    By David Divers, Chris Mayo, Nathalie Cohen and Chris Jarrett, 2009
    ISBN   978-0-9542938-7-1

9   On the Boundaries of Occupation: Excavations at Burringham Road, Scunthorpe and Baldwin Avenue, Bottesford, North Lincolnshire
    By Peter Boyer, Jennifer Proctor and Robin Taylor-Wilson, 2009
    ISBN   978-0-9542938-8-6

Contents

Contributors

Principal author (archaeology)	Frank Meddens
Principal author (historical research)	Gillian Draper
Volume manager	Victoria Ridgeway
Project manager	Gary Brown
Graphics	Hayley Baxter
Finds illustrations	Cate Davies, Helen Davies, Michael Miles
Photography	Strephon Duckering, Cheryl Blundy, Frank Meddens
Medieval and post-medieval pottery	Chris Jarrett
Animal Bone	Philip Armitage
Metal Finds	Geoff Egan
Coin Catalogue	Barry Cook, Richard Kelleher
Timber and woodworking	Damian Goodburn
Fishing Implements	Ian Riddler
Flint objects	Barry Bishop
French translation	Nathalie Barrett
German translation	Sylvia Butler
Series editor	Victoria Ridgeway

Figures

Tables

Summary

This publication was inspired by archaeological investigations at the Southlands School site, New Romney, in preparation for the construction of a new superstore. Although the town now lies approximately two miles from the coast, the sea was crucial to New Romney's medieval development and prosperity and these excavations, located in an area that formed part of New Romney's long beachfront in the medieval period, provided an opportunity to explore that relationship. This monograph investigates the association between town and sea by linking the results of excavation to the wider history of New Romney as a whole.

Beginning with a consideration of the early origins of the town, New Romney's role as a Cinque Port is explored, this being fundamental to any examination of its subsequent growth. The examination of cartographic and historic records, standing medieval buildings and the results of earlier excavations has allowed a picture to be built up of how the street layout developed challenging the theory, propounded by Beresford in the 1960s, that New Romney was a planned town. In the medieval period New Romney was provided with a sheltered haven, or port, as well as a long strand, upon which boats were beached, unloaded, broken or mended, where fishing took place and a market developed. Both port and strand were critical to the medieval town's commercial success and its function as a Cinque Port. Fishing, trading connections, the town's involvement in piracy, including licensed skumerie, town government and welfare provision are all considered through the study of contemporary sources. However, the sea also ultimately contributed to the town's decline: a series of calamitous storms ravaged this part of the coast particularly through the 13th century, the harbour began to silt up and, although measures were made to keep an open flow of water out past the strand to the sea, the settlement became land-locked and the community increasingly turned to the marsh, where sheep could be grazed, for its income. Although the town continued to be relatively prosperous the effect of the storms, increasing bad weather and the Black Death led to a decline in the population.

The excavations, sited on what had once been medieval foreshore, revealed forceful evidence of the power of those storms, culminating in the destruction of a building at the water's edge. The recovered pottery assemblage provides evidence for local production and exchange networks as well as more distant trade; while ceramic ventilators and louvers evince local medieval building traditions. The archaeological evidence demonstrates movement and displacement of artefacts as deposits were ripped through by surge tides and then redeposited. Nevertheless a remarkable metal finds assemblage was retrieved, not least as a result of the efforts of local detectorists, and this sheds new light on the everyday life of the inhabitants of this area of town. Among the metal finds recovered were rovenails, indicative of ship breaking or repair as well as fishing hooks and weights, which testify to the range of fishing methods employed, this variety being borne out by the fish bone recovered from the excavations. This information has been drawn together to provide a comparison of fishing vessels, techniques and catches from around the southeast coast.

The authors conclude by expressing the hope that this book will play a part in wider study of the Cinque Ports as distinctive and early medieval towns and also contribute to understanding the characteristics of early borough and market settlements in southeast England. Although rich in surviving medieval structural remains, few historic buildings surveys have been made of New Romney and this publication points the way to further study of these in the future and highlights the importance of continued excavation in the town.

Acknowledgements

The authors wish to thank Sainsbury's plc for funding the work, Duncan Hawkins of CgMs Consulting for his input and Wendy Rogers of Kent County Council for her monitoring of the project. Many thanks are extended to Helen Clarke, Mark Gardiner, Gustav Milne, Steve Rippon, Jane Sidell and David Rudling for their comments and suggestions, and to Luke Barber, Adrian Gollop and Ian Riddler for their ideas and providing access to unpublished information. Gary Brown and Josephine Brown are thanked for their support and comments. Thanks to Helen Davies, Cate Davies and Michael Miles for their work on the finds illustrations, Hayley Baxter for her hard work on the line illustrations, Cheryl Blundy and Strephon Duckering for photography and to Jake Lunt-Davies for the reconstruction drawings. Many thanks to Jonathan Butler and Saskia Meddens for proof reading copies of this text.

Many thanks also to Malcolm Dyer for helping us get access to relevant properties in New Romney and his enthusiastic support; to Gillian Hutchinson for assisting us in accessing relevant parts of the National Maritime Museum archives and collections; Barry Cook and Richard Kelleher of the British Museum for their detailed assistance with the coin identifications; Helen Keeley for her ideas on aspects of the depositional processes involved in the site formation; Mrs Valerie Tully in helping us in accessing the town hall and parts of its archive. Kevin Wooldridge and Elliot Wragg are thanked for their supervision of the fieldwork, the field staff for all their hard work and Victoria Ridgeway for her dedication, input and commitment to the project. Many thanks to the Romney Marsh Metal Detectorists Club for their help in retrieving metal finds from the site.

Gill Draper is grateful to Lynne Bowdon, M.A., for a copy of her unpublished paper and of her collection of data on maletolts, cesses, appraisers, new advocants, jurats and distraints from the court books of New Romney, on taxation exemptions from 1489 onwards and on wills from the 1430s onwards. Thanks are also due to Chris King, University of Reading, for a copy of his unpublished paper. Many thanks are due to members of the Romney Marsh Research Trust for their data collection from the civic records of New Romney in *Historic Manuscripts Commission, 5th report*, the printed calendars of royal records, and manuscript material.

Chris Jarrett would like to thank John Cotter for identifying the pottery and for his help and assistance in writing this report. Damian Goodburn is grateful to Kevin Wooldridge for liaising over the project and to Dana Goodburn-Brown for drawing the author's attention to the X ray sheets from both Smallhythe and Southlands School. Thanks are also due to Gustav Milne and K. Ayodeji for providing access to the unpublished preliminary study of the nails found at Smallhythe. The contributions of Channel 4's Time Team, and assistants John Minkin and Ryzard Bartokowiak, must also be acknowledged.

Chapter 1 Introduction

The initial inspiration for this publication came from archaeological work carried out by Pre-Construct Archaeology on the Southlands School site in New Romney, Kent. It soon became clear to the authors that the results of this work could best be understood through a detailed analysis of the historical background of the town's development and in the light of other recent archaeological excavations, most of which remain unpublished. Thus, the resulting monograph focuses on the development of New Romney from its 8th-century origins through its medieval prosperity and decline, and into the early post-medieval period, while the results of excavation help to illustrate the development of the beachfront strand, to the northeast of the town, and reflect the severe storms which ravaged this part of the coast during the 13th century.

Archaeological fieldwork was undertaken at the Southlands School site (site code NFR 01), centred on National Grid Reference TR 0675 2510, in advance of the construction of a new Community Store by Sainsbury's plc (Fig. 1). Following an initial Desk Based Assessment (Hawkins 2000) an evaluation undertaken in February 2000 by Wessex Archaeology identified the site as having a high archaeological potential, particularly for the medieval and post-medieval periods (Wessex Archaeology 2000). Subsequently Pre-Construct Archaeology (hereafter PCA) undertook a series of excavations, the first phase of which took place between February and March 2001, and the second in June and July of the same year. Prior to its redevelopment the site was occupied by a secondary school and associated grounds, the earliest elements of which probably dated to the late 19th century.

An archaeological mitigation strategy for the site was developed following consultation between Duncan Hawkins of CgMs Consulting, acting on behalf of Sainsbury's Supermarkets plc, Simon Mason and Wendy Rogers, Archaeological Officers of Kent County Council, and Shepway District Council. A specification for an archaeological investigation of the site was prepared by Duncan Hawkins to mitigate the impact of the proposed development by fully excavating and appropriately recording any archaeological remains which could not be preserved *in situ* and properly protecting any remains which were to be preserved *in situ* and not impacted upon by the development (Hawkins 2001).

In May 2002 PCA undertook further fieldwork in the area, in the form of an evaluation on land adjacent to the initial Southlands School excavations to the north and east (site code NCR 02) again commissioned by Duncan Hawkins on behalf of Southlands School (Wragg 2002).

Fig. 1   The site location (scale 1:80 000)

The excavation of this site was subsequently undertaken by Archaeology South-East and thus the results of the evaluation are not reported on in detail here, but are referenced where relevant in relation to the findings of the excavation.

Format of the publication

Within this publication the historic background to
New Romney is presented thematically rather than as a
chronological narrative. This chapter (below) provides
the background to the project, comments on the local
geology and topography, provides a gazetteer of local
archaeological interventions and the remains of historic
buildings within the town with an accompanying
discussion of these and provides a discussion of the
sources of information that inform this publication.
Chapter 2 provides a narrative of the town's origins,
its development and role as a Cinque Port. The layout
of the town is then explored through a consideration
of its ecclesiastical buildings, their attendant parishes
and the trades carried out in them (Chapter 3). New
Romney's relationship with, and use of, the sea is then
explored (Chapter 4) followed by a consideration of the
contribution it made to ship service as a Cinque Port, its
trade connections and evidence for piracy (Chapter 5).
The role of local government in the town and evidence for
associated buildings is discussed (Chapter 6), followed
by a consideration of the hospitals, welfare provision
and local traditions culminating in a discussion of the
town's eventual decline (Chapter 7). This decline was
largely brought about by a series of calamitous storms,
which ravaged the coast during the 13th century leading,
eventually, to the silting of the harbour and associated
waterways. The archaeology of Southlands School is then
described (Chapter 8), presenting evidence of the nature
of occupation and activity along the foreshore and also
the storm impact which led, eventually, to the silting of
the harbour and associated waterways resulting in the
diminishing importance of the town as its access to the sea
dwindled. Discussions follow of the pottery assemblage,
revealing evidence for local production and exchange as
well as more distant trade links (Chapter 9), the metal
finds assemblage (Chapter 10), rovenails, indicative of
ship-breaking or building, fishing hooks and weights and
the recovered fish and animal bone assemblage (Chapter
11). The volume concludes with a discussion of the
findings as a whole (Chapter 12).

Methodology

The archaeological excavations

The site, covering an area of approximately 1.3 hectares,
is bounded to the northwest by Fairfield Road and
Cannon Street, to the southwest by George Lane and
to the southeast by Dymchurch Road with a short
northeast frontage backing onto existing properties
behind Cannon Street. The mitigation strategy employed
resulted in the excavation of one large, open area
measuring approximately 700m² in an area formerly
occupied by Tennis Courts (henceforth referred to as
Area A), in advance of construction of a new access
road from Dymchurch Road into the site, and was

excavated down to the formation level for the road.
Elsewhere, interventions covering a much wider area to
the southwest (Area B) were much more limited in size.
The foundation footings for the new community store
were excavated as 56 foundation pits measuring from
1.3m by 1.3m to 4m by 3m and a new drainage system
as 12 pits measuring up to 4m²; the total area of these
pits being 425m². The northern and western boundary
walls of the site adjoining George Lane and Fairfield
Road were excavated as a discontinuous trench (Trenches
1–9) measuring 110m², giving an overall archaeological
excavation area of *c.* 1235m², equalling only 9.5% of
the total area of the development site (Fig. 2). The most
archaeologically significant features were found in Area
A and within the excavation of the boundary trench,
specifically in Trenches 1, 2, 3 and 5, (Fig. 2: T1, T2, T3,
T5) although this may be largely a factor of the area and
depth of these interventions, rather than a true reflection
of the distribution of archaeological remains. The most
meaningful data was obtained from the open area
excavations in Area A, which allowed for a significant
area to be examined in plan.

In those trenches that were archaeologically excavated
the overlying made ground and low-grade deposits were
generally removed by earth-moving machinery under
archaeological supervision, except for the boundary
trenches which were excavated completely by hand. When
significant archaeological horizons were reached all
subsequent investigation was by hand employing standard
archaeological excavation techniques and recorded
using a single context recording system. All features and
deposits were levelled relative to the Ordnance Datum
mean sea level at Newlyn, in Cornwall.

During the post-excavation analysis the stratigraphic
information was organised into chronological periods
based on stratigraphic and dating evidence (Meddens
and Wooldridge 2002). In this text individual context/
feature numbers appear in square brackets (eg [100]) and
registered (small) finds are referenced as <15> throughout
in order to provide access to the archive.

The project was given a unique reference code by
PCA of NFR 01. For the archaeological evaluation the
site records and finds were allocated a site code by
Wessex Archaeology of 47707. The project was managed
for Pre-Construct Archaeology by Gary Brown and the
archaeological fieldwork supervised by Kevin Wooldridge.

Further archaeological interventions were also
carried out elsewhere on the site of Southlands School:
an evaluation was carried out adjacent to these
excavations to the northwest by PCA in 2002 and given
the site code NCR 02: this was followed by excavation
by Archaeology South-East. During the evaluation the
most archaeologically significant features were found in
Trenches 1, 2 and 5 (Fig. 2: NCR 02 T1, NCR 02 T2, NCR
02 T5) and these are reported on below. To distinguish
between these interventions and those that form the
basis of this report the later evaluation and excavation is
referred to below by name and site code as Southlands
School, Dymchurch Road (NCR 02).

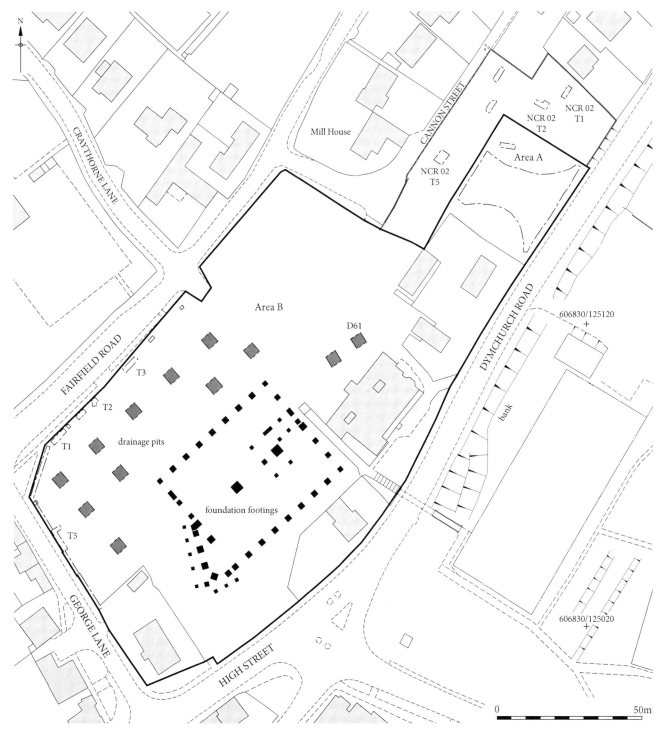

Fig. 2   Areas of archaeological excavation (scale 1:1250)

The historical evidence: sources consulted

There are extensive records revealing the medieval and early-modern history of the town, which have been used as source material for this study, notably the deeds of the Hospital of the Blessed Stephen and Thomas of *c.* 1170 onwards, and the town or chamberlains' records and accounts of 1340 onwards. The earliest surviving town accounts of New Romney date to the mid-14th century and were printed in *Collections for an History of Sandwich in Kent with Notices of the Other Cinque Ports, etc.* (Boys 1792) and later ones by the Historic Manuscript Commission (HMC V). Data on wills from the 1430s onwards, and on maletolts, cesses, appraisers, new advocants, jurats and distraints from the court books of New Romney, and on taxation exemptions from 1489 onwards, has been generously provided by Lynne Bowdon (East Kent Archive Office, New Romney: EKAO NR/JB2, 1454–1482; NR/RTt 1–8).

One of the major sources consulted was the mid- to late-14th century register of the town clerk Daniel Rough, which incorporates an earlier table of maletolts, the customary taxes levied by New Romney on commodities bought or sold there (*Rough's Register*, 28–35). Comparison with other documentation from the New Romney locality places the town's listing of the maletolts before, and probably well before, the early 13th century. However, the table of maletolts may have been updated until the mid-14th century as the town's economic activities expanded, and also as a result of contact between New Romney and the other towns which also levied maletolts; early coastal towns or ports including London, Sandwich, Fordwich, Ipswich and Norwich, also have such lists. A large-scale manorial survey made in 1283–85 of Archbishop Pecham's holdings in and around the town was analysed to distinguish the town centre quarters from those outside (*Pecham's Survey*, 231–233).

Cartographic sources have been instrumental in helping to compile a series of maps charting the development of the town and these include the New Romney tithe apportionment and map, various editions of the Ordnance Survey as well as a 1683 map of the liberty of New Romney. Taken together these sources allow a view of the commercial and corporate functions in the town centre, including those based in its taverns and on its pilgrimage trade. In addition, Domesday Book and the evidence of the parish churches demonstrate the beginnings of urban activity at New Romney in the 11th century. Royal records reveal the interaction between the monarch, New Romney and the other Cinque Ports in the provision of ship service, and how this altered over time with changes in the size of vessels and the gradual deterioration of the town's harbour.

Geology and Topography

The Holocene geological deposits of New Romney comprise wind-blown sand over storm gravel beach deposits and marine alluvium. These seal Hastings Beds dated to the early Cretaceous period of *c.* 145–100 million years ago. Romney Marsh was originally a low lying area which, as a result of being cut off from the sea by the formation of shingle ridge banks along the seaward side, turned into a shallow freshwater lake. This eventually transformed into a marsh, and was crossed by a number of streams draining off the Weald. The marsh was largely protected from inundation on its seaward margin by the shingle banks and ridges.

New Romney's importance during the medieval period is linked to its origins as a fishing village, which developed into a coastal port. The story of the town's development is inextricably linked to its proximity to the sea; any understanding of its role as a medieval port needs to account for its shifting coastline. Today, however, the town lies approximately 1 mile inland from the coast at Littlestone-on-Sea. Much of the Saxon, medieval and later history of the town is linked to its dynamic environment, including the shifting course of the River Rother, the gradual silting of the harbour and bay to the east and the destructive effects of storms depositing great quantities

of sand and shingle whilst also eroding earlier deposits and structures. Alongside these indications of natural intervention is evidence for human action to stabilise and consolidate the landscape. The ground levels of the development site rise from about 5m OD in the southwest (George Lane) corner, to close to 8m OD in the northeast (Tennis Court) area as a result of the natural site formation processes. This elevation constitutes the highest point above sea level in the town and its immediate vicinity.

Archaeological Background

Within this volume the history of New Romney is explored in some detail, and that history provides the backdrop for the archaeological investigations at the Southlands School site. Since the early 20th century a series of archaeological excavations have been undertaken in New Romney. The frequency of archaeological interventions has increased in recent years, particularly since the introduction of Planning Policy Guidance notice 16 (PPG16) in November 1990, which resulted in a number of planning-driven excavations. Of the fifteen archaeological projects completed (excavations, evaluations, watching briefs and surveys), with the exception of the outcome of the Southlands School excavation detailed in this volume, few of the others carried out in order to meet planning conditions have seen their results published so far. The gazetteer presented below provides a brief synopsis of these interventions and locates them within the modern town (Fig. 3). The following provides a very brief background to these archaeological interventions and sets previous archaeological findings from New Romney in context as well as detailing the elements of medieval buildings still visible in the modern town.

Saxon

New Romney's Anglo-Saxon origins as a fishing village are clearly demonstrated by the documentary evidence; there was a mint at Romney by the late 10th or early 11th century, although there is comparatively little archaeological evidence from New Romney itself to substantiate it. What there is comprises surface finds and material resulting from metal detecting activities, including two coins of Cnut dated 1016–1035 and one of Edward the Confessor dated 1044–1046 (Tyler 2007). Coins minted at New Romney are better known from findspots outside the town, with a single example from Minster-in-Thanet, in Kent, a small group of the 'Expanding Cross' type forming part of a coin hoard from Appledore as well as less well-provenanced examples held in the Fitzwilliam Museum, Cambridge and the British Museum. Pins, straps and fittings including a harness fitting, dress fasteners, four brooches, a finger ring and some pottery dated to the 7th to 11th centuries have also been recovered from around the town. Most of the Saxon material belongs to the period AD 800–1100, with a small group of earlier material comprising a dress fastener, a

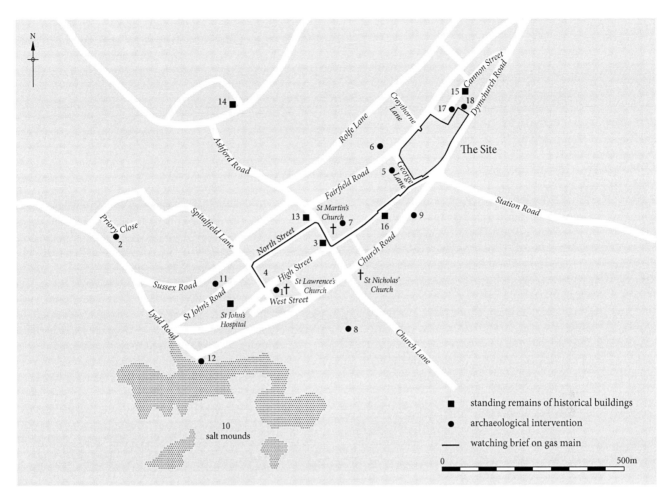

Fig. 3   Previous archaeological interventions and visible remains of historic buildings in New Romney (scale 1:10 000)

Gazetteer of sites shown in Fig. 3

1   The remains of the late Saxon church of St Lawrence, apparently pulled down in 1539. *In situ* structural remains comprising foundations and glazed floor tiles were uncovered, interpreted as elements of the church of St Lawrence and probably representing a 12th-century, or later, rebuild of the church (Willson and Linklater 2002).

2   The remains of a building, interpreted as the chapel of the leper hospital of the Blessed Stephen and Thomas, founded in the late 12th century, were uncovered in the 1930s, along with a domestic structure, probably a timber hall, and evidence of an associated graveyard (Rigold 1964).

3   The 13th-century Cistercian alien priory of Pontigny Abbey. The remains of (much modified) wall fragments, incorporating niches, doorways and windows as well as parts of a cellar, remain *in situ*.

4   An archaeological watching brief along the line of a gas main revealed evidence for 12th and 13th century road metalling, dumps and flood deposits (Canterbury Archaeological Trust 2005).

5   Excavations at Prospect House on the south side of Fairfield Road: 12th–13th-century building remains with evidence of a hearth and artefacts associated with textile manufacture, overlain by evidence of 14th-century domestic occupation (Linklater 2001a; Willson 2003).

6   A watching brief at Melaine in Fairfield Road: rubbish or cess pits dated 1250–1325 and a compacted gravel surface overlain by later 14th-century soils indicating use of the area for arable farming (Linklater 2003).

7   Two inhumation burials associated with the graveyard of St Martin's Church (Boden 2006).

8   13th-century building remains and flood layers interpreted as being deposited during flood events were found overlain by alluvial deposits during an evaluation of land to the rear of the Old School House on the south side of Church Lane (Thomason and Stafford 2001)

9   A watching brief on the edge of the town, found building remains fronting onto the southeast side of Church Road. Sand and shingle deposits were indicative of frequent flooding events (Willson and Linklater 2003).

10   Three low salt mounds, still visible in the landscape and on aerial photographs, are part of a much larger number mapped as part the soil survey of Romney Marsh (Green *et al.* 1966).

11   The site of the burial ground of St John's hospital: marked as such on the Tithe map, suggested by excavation in the 1920s (Teichman-Derville 1929) and confirmed by work in 1995, which revealed structural remains and inhumation burials (SMR TR02 SE4, KCC).

12   An evaluation of land on the southwest side of Church Road produced evidence for a small number of pit cuts, linear features and dumps dating to the late 13th and 14th centuries and a few fragments of animal bone and shell with possible evidence for storm deposits (Priestley-Bell 1999).

13   The remains of a wall and house to the south and east of Dolphin Spot in North Street, attributed to the 14th century.

14   A gold noble of Edward III, struck between 1369 and 1377 was found as a result of metal-detecting at the former borough rubbish dump at Hope Cottages.

15   Frogs Hall: contains surviving structural elements of 15th-century date.

16   Mittel House: contains surviving structural elements of 15th-century date.

17   An archaeological evaluation adjacent to Southlands School by PCA (NRC02, Wragg 2002)

18   An archaeological excavation adjacent to Southlands School by Archaeology South-East (NRC02, Stevenson and Hunter 2005)

hooked tag, and a heart-shaped plate dated to AD 410–800 (Tyler 2007).

As discussed further below (see Chapter 2) the oratory of St Martin was established in the locality by AD 740, and St Martin's Church (now demolished) probably by the late 11th century (Ward 1933, 60, 74). Archaeological evaluation trenches excavated in advance of construction work for a sewerage scheme by the Canterbury Archaeological Trust in 1996 uncovered evidence for two inhumation burials, part of the cemetery associated with St Martin's Church in the field on the junction of Ashford Road and Fairfield Road, known as St Martin's Church Yard (Fig. 3.7). Finds from these two trenches dated between 1175 and 1400, and some of the deposits encountered comprised demolition debris probably deriving from the pulling down of the church in the 16th century, although no finds of Saxon date were recovered (Diack and Boden 2004).

The remains of the late Saxon church of St Lawrence, apparently pulled down in 1539 (Parkin 1973, 119), may have been found between the High Street and Church Road, north of Lions Road (Fig. 3.1). *In situ* structural remains comprising foundations and floor tiles were uncovered in the 1930s (Willson and Linklater 2002, 2). As the latter were reputedly glazed, if they formed part of the church of St Lawrence they clearly constituted a rebuild or modification to the church fabric of the 12th century at the earliest but more likely 13th century or later.

Medieval

Two isolated 11th-century stirrup mounts have been found through metal detecting work while coin evidence for the New Romney mint at this date has been recovered from outside the town. The Denge Marsh hoard, found in 1739, comprised several hundred silver coins, which may have been held in a silver pot. All of these were minted by Wulfmaer and many were of the William I profile left type, dated to between 1067 and 1069 (Purefoy 2005). Other single coins are known from Barham in Kent, one from William I and minted by Wulfnoth, the other of William II from the Essex/Hertfordshire border.

As discussed in greater detail below, the seafront of the medieval town of New Romney is likely to have been centred along the east sides of the present Church Road and Dymchurch Road and historical and archaeological evidence for New Romney during the 13th century is plentiful. The frequency of material of this date in the archaeological record and the extent of the area of the town over which remains of this date can be identified supports the assertion that New Romney reached its maximum influence and importance during the 12th and 13th centuries. However, as the archaeological work carried out in New Romney has been linked to re-development, construction work and chance finds, it may be that the comparative lack of earlier finds is partly influenced by chance, rather than necessarily mirroring the relatively small size and lower ranking status of the settlement during this period.

The church of St Nicholas, possibly in existence by the 11th century and certainly present by the mid-12th century (Fig. 3), remains standing on a former promontory on the southeast side of the town. Its entrance in Church Road is around 1m lower than the road itself (Fig. 4), suggesting the deposition of a considerable body of material in this area subsequent to the construction of the building. The tower has a Norman doorway with an archivolt and triple jamb-shafts, is of a square type and is located on the west end of the church. The original Norman pillars supporting the arcade along the nave alternate between being round and octagonal and are of Caen stone (Fig. 5); the chancel appears to have been added in the 14th century (Parkin 1973, 121). Leland, writing towards the middle of the 16th century wrote that:

'Rumeny is one of the cinque ports, and hath bene a netely good haven, yn so much that withyn rememberance of men shyppes have cum hard up to the town and cast ancres [anchors] yn one of the church yards' (Toulmin Smith 1964, vol. 4, 67).

The churchyard referred to seems most likely to have been St Nicholas' (though may conceivably be St Lawrence's) suggesting vessels were beached on a strand and anchors cast over the wall (Fig. 6).

Remains of the chapel of a leper hospital, dedicated to the Blessed Stephen and Thomas, and founded in the late 12th century in the parish of St Lawrence were uncovered in 1935 and again in 1959 (Rigold 1964, 47–69; see Fig. 3.2; and see Chapter 7). The chapel measured 9.75m wide by 14.94m in length externally with a suspected 2.44 m wide aisle running along its north side. The earliest walling was constructed of cobbles set in clay mortar and two building phases were represented; a new floor and a tile roof replaced a slate predecessor, the excavators interpreted these modifications as having been made sometime in the 13th century. Burials were found on the outside along the north and south walls, and a single brick lined east-west orientated grave was found inside the structure on its east side. Elements of a domestic structure, probably a timber hall, were also revealed. Finds included a fragment of a calcareous headstone cross, a whetstone and an early to mid-15th-century French jetton. The pottery assemblage included Wealden wares, and Ashford/Wealden as well as Rye type wares. Oyster shell was found in associated midden deposits. The leper hospital was re-founded as a chantry chapel *c.* 1363, but had probably fallen out of use by the 1490s. However, the excavated remains largely predate its 14th-century re-founding (Rigold 1964, 47-69).

In the 13th century a Franciscan Friary was reportedly in existence in New Romney, probably founded before 1241 but this no longer survived by 1331 (Little 1939, 151–152). To date no remains that could be linked to this friary have been identified on the ground. However, elements of the Cistercian alien priory of Pontigny abbey, of 13th-century date, are located on the corner of Ashford Road and the High Street, in the parish of St Lawrence (see Fig. 3.3). Much-modified wall fragments, including details of niches, including two with simple two stone

Fig. 4 The entrance to St Nicholas' Church on Church Road

Fig. 5 The interior of St Nicholas' Church

Fig. 6 The south side of St Nicholas' Church with the wall alongside which ships landed and over which ships' anchors are said to have been laid

abutment arches, doorways and windows as well as parts of a cellar, remain *in situ* (Fig. 7, Fig. 8, Fig. 9).

An archaeological watching brief carried out along the line of a new gas main running from North Street, down West Street, along the High Street to the intersection with Station Road was carried out during 1996 by the Canterbury Archaeological Trust (see Fig. 3.4). This revealed horizontal stratigraphy, representing road metalling, and dump and flood deposits. Most of the datable deposits came from the lower levels at the northeast end of the High Street and these dated to the late 12th and 13th centuries, particularly the period between 1200 and 1250. The small ceramic assemblage included Ashford Potter's Corner-type jars, possibly representing locally produced wares, a Rye ware vessel or copy thereof and imported wares such as North French/Flemish Shelly wares, Saintonge Whiteware and an example of an Aardenburg jug form. Overlying these layers were two deposits of a silty sand with a high gravel content devoid of cultural material, possibly associated with a storm event (Herdman and Jarman 1996).

The remains of buildings were revealed in excavations at the rear of Prospect House, on the south side of Fairfield Road in the parish of St Martin (see Fig. 3.5). The earliest remains comprised laminated floor and occupation deposits with a centrally placed hearth. Associated finds include pottery, dating from the late 12th to late 13th century, fragments of two siltstone spindle whorls, a limestone polishing tool, a stone hone and a glass cloth smoother, interpreted as pertaining to a trade linked with textiles, though a medieval fish hook was also recovered (Linklater 2001a). A sub-square oven or furnace and various pits and ditches were associated with this phase of

site occupation (Linklater 2001a; 2001b). The remains were overlain by alluvially deposited grey silty sands (Linklater 2001b). Presumably these deposits again represent storm deposits and similar layers were found during a watching brief at Melaine in Fairfield Road (Fig. 3.6), sealing the remains of two rubbish or cess pits, and pottery from these dated between 1250 and 1325. Overlying these deposits a compacted metalled surface may have represented a track or hard standing to the rear of a medieval building, possibly fronting onto Fairfield Road. This surface was sealed by a fine grey topsoil which may represent the use of the site for arable farming in the later 14th century (Canterbury Archaeological Trust 1996, 271–272).

At the Prospect House site (Fig. 3.5), the 12th- to 13th-century features were replaced by a later building evidenced by robbed out wall foundations, constructed on a southeast alignment, associated with numerous pits and a ditch cut. The features may represent the remains of auxiliary edifices associated with a building formerly fronting onto either the medieval predecessor to the High Street or to Fairfield Road. Alternatively they may be the remains of buildings fronting George Lane located

Fig. 7   Remains of the alien priory of Pontigny on Ashford Road

Fig. 8   Remains of the alien priory of Pontigny on Ashford Road, looking towards the High Street; St Nicholas' church is visible in the background

between, and parallel to, the High Street and Fairfield Road. The finds associated with these remains date from the late 13th- to the late 14th-centuries and include pottery (Rye-type and Ashford Wealden sandy wares and a little Dutch grey ware and material from Yorkshire), ceramic and stone building material, shell and animal bone.

An evaluation of land to the rear of the Old School House on the south side of Church Lane by the Oxford Archaeological Unit (Thomason and Stafford, 2001) revealed structural evidence comprising post holes, a narrow slot, the remains of a possible chalk and flint foundation, associated with surfaces showing evidence of heating and burning and cobble-built structural elements (see Fig. 3.8). Sediments characteristic of deposition in a high-energy environment, interpreted as evidence of a storm event, overlay much of the archaeology and overlying this material was a sequence of alluvial deposits, laid down in a lower-energy depositional environment. The finds included mostly ceramics of early to mid-13th-century date with a single late 13th-century sherd; two fragments of copper-alloy and a silver coin were also identified along with an animal bone assemblage comprising the common domesticates, cattle, sheep/goat/pig and horse. A large quantity of fish bone and marine shell was also found (Thomason and Stafford 2001, Scott 2001). The carbonised plant remains included fragments of charcoal in particular oak, hawthorn/pear/apple, beech and alder/hazel, and charred grains, namely wheat, barley and oats, as well as pea/vetch and grasses; chaff and weed grains were not present suggesting the material constituted food remains (Challinor 2001).

As described above, subsequent to the investigations at the Southlands School site in 2001 further archaeological evaluation was carried out by PCA at the Southlands School site to the northeast of the main excavations (Wragg 2002; see Fig. 3.17) and succeeded by excavations by Archaeology South-East (Stevenson and Hunter 2005, 24–26; see Fig. 3.18). Evidence for storm deposits was again encountered, along with remains of a possible medieval road, a pottery kiln and evidence for fishing in the form of artefacts and faunal remains; the

Fig. 9   Remains of the alien priory of Pontigny on Ashford Road: detail above doorway

results of these interventions are discussed in greater detail below, in relation to the archaeological sequence revealed in 2001 (see Chapter 8).

A watching brief on the edge of the town, on the southeast side of Church Road revealed fragments of two buildings of medieval date (see Fig. 3.9). The earliest structure was timber built, with its gable end facing the road and aligned at right angles to the street; a later masonry structure was erected on a parallel alignment to the road. Both buildings contained sequences of clay floors and deposits of sand and shingle demonstrated that the site had been affected repeatedly by storm events throughout this period. No evidence to date the site more precisely than to the medieval period was identified although pottery recovered from a pit which cut the floors of the building was dated to 1475/1500–1550. This was part of a series of modifications to this building, which was finally abandoned following a flooding event sometime during the 16th century (Willson and Linklater 2002).

Three relatively low but sizable mounds, visible in the landscape and on aerial photographs and located to the south of New Romney and outside the settlement proper, may represent Medieval salterns or salt production sites (see Fig. 3.10). These are the remnants of a much larger number mapped by R. Green (see Chapter 4) and subsequently largely removed by agricultural processes over the last few decades.

The site of the Hospital and chapel of St John the Baptist has been identified on the south side of St John's Road, with the churchyard on the north side of the road in the parish of St Lawrence (see Fig. 3.11). This was established in 1929 (Teichman-Derville 1929, 170) and again in 1995 when foundation remains and inhumation burials were uncovered during construction work. Structural elements of 14th-century date, comprising stone walling and a substantial fireplace survive in 'Old Stone Cottage', West Street (now 3 Old Stone Cottages and Plantagenet House). Slightly earlier building remains are incorporated in this building.

An evaluation of land on the south-west side of Church Road by Archaeology South-East (Fig. 3.12) produced evidence for a small number of pit cuts, linear features and dumps, which produced a finds assemblage comprising a small number of pot sherds, tile fragments, some burnt clay all dating to the late 13th and 14th centuries and a few fragments of animal bone and shell. Some evidence for deposition of possible storm deposits was also uncovered (Priestley-Bell 1999).

The remains of a wall and house to the south and east of Dolphin Spot in North Street (Fig. 3.13) have been attributed to the 14th century.

There are surviving structural elements of 15th century date reported in a number of standing buildings in the town, such as Frogs Hall in Cannon Street (Fig. 3.15), Mittel House between Church Road and the High Street (Fig. 3.16), and a string of properties (numbers 17, 18, 19, 20, 21, 28, 30 and 43) along the High Street.

Chance and metal-detected coins of 11th–13th-century date from New Romney are numerous. Additionally a small number of coins of Henry I's reign (1100-1135) minted at Romney have been found in Lincoln, and one is known to have come from Seasalter in Kent. A relatively large number of lead, and smaller number of bronze, seal matrices have been recovered from the town and these are discussed further below, as well as two bronze casket keys dated 1100-1300. These

items clearly demonstrate the importance of trade items to the town at this time, although whether through its legal trading activities or licensed piracy is perhaps less clear. Other finds include a range of fittings and dress accessories which are less well dated but which can be broadly classed as medieval, including strap ends, horse trappings, a harness mount and pendant and several thimbles. Lead seal matrices have been found in relatively high numbers in New Romney and these finds include: one vesica shape, with star motif, (+ S' Ioh: [-]T[---]C) (1100–1199); a vesica, with fleur de lys motif, (S' ADE F'ERIC) (1100–1199); a vesica (S' EMME [---] PETRI) (1200–1299); a vesica (S' EMME [---] PETRI) (1200–1299); one vesica with eight-pointed star motif; (S' SIGPI[--]I . IohIS) (1200–1299); one circular shaped with a star motif, (S' RADULFI FIL RICARDI) (1200–1299) and one vesica shaped with a cross motif, (S'[-]hERd dEPSER) (1299–1300). There are also some bronze seal matrices, one five-pointed in shape with a running, spiral motif (1200–1300), a second one which is elliptical in shape with an armoured knight motif (MATTHEW VICKERY OF IVYCHURCH) (1100–1400), and a third which is circular with six-petal flower motif (1200–1300).

Three silver coins of Edward II (1307–1327) three silver coins of Edward III (1327–1377), dated 1351–1361, a silver coin of Richard II (1377-1399) a harness pendant, two bronze buckles, two strap fittings, a silver stirrup finger ring, a scabbard, a bronze spur, a bronze beehive shaped thimble, and a harness mount constitute finds for the 14th century recovered during metal-detecting activities. A 106mm long iron arrowhead, of Ward Perkin's type 14 dating from the 14th to the 16th centuries and associated with hunting came from allotment gardens along Sussex Road (Grove 1967, 296), and a gold noble of Edward III, struck between 1369 and 1377 was found at the former borough rubbish dump at Hope Cottages (Fig. 3.14).

A silver ring of 15th-century date, a silver coin of Henry V, 1413-1422, a silver half penny of Edward IV from the Canterbury mint dating to 1460-1471, and a second silver, Edward IV coin dating to 1461-1470, and an oval seal matrix ('S EADMUNDI FIL STEPHANI CLERICI) dated 1400-1500, constitute chance and metal detector finds.

A crucifix found during road works in the High Street is of particular interest, perhaps being part of a processional cross and arguably deliberately buried in 1568, prior to the High Street being paved for the first time (see Chapter 7).

Chapter 2 New Romney's Origin, Development and Role as a Cinque Port

New Romney originated as a fishing settlement that, in part because of its shelving beach and good anchorage, developed into a port. In Saxon times the port comprised a beach market; trading vessels were comparatively small, had a shallow draught and could easily be floated on and off the beach. Subsequently an anchorage in the estuary was used for larger vessels. As a result of its growing strategic and economic importance Romney joined the confederation of the Cinque Ports under Edward the Confessor; this increasing significance is confirmed by the fact that it had a mint by or in the early 11th century (Ward 1952, 21–22: *Rough's Register*, 32–33). By the mid-12th century the presence of St Nicholas' church on the southeast margin of New Romney indicates that New rather than Old Romney was by then the settlement of growing significance (Tatton-Brown 1987, 344; Harris 1990, 6–7). Its hinterland was increasingly of agricultural importance and the town had significant links to the national and cross-Channel trading systems and financial markets (Barber 1998, 105; Gardiner 2000, 92). Documentary evidence, supported by archaeological data, suggests that the agricultural hinterland of Romney Marsh proper was dedicated to arable farming rather than pasture with the focus of the coastal communities being on fisheries, from the 7th through to the 10th and 11th centuries (Allen 2002, 124). From the mid-11th to the mid-13th centuries Romney Marsh saw a dramatic increase in population and from the mid-12th century onwards land claim started in the Walland and adjacent marshes with occupation densities there, and on Romney Marsh, reaching approximately one house for every 2.4 ha. By the 14th century imports into New Romney included timber, building stone and garlic (from the Mediterranean) and exports comprised among others fish, corn and dairy produce (Eddison 2000, 20, 65–71). From the late 14th to 15th centuries onwards a rapid population decline commenced and by the mid-17th century the marsh was one of the least populated areas of Kent and had been largely turned over to sheep pasture (Dobson 1998, 170; Reeves and Eve 1998, 193–194). New Romney's population in the later 17th century was about 450, and only two men earned a living from maritime activity: a fisherman and a ripier, ie one who organised the transport of fish to London and inland towns. By then fully one-third of the town's known poll tax payers were occupied in grazing sheep on Romney Marsh for wool or meat, some making a substantial living; the rest were otherwise occupied in the local agricultural economy (Hipkin 2002, 177–178).

In considering the development and importance of New Romney as a medieval town, it is crucial to consider its status as a Cinque Port. The Cinque Ports need to be understood not in terms of familiar arguments about urban growth and decline but by investigating their port functions and the effects of physical change on their harbours and seafronts. The particular nature of the small but important early port of New Romney is examined in this chapter through the economic, social, religious and cultural history of the town, based on an investigation of its various records, quarters and buildings. New Romney had several important buildings and institutions commonly found in towns such as hospitals, and their origins in the late 12th and 13th centuries are reviewed, as are the ways in which the townsfolk adapted them to their own purposes and economic circumstances over the subsequent centuries. Contrasts are noted between the hospital associated with the town government, St John's, and the Hospital of the Blessed Stephen and Thomas, which became increasingly associated with people of gentry status. Both had important chantry functions and were linked to education and literate activities. Record-making was an integral part of this urban culture at New Romney from an early period, as it was at other towns such as Rye which were members of the Cinque Ports confederation (Draper 2008).

The Port and the Harbour; the Southlands School Site in Context

At New Romney it is important to distinguish between the medieval port or harbour and the beachfront. They were in separate locations and had different functions. The port or harbour lay to the southwest of the town and the beachfront lay between the central and the northeast side (see Fig. 12). The harbour lay close to the intensively used commercial quarter of New Romney. The beachfront was an area of much more extensive sea-, ship- and shore-based activities more distant from the commercial quarter. The Southlands School excavations have been critical in demonstrating archaeologically the existence and nature of this beachfront and the historical sources, especially Daniel Rough's Register (*Rough's Register*), have confirmed and broadened our knowledge of economic activity there.

As will be demonstrated below the sources indicate that rather than being a town planned and set out on a grid plan before the Conquest, the street layout developed and was modified over time in response to the underlying geology and coastal changes. This argument bears on the early history of the settlement at Romenal and the oratory of St Martin, which is reviewed along with past work on the relationship between Old and New Romney. The nature of the Rumenesea and its relationship with the Rhee is critical to this, since recent geomorphological study has challenged some of the basis of previous work.

The origins and development of the Cinque Ports

The Cinque Port confederation was a group of Kent and Sussex coastal towns with direct access to the English Channel and thence continental Europe (Fig. 10). The towns of the confederation all had their urban origins in or before the 10th century (Gardiner 2000) and only later became known as the Cinque (meaning five) Ports (also known as 'head' and consisting of Sandwich, Dover, Romney, Hythe and Hastings) and two 'ancient towns'

(Rye and Old Winchelsea). The towns of the confederation made a living from the sea and foreign trade. In exchange for the use of their ships and sailors by the crown, these towns received significant trade concessions and rights to run their own legal affairs. They jointly extended the monarch's power along the southeastern coast onto the open sea and the lands beyond. They represented the medieval predecessor to the Royal Navy and as a result their influence on regional affairs was considerable.

Coins were minted at Romney in the reigns of Æthelred II (the Unready) (978–1016) and Cnut (1016–1035), seven coins are known from the reign of Æthelred and more from that of Cnut (www-cm.fitzmuseum.cam. ac.uk/coins). Romney is the most likely identification of the 'port called Ruminella' and all that belonged to it, ie mills, fisheries, cultivated and uncultivated land, and rents which appear in a charter, datable between 1023 and 1035, of 'Edward, King of the English', granting the property to Mont-St-Michel. The charter probably represents a 'wishful thought' on the part of Edward, although he may have 'considered himself empowered to grant land in England' including apparently Romney, 'an important port on the south coast' (Keynes 1990, 191–193, 204). By the time Edward reigned as the Confessor (1042/3–1066) Romney provided men and ships for service at sea when required by the crown, for which it, along with Dover and

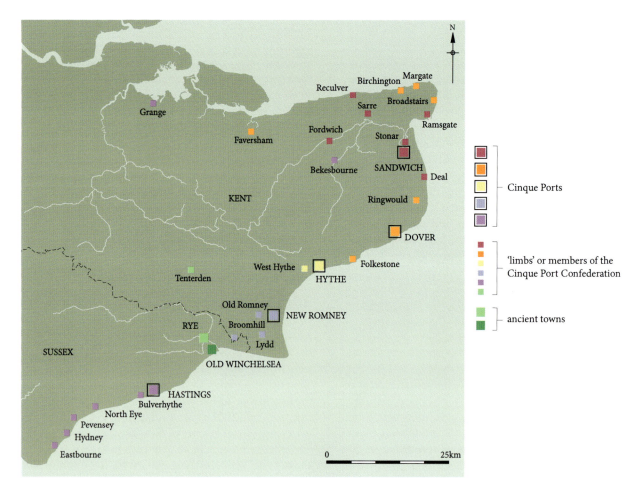

Fig. 10   The Cinque Ports (Sandwich, Dover, Romney, Hythe and Hastings) and their limbs, and the two 'ancient towns' of Rye and Old Winchelsea (scale 1:750 000)

Sandwich, later received privileges (*Domesday Book: Kent*, D2; 5,178; 2, 2; D22, 24, Morris 1976). The port of Romney was significant by 1053 when Earl Godwin and his allies entered the harbour 'and led away all such Ships as they found' there (Jeake 1728, 108). After the invasion of 1066, Duke William and his forces travelled from Hastings via Romney and Dover to London, rather than taking a more direct route. This was to subdue these towns and keep his forces within reach of his ships (Banyard 2004, 34–35).

Development at the time of Domesday Book

By the time of Domesday Book (1086), the urban development of the Cinque Ports is evident in the large number of burgesses (townspeople) in these towns: Romney had 156 burgesses and Rye had 64 (Rye can best be identified with the 'new borough' in the manor of Rameslie, Sussex, *Domesday Book: Sussex*, 5, 1, Morris 1976). Sandwich had 383 'habitable dwellings' and Dover already had a burgesses' guildhall. Domesday Book describes Romney (Romenel) as a borough and port, setting it apart from royal boroughs such as Dover, Canterbury and Rochester and putting it in the same category as Sandwich, Hythe and Fordwich. These were under the control of lay and ecclesiastical lords rather than the crown, but also had their own privileges and obligations as they developed as Cinque Ports (Murray 1935b, 5). The lordship of Romney was in the hands of the Archbishop of Canterbury and Robert de Romenal, apparently an Anglo-Norman layman (*Domesday Book: Kent*, 2, 25, 43; 5, 178, Morris 1976). The relationship of the Cinque Ports with the crown gave them a much greater independence from such lords than was the case in seigneurial or monastic boroughs elsewhere in the country. That relationship was expressed in the honorific title of (com)baron, or occasionally combaroness, given to the townsfolk of the Cinque Ports (*Rough's Register*, li).

Romenel is referred to in Domesday Book and the identification of Romenel with Old or New Romney as applied to the two separate settlements which exist today, and which are about 3km (1.86 miles) apart, cannot be substantiated in archival data until the mid-12th century (Gardiner 1994, 339), as discussed below. The Domesday references of 1086 to Romenel were probably to the whole entity which constituted Romenel as it had by then developed; that is, feudal landholdings, urban rights, the port liberty, areas of settlement, trade and other economic activity, and exploitation of the maritime resources. Old and New Romney continued to be referred to as Romenal, Rumenhale or similar in the medieval sources, indicating their origins as a single unit.

The royal boroughs, Dover, Canterbury and Rochester, had defensive works at the time of Domesday Book. The defences were greatly strengthened and renewed after the Conquest because these boroughs were significant entry points for invasion and on routes leading to London and the rest of the country. The other boroughs were essentially places based on trade and maritime activity.

The town walls of Sandwich were apparently built in the 14th century in response to French raids and possibly also to fashion (Clarke 2005). Similarly the town wall of the Sussex Cinque Port of Hastings was probably not built until the later 14th century (Rudling *et al.* 1993, 75). There is no evidence of defences at New Romney at any period, apart perhaps from a mention of a 'strong ditch' (*foveam fortem*). *Rough's Register* mentions a messuage lying between king's highway and the strong ditch in the mid-14th century, which lay in St Lawrence's parish, ie towards the port side of the town, where there was low-lying and boggy ground (xxxvi, 132). In the context of Romney Marsh where ditches and walls were used to drain land however, this ditch is just as likely to have been connected with reclamation as defence.

The significance of the Cinque Ports in 11th- to 13th-century England was marked by their possession of early markets and by the monastic and other ecclesiastical houses, such as hospitals and friaries, which were founded in them at this time (McLain 1997; Draper 2004b, 56–57; Sweetinburgh 2004a, 2004b). The links of the Cinque Ports with France and the Norman archbishops are reflected in the extensive rights of Pontigny abbey at Romney and Fécamp abbey at Rye. Most of the Cinque Ports had more than one parish church to cater for their relatively large populations at the height of their prosperity.

Ship service in the Cinque Ports

The Cinque Ports supplied 57 ships to the monarch for a limited number of days per year: Dover supplied twenty ships for fifteen days a year in 1086, and similarly Sandwich. The numbers supplied by the other Ports was not specified at this time (*Domesday Book: Kent*, 2,2; 2,25; 2,43; 5,178; D2; D8, Morris 1976). However from the early 13th century when the fortunes of the various ports, and also the sizes of ships, were changing, these numbers were recorded: Hastings (including Old Winchelsea and Rye) twenty-one ships, Romney five ships, Hythe five ships, Dover twenty-one ships, and Sandwich five ships. These were mainly used for cross-Channel transport, 'keeping the seas' or suppressing piracy. Payment for the latter comprised the pirate ship and cargo taken in prize. In effect therefore actions against pirates often involved piracy in its own right. 'Limbs' or members of the Cinque Port confederation assisted the head ports and ancient towns in supplying ships in return for some privileges of self-government. The town of Lydd, for example, a member of Romney, supplied one of Romney's five ships. Each Cinque Port supplied 21 men and one boy or steersman (*garcione*) with each ship from the 11th to the 13th centuries (Parker Library, Corpus Christi College Cambridge, ms. 189, 35). With the general increase in the size of vessels, the crown subsequently requested half the total number of vessels but 'with the same number of men and the same amount of equipment' as for the full service (Murray 1935b, 129, 143–145; Lawson 2004, 52). The ship service was carried out using craft normally engaged in the Ports' primary activities of fishing, coastal and cross-Channel trade; for example, goods from the Mediterranean were trans-shipped at Sandwich, and Romney and Hythe supplied salt to London. The Cinque Ports controlled the major herring fair and fishing at Yarmouth in Norfolk via their Cinque Port court of Brodhull. Romney played an important part in doing so in the 11th to the 13th centuries, when this court was held at Brodhull at Dymchurch to the northeast of the town. Romney also traded with and fished at Scarborough, as evidenced by the finds of Scarborough Ware pottery from the excavations at Southlands School.

The Origins and Development of Medieval New Romney

The early origins of the town

The earliest documentary reference to New Romney, although not by name, is in a charter from king Æthelbert of Kent dated to AD 740 (Ward 1952, 12–25). In it he granted his fishery at the mouth of the Limen river, the former name of the River Rother, and part of the field in which an oratory of St Martin was located, as well as the fishermen's houses and some plough land there to the Minster at Lyminge. The dedication of the oratory indicates its general location at or near New Romney where there was a later manor and church of St Martin. A charter dated to *c.* AD 914 refers to a channel reaching the sea named Rumenesea from which the name Romney, earlier Romenel or Romenal, derives (Gardiner 1994, 339; Eddison 2000, 60–61). The geomorphological evidence

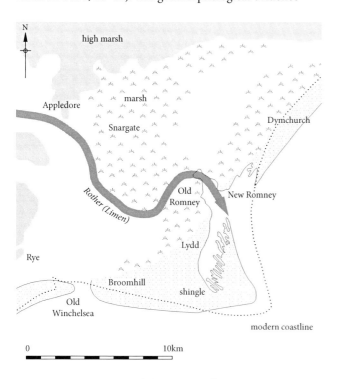

Fig. 11   New Romney and the estuary of the River Rother in the 11th century (based on Green 1988, 14.2-3) (scale 1:250 000)

suggests that before around AD 700–800 a shingle barrier probably extended uninterrupted from Lydd to Hythe providing the conditions under which the peats inland of Romney, and those around Scotney to the southwest, developed. The estuary of the Rumenesea and Rother, a tidal inlet, probably developed at Romney sometime after the end of peat formation around AD 700–800 (Long *et al.* 2007, 199–201).

A charter of 741 recorded fishing rights at the mouth of the Limen and fishermen's houses there, and an associated early oratory. This location may represent the origins of the port of Romenal (see Gardiner 1994, 339–340, 343–345). The early course of the Limen or Rother across Romney Marsh, and various tidal inlets on the Marsh, bear on the development of the port of Romney. However, they remain a matter of current debate, although one point of fairly general agreement is that the Limen(ee), Ee or Rhee, Rother or the river of Newenden are all names for an important watercourse or courses draining the southeast Weald near Appledore across the medieval Marsh to an exit to the sea at what became the port of Romenal (eg Allen 2002; Reeves 1995; Rippon 2002; Gardiner 1994, 339; Vollans 1988, 132).

The early oratory of St Martin

The early oratory at the mouth of the Limen was dedicated to St Martin and this is the basis of the identification with the later site of (New) Romney, which is the only place on the Marsh with a parish church of this dedication. Gardiner (1994, 339) suggested that 'the reference to the mouth of the Limen' in connection with a fishing settlement, appears to be 'appropriate for that location', ie St Martin's parish church at New Romney. The recent archaeological and historical work confirmed fishing activity in St Martin's parish and particularly St Nicholas' parish of New Romney from the 13th century. However, any simple identification of the site of the early oratory of St Martin with that of the later St Martin's parish church in the centre of New Romney is problematic for three reasons. Firstly, the physical environment and the topography of the area between the 8th and the 13th centuries underwent continuous modification by the sea, weather and human activity. Fishing on the Marsh took place widely on the shingle beach areas and not necessarily in or near a town or its haven (B. Coatts, pers. comm.). Secondly, in 1291, a church of St Martin existed at New Romney, but also the chapel of St Martin de Northne, with Northne being an area 'which stood on the north bank of the old channel of the Rother'. In the 13th and the 14th centuries, the church of St Martin was separate from the chapel of St Martin de Northne. Rough's record of the salary of four chaplains at New Romney and of the livelihood of the parish priest for St Nicholas' Church in 1354 accords with a listing of clergy in the deanery of Lympne which shows this arrangement (Draper 2000, 6–8, *Rough's Register*, xxxix, 296; Canterbury Cathedral Archives (CCA), DCc CA S425). Thirdly, St Martin's parish church was demolished in the 16th century and there is not a complete record of its form. However, it was a large church which had a major place in the central rectilinear part of New Romney which was laid out probably in the early 13th century, to the northwest of the new High Street and close to the buildings of the alien priory of Pontigny to which St Martin's along with the other parish churches belonged. It is therefore impossible to say that the site of the early oratory of St Martin is that of the later parish church of St Martin, although it might be; equally possible is that the dedication of a sacred place to St Martin was transferred to a new site and new building at some point.

The Street Layout of New Romney

The layout of the havens and towns of most of the Cinque Ports was profoundly affected by environmental and other changes over the medieval period, particularly in the configuration of the estuaries on which some lay, in the size of ships and economic and mercantile conditions. At Sandwich current research indicates that there was an early settlement to the east of the later town, and that the present town grew up on a new but nearby site sometime after *c.* 1000, with subsequent changes in emphasis in the location of the commercial centre and internal topography (Clarke 2005; Helen Clarke, pers. comm.). Martin postulated that 'new Hastings', now called the Old Town, replaced the original, possibly Saxon, settlement on a new site from the 1180s (Martin 1993, 72–77). Old

Winchelsea in Rye Bay was finally washed away by storm activity, which commenced in the mid-13th century, and was replaced by New Winchelsea as a planned royal town in the 1280s. The town was set out with a grid plan on a nearby hill, with 79 merchant quays at the foot of the hill. New Winchelsea's royal patronage, trading privileges and situation made it the most important of the Cinque Ports between *c.* 1290 and 1330 (Martin 1999, 44–45) and was exceptional in medieval England in being laid out simultaneously on a grid plan (Hindle 2002). Beresford (1967) has also suggested that New Romney had a grid pattern and was 'one of the few towns in England known to have been "planted", or town-planned before the Norman Conquest' (quoted by Parkin 1973, 118). Beresford's suggestion is however challenged by the archaeological and historical evidence presented here. Rather than being a town planned and set out on a grid plan before the Conquest, the street layout developed and was modified over time in response to the underlying geology, commercial changes and the presence of the beachfront and harbour. Although the 'port of Ruminella' may have existed by 1035, it is argued that New Romney originated as a fishing village and had a beach market between the central and northeast side of the town with a sheltered haven to the southwest of the town formed from the estuaries of the Rother and Rumenesea (Gardiner 1994, 329–330). There were probably merchants' quays sited there by the early 13th century, at which period a notable reconfiguration of the town layout occurred.

At first glance New Romney's medieval street plan appears to form a well-defined grid pattern. The town

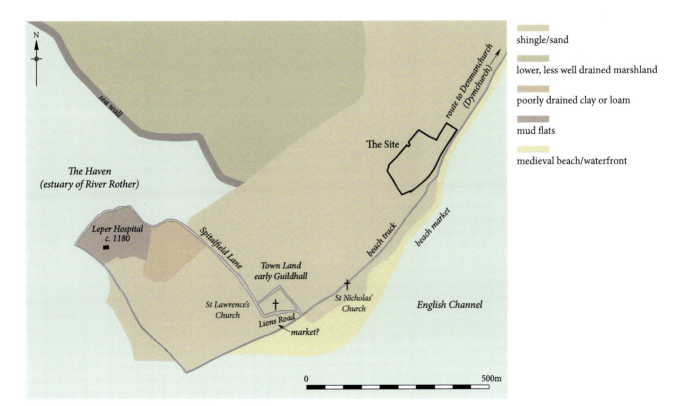

Fig. 12   Schematic reconstruction of the probable layout of New Romney in the 12th to early 13th centuries (scale 1:10 000)

therefore has the appearance of having been laid out following a pre-planned design. This impression is reinforced by historic maps, but these in fact represent the culmination of centuries of town development at New Romney. These include Hasted's map (Hasted 1797–1801, vol. 8), the map of 1683 (see Fig. 22) and the tithe map of 1840 (Fig. 13). The known early origins of the town together with the apparent grid plan led Beresford (1967) to suggest it was an Anglo-Saxon planted town. The town layout is however the result of modifications over the medieval period. Two main phases can be identified from the archaeological, historic and buildings record. These are illustrated in figures based on the tithe map (Fig. 12, Fig. 14). The town layout is underpinned by the shingle on which New Romney lies and was also influenced on its southeastern, seaward, side by storm events, including ones which apparently occurred before those documented from 1236 onwards.

To understand the early layout of the town the few early surviving or known buildings and structures dating to the late 12th and 13th centuries need considering. These include St Nicholas' Church, the leper Hospital, St Lawrence's Church and the early Guildhall, which was sold by the town before 1234. Some or all were built in stone and were grouped in the west-central part of the town. St Lawrence's Church was on a small triangular site, which is still evident, possibly with a small market on the sea side (*Rough's Register*, xxxvi–xxxvii). The locations of these early buildings do not suggest a grid plan. There was one main highway, the beach track (subsequently the old High Street and now Church Road, leading to Dymchurch

Road). It linked the shelving beach, with its fishing boats and beach market, to the town centre buildings and led on to the harbour area to the southwest (Fig. 12). This beach track, following a sinuous line, has parallels with those at other ports such as King's Lynn, Hull and Sandwich (Clarke and Carter 1977, 417; H. Clarke, pers. comm.). From the northeast side of New Romney the beach track (now Dymchurch Road) led to the important early church and settlement of Dymchurch. There was also a road or track between the leper Hospital of *c.* 1170 and the town centre (now Spitalfield Lane). There may also have been a road leading from near St Lawrence's church to the port area, which could have been a link between Lion's Road and the current Lydd Road. Recent work in the town by the Canterbury Archaeological Trust has revealed that medieval house plots crossed over the intersection linking Lydd Road with the new High Street, demonstrating that this road link did not exist until later medieval times (A. Gollop, pers. comm.). By the early 13th century the port location would have been of increasing importance and additional road links would have been useful.

In the second phase of New Romney's development, the beach trackway became known as the old High Street. A new High Street opening out into a long and wide market area was laid out on the former site of the Town Land and the early Guildhall, which was sold before 1234 (Fig. 14, *Rough's Register*, 4); the new High Street did not link up with Lydd Road until later in the town's development. The framework of New Romney's so-called grid plan was established at this period with four long streets: the Old and new High Streets, Fairfield Lane and Rolfe's Lane.

Fig. 13   Detail from the Tithe Map of New Romney 1840

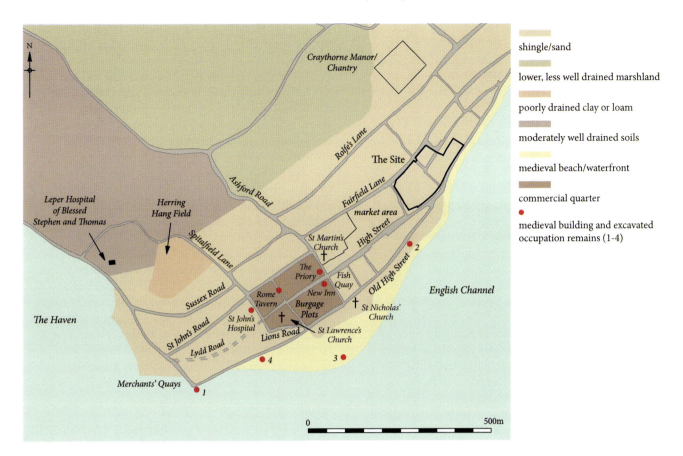

Fig. 14   Schematic reconstruction of the layout of New Romney in the 13th to 15th centuries, showing the haven and the estuary of the Rother open (scale 1:10 000)

None of these long streets is straight, and the courses of the old High Street and Rolfe's Lane depend upon the edge of the underlying shingle. Rolfe's Lane, which joined Ashford Road where it left the town, marked the parochial and liberty boundaries by the early 13th century (see Fig. 15). It runs along parallel to the boundary between the shingle on which the town stands and the lower-lying marshland to the northwest, where lay the moated manor and chantry chapel called Craythorne manor, known from the 1240s (Draper 2004a). Fairfield Lane, the site of the fair, appears to have been set out roughly parallel with the new High Street and behind the site of St Martin's Church, which was probably new at this period.

Burgage plots were created in a rectangular block along the new High Street to the southwest of the new market area formed by the widening out of the High Street in the area where the early Guildhall and Town Land had lain before 1234. The burgage plots along the new High Street were delimited on the northwest side by Victoria Street and Rome Road and on the northeast side by Ashford Road. The burgage plots backed onto a short new street, North Street, to the northwest of which there may have been further burgage plots. Other ones may be represented by the plots on the southeast side of the market area of the new High Street adjacent to Tritton Lane (see Fig. 17). This lane itself also constitutes a later medieval development after the new High Street and market area were set out, as demonstrated by work by the Canterbury Archaeological Trust (A. Gollop, pers. comm.). A total of

about 45 remnants of plots can be identified from the tithe map (Fig. 13). This number of plots is far fewer than the 156 burgesses at Romney in Domesday Book. However Domesday Book records people granted burgess rights at Romney (both Old and New), and not plots *per se*. Some plots may also have been lost by amalgamation since New Romney's urban peak.

Two early short streets next to the churches of St Lawrence and St Nicholas led into a new rectilinear area of the burgage plots. The road now called Church Approach ran from St Nicholas' church to the new High Street and was adjacent to the fish quay area. It led on into Ashford Road, which became a second route out of town in addition to Spitalfield Lane. Spitalfield Lane would have been the main route into the town from the Romney Marsh direction, and by *c.* 1260–1270 included the bridge of Romenal (below) where the hospital inmates would have begged for alms (Sweetinburgh 2004b, 44; *Magdalen College Muniments (MCM) Oxford, Romney deed 39*). Ripiers carried the town's major commodity, fish, out via this route certainly by the 1340s and probably by the 1220s. There is a possible merchant's house and undercroft in Church Approach leading to St Nicholas' Church, which may be dated to the 13th century (Harris 1992, 5).

The streets around the new burgage plots formed the core of the new rectilinear pattern of the town streets. In addition, to the southwest of Rome Road and the burgage plots, there was another block delimited by West Street where the 13th-century St John's Hospital lay (Fig. 14, see

Fig. 17). West Street was part of the earlier Spitalfield Lane. It had a southerly continuation to the old High Street, which was closed in 1829 as no longer needed (East Kent Archives Office (EKAO), NR/JQF/8/2). This continuation formed another cross street between the long streets of the so-called grid pattern.

The west-central end of the new High Street was the focus of the commercial area, which included at least two of the town's medieval taverns, the Rome tavern and the New Inn (which is still standing and in use). The commercial area was flanked by the three parish churches and the building and precincts of the alien priory of Pontigny in Ashford Road (Fig. 14).

On the western side of the town, two more streets developed or were set out: one curving, Sussex Road, and one straight, St John's Road, which ran between St John's Hospital and its churchyard. These roads led travellers and residents between the town centre and the harbour. Those who used St John's Road and then West Street passed along two sides of St John's Hospital precincts, perhaps giving them the opportunity to give alms to the hospital inmates. The land in this western part of the town was low-lying, and associated with salt pits and the drying and soaking of herring at Herring Hang field.

To the northeast of the central rectilinear area of New Romney, there was a further area where the long streets and cross streets leading inland from the beachfront and strand formed a sub-rectangular pattern, including the area covered by the Southlands School excavation site. Here the Old and new High Streets joined each other at the point where the new High Street narrowed as it ran in a northeasterly direction. In this part of the town there were thus only three long streets. The course of the old High Street (Dymchurch Road), which ran along the edge of the shingle, may have been modified by storms. Rolfe's Lane provided an alternative route towards Dymchurch on the landward side of the shingle area but was effectively outside the town centre. Along Fairfield Lane there is archaeological evidence of the textile trade and its associated buildings between the 12th and 14th centuries (with this trade also evidenced in the historical sources of this date), and also of metalworking. The table of maletolts shows the presence of weavers and cloth finishers in the town, although not in a specific location, and a smith is known in the town in *c.* 1260–1270 (*Rough's Register*, 28–35, MCM Romney deed 39). In this vicinity, outside the built-up area of town, the cross streets such as Craythorne Lane and George Lane took short direct routes between the three long streets of the town. They were not precisely straight roads suggestive of laying out on a grid plan. Craythorne Lane may have developed as the routeway to Craythorne manor and George Lane around the buildings and needs of the industrial activities carried out in that part of New Romney.

Two aspects of the dynamics of the town's topography are of some importance to the distribution and spread of the settlement during medieval times. Along the southern and therefore seaward side of the town the results of four excavations (see Fig. 3, Fig. 14) have demonstrated the presence of medieval occupation remains south of the line formed by the old High Street/Church Road, namely those located on land to the southwest of Church Road (Priestley-Bell 1999) (see Fig. 3.12, Fig. 14.1), at the northeast end of Church Road (Willson and Linklater 2003) (see Fig. 3.9, Fig. 14.2), at the rear of the old School House along Church Lane (Thomason and Stafford 2001) (see Fig. 3.8, Fig. 14.3), and at Butt field, south of Church Road (Fig. 14.4). In addition the plotting of the town's natural surface topography, using available Ordnance Survey data and evidence from the excavated sites, demonstrates that a natural promontory projects southeast from Church Road along Church Lane. The old High Street/Church Road runs along an easily observable shingle ridge, which still stands proud of the land to the southeast (see Chapter 8, Fig. 29, below). The archaeological evidence for extensive truncation and flooding events from the northeast end of Church Road and the rear of the old School House along Church Lane (Fig. 14.2, Fig. 14.3) indicates that medieval New Romney extended beyond the line of the elevated shingle ridge now defined by Church Road and that this area was rendered uninhabitable by the 13th-century and later storm events.

The 13th-century weather: storms and the problems of the port (haven)

Of particular relevance to the excavations at Southlands School are the poor weather conditions documented in the 13th century. These include disastrous storms in 1236 (Scott Robertson 1880, 241) 1250 (1 October?), 1252 (October?), 1261 (?), 1271, 1287 (December) and 1288 (January?), which affected extensive parts of the reclaimed land of the Walland marshes and led to the abandonment of the port of Old Winchelsea to the sea (Eddison 2002, 130). The absence of documentary sources for earlier storm activity does not mean that it did not occur, and recent geomorphological research shows that this area has evidence for inundations after about AD 700–800, following an extended period of saltmarsh formation.

Additionally at New Romney the increases in the sizes of the ships needing to land and load cargoes resulted in a requirement for deeper water. With the introduction of cogs in the 13th century (Crumlin-Perdersen 1972, 190), quays and even cranes would have been needed to load and unload goods. This, combined with the partial silting up of the estuary and tidal inlet along which New Romney was located, resulted in responses to mitigate the changed conditions, primarily the construction of the Rhee as argued by Eddison (2002). This comprised a 7.5 mile (12km) long embanked channel running from Appledore to New Romney, through which tidal water, river water and runoff was fed, to flush out the silts being deposited in the New Romney inlet (see below and Fig. 18) (Eddison 2002, 127–128, 137–138) although ultimately even this failed to keep the port open. If the final phase of its construction dates to around 1258 as Eddison (2002, 128) suggested, the primary motivation for the building of the Rhee may have been the doubling of the depth of water required by ships to be able to enter the port over the first half of the 13th century, from 5 feet to 10 feet (Crumlin-Perdersen 1972,190). The silting of the harbour became of increasing concern during the second half of the 13th century. Although the earliest documented storm occurred at Martinmas (November 11) 1236 and is known to have affected New Romney, Appledore and Old Winchelsea (Scott Robertson 1880, 241), the frequency and intensity of storm activity noticeably increased after *c.* 1250. The planning of an engineering project the size and complexity of the construction of the Rhee as well as the implementation of the scheme itself would have involved considerable time and resources. A timespan of at least a decade or more from initial concept to completion would not seem unreasonable.

Nevertheless, in spite of these efforts, access to the port of New Romney from the sea is thought to have been greatly impeded by 1258 (Eddison 2002, 137–138), presumably as a result of the 1250 and 1252 storms and perhaps other undocumented events. The silting up of the harbour led to the gradual decline of the town (Eddison 2002, 80–84). An exceptionally heavy storm in December 1287 appears to have affected New Romney in particular, destroying much property in the process. This 1287 storm was one of truly epic proportions with a surge tide, which dramatically affected the coasts of Germany and the Netherlands (Fagan 2000, 65) as well as bringing floods to East Anglia. What remained of the main channel forming the New Romney harbour is recorded as ending up choked with material deposited during this event. The flooding is also thought to have left extensive deposits throughout the town (Teichman-Derville 1929, 155–156; Parkin 1973, 117–128). The Rhee continued to function and facilitated some use of the port of New Romney until 1400 or possibly even as late as 1430 (Eddison 2002, 137).

The problems of the port were greatly exacerbated by the increases in draught and sizes of vessels from the typical early medieval types which could be drawn up

on the beach to the later medieval ones which required a quayside. Access to the beach area from the sea, by shallow draught vessels, would have continued until this had silted up too, as is evidenced by the archaeological evidence from Southlands School. The historical evidence of the 14th century (below) suggests that open access to the beach was replaced by a course of water running from the harbour in a northeasterly direction past St Nicholas' churchyard through sandbanks. By 1518/19 this course was referred to as the 'Havene stremes' and was silting up (HMC V, 553), although as discussed below a map of New Romney dated 1683 shows that this watercourse still existed in some form into the 17th century (see Fig. 22).

Continued decline of the town

Crop failures between 1315 and 1322, the Black Death in 1348–1349, and further epidemics in the later 14th century followed the storms. Population levels nationwide fell by possibly as much as 60% as a result of the plagues and the population level in New Romney does not seem to have recovered from this period onwards (at nearby Rye, population fell by 40% among the well-fed and comfortably-housed town elite and possibly more among the poorer townspeople, Draper *et al.* forthcoming). The increased storminess of the late 13th century and the catastrophic rains of the early 14th century have been linked with the onset of the 'Little Ice Age' (Fagan 2000, 29–44). Storms are also documented at the start of the 15th century, continuing to affect the coast around Romney Marsh, including Dover and Hythe, and the Thames/Medway estuaries as far as Rochester (Mercer 2005, 49, 63, n.10). Changes in agricultural practices were triggered by the wetter and colder climate with marginal land being abandoned (Mercer 2005; Fagan 2000, 32–41). It is likely that the changes observed in Romney Marsh from a mixed farming economy to one rooted in sheep farming were initiated by these changing environmental and demographic conditions.

Chapter 3 Medieval Elements of the Town, its Layout and Trades

By the 12th century New Romney supported three parish churches, a chapel and a hospital for lepers. By or during the 13th century a further hospital, a Franciscan Friary and a cell or sub-unit of an alien Cistercian Priory were established, as well as a substantial moated manor, Craythorne, on the outskirts with its own chantry chapel (Draper 2004a). The boundaries of the town's parishes, which were lost after the medieval period, have been reconstructed below, and the economic activities of each analysed. Much of the information on which this reconstruction of parish boundaries is based comes from information in *Rough's Register*, which locates property in New Romney by the parish in which it lay.

The Ecclesiastical Buildings and the Parishes

The parishes making up the town were St Nicholas', St Martin's, and St Lawrence's, while Hope All Saints parish lay just outside New Romney proper. The boundary between Hope All Saints parish and New Romney in the

13th century was Rolfe's Lane. This was also the borough boundary, and the approximate line of the northwestern edge of the shingle bank on which New Romney stands, beyond which lies poorly-drained land (Draper 2004a). The southeast boundary of St Nicholas' parish was where the edge of the churchyard and the old High Street met 'le Strond' or beachfront, as indicated on the tithe map. In the mid-14th century, Rough described le Strond as extra-parochial, outside St Nicholas' parish, although at an earlier period, before the storms of the late 13th century, there were buildings along the natural promontory which projects southeast from Church Road along Church Lane, and this may then have been within the parish. Only part of St Martin's parish can be identified firmly, and one part conjecturally, which could alternatively be part of St Nicholas' parish. Of particular relevance to the Southlands School excavation site is a 1.2 mile (2km) extension of New Romney along the line of the shingle bank to the northeast. On the Hope All Saints' side this would have been part of St Martin's parish and the area fronting on the sea, ie along Dymchurch Road, the continuation of the High Street, was part of St Nicholas' parish (Fig. 15);

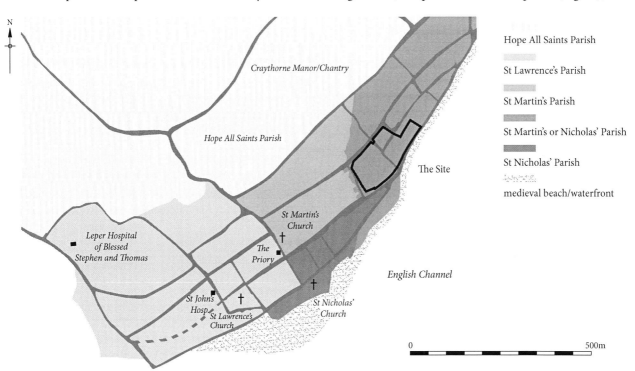

Fig. 15   Reconstruction of the medieval parishes of New Romney, based on the Tithe map (scale 1:10 000)

the nature of economic activity there was expressed in the church's dedication to the patron saint of maritime causes.

St Martin's parish and manor had the same dedication as the early oratory, but the site of the medieval church of St Martin cannot be identified precisely with the location of that oratory in this changing environment and St Martin's church may have been built on its large site in the town centre as the town expanded. St Martin's parish included the northeast side of the High Street, but the north and northeastern parts of the parish were areas of extensive rather than intensive activity, with the site of the fair lying to the northwest of the church and graveyard along Fairfield Road.

St Lawrence's parish, on the port side, was the area of concentrated commercial functions, and the location of many burgage plots (see Fig. 17). The important hemp, butter, poultry and meat markets were held in St Lawrence's parish (*Rough's Register*, xxxvii). The leper Hospital founded *c.* 1170 and Spitalfield Lane (Spitelstreet) were also in St Lawrence's parish but well on the northwest outskirts of the town (*Rough's Register*, 87). Similarly St John's Hospital and its large churchyard, used for the burial of parishioners of St Lawrence's, were on the edge of the commercial quarter (*Rough's Register*, xxxvi). St Lawrence's Church, removed by 1539, was apparently between the High Street and Church Road, with 'a small market on its south [ie shore] side' (Parkin 1973, 122); Tatton-Brown (1987, 346) recorded a new building of August 1987 as being built on the probable site of St Lawrence in the High Street. Murray's introduction to *Rough's Register* (xxxvi, quoting Scott Robertson 1880, 244–245), says St Lawrence's Church 'stood a little inland on a triangle of land between streets in a crowded part of town'. This may be based on the tithe map, which has the words 'St Lawrences' in this location, although it might indicate the general area or the parish rather than the actual site. Civic and charitable functions were also located in St Lawrence's parish in the 13th century (*Rough's Register*, xxxvii, 167).

The cell of the alien priory of Pontigny lies in Ashford Road on the boundary between the medieval parishes of St Lawrence and St Martin, and is known as 'The Priory'. Such alien priories administered the English property of monastic houses in France or Flanders. At some there was a 'truly conventual house', at others merely an administrative centre (Hughes and Stamper 1981, 24). At Lewisham, for example, there was a cell of the alien priory of the Benedictine Abbey of St Peter's Ghent, Flanders. Apparently here there was 'the prior's own residence with room perhaps for one or two companions', and possibly 'a small chapel for their own use', and farm buildings including a barn for tithes in kind. It may have been close to the parish church (Egan 2003, 236). The 'Priory' building and precincts at New Romney have not been surveyed, and little is known about the nature of ecclesiastical or organisational activity there. The Priory lay very close to St Martin's Church, with this church being part of Pontigny's possessions in the town. Pontigny Abbey sheltered Thomas Becket when

he attempted to flee to France in 1164, via New Romney. Subsequently Pontigny Abbey received the advowson and patronage of the churches in New Romney and set up the cell or alien priory to administer its property there. The link with Pontigny was first severed by the crown during the 14th-century wars with the French, when the king took control of such properties and leased them out. The property in New Romney was finally formally seized in 1415 along with the holdings of other alien priories in England, and it was ultimately granted to the warden of the College of All Souls in Oxford in 1438–1443 (Draper 1998, 111, 113).

One of the greatest sources of information on the layout and trades of the town is *Rough's Register*, compiled in the 14th century. It is an important historical source for the medieval beachfront area of New Romney revealed by the Southlands School excavations and includes a chronological register of land transactions in the town (1357–1380). These were often concerned with the inheritance-rights of women, particularly married daughters, to land, rents and family business activities, including fishing and milling. Sequences of land-transactions reveal the nature and location of trade, fishing and maritime activities of many individuals and families.

Different kinds of real property were carefully distinguished in the land transactions in *Rough's Register*. These included houses (*domus*), shops and inns. The terms tenement (*tenementum*) and 'messuage (*messuagium*) and appurtenances' were used, the latter indicating pieces of land with one or more buildings on it, usually including a house. References to plots (*placia*) or pieces (*pecia*) of land indicated vacant lots within the built-up area. Real property was occasionally described as 'land' (*terra*), suggesting it lay outside the fully built-up area, although within the bounds of the town. These distinctions help reconstruct the quarters of the town. They allowed the old High Street, repeatedly mentioned by Rough as abutting various lands, to be located.

Rough located real property by the parish in New Romney in which it lay. Notably property *super le Strond*, on the beach, was extra-parochial. The Strond was 'land abutting on the sea, a river, or other body of water, a shore, bank, coast' (Middle English Dictionary, University of Michigan quod.lib.umich.edu/m/med/). It could also be used specifically in relation to fishermen's rights to use the shore and inlets, in the phrase 'den and strond', as in those rights of Cinque Port men to do so at Yarmouth. Property on le Strond was not recorded as being in any parish. Rough also distinguished the beach (le Strond) from the sea shore (*litus maris*).

References to 'the course of water of the port' (*cursum aque portus*) or 'the course of the sea' (*cursum maris*) indicate that in the mid-14th century, the entrance/exit channel of the port ran alongside St Nicholas' Church and northeast towards sandbanks or similar at Le Helmys near modern Littlestone (*Rough's Register*, xxxvi, 40, 153, 185–186, 199, 243). Ships may still have been able to tie up close to St Nicholas' Churchyard in the 16th century

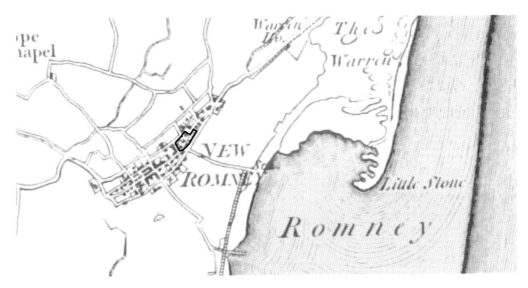

1801 OS map

1877 OS map

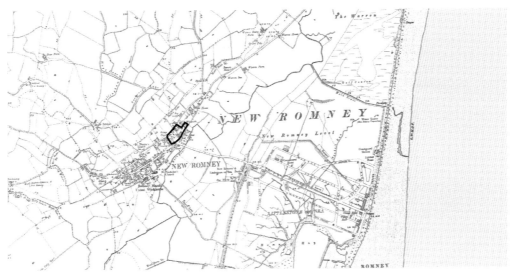

1899 OS map

Fig. 16   Ordnance Survey maps of 1801, 1877 and 1899 showing the speed of silting of the coastline adjacent to New Romney through the 19th century (scale 1:32 000)

(Toulmin Smith 1964, vol. 4, 67). Extensive deposition of sand subsequently occurred to the southeast of New Romney beyond the medieval beachfront; the OS maps of 1801, 1877 and 1899 graphically illustrate the speed and impact of the silting process in the 19th century.

Rough's Register allows commercial, port, shore-based and trade activities, including fishing, to be located by parish within medieval New Romney. The quarters of the town are often described by the term 'hope' in the medieval sources, eg Archbishop Pecham's survey, 1283–1285, which enables 'hopes' inside and outside the town centre to be distinguished (*Pecham's Survey*, 231–233). *Rough's Register* located hopes such as the Kidelmanhope, the hope or quarter associated with the shore (or kiddle) fishermen, by parish. Detailed reconstruction of holdings, beach and seashore allowed the Kidelmanhope in particular to be identified with the Southlands School excavation area. Street names and personal names further link the economic activity of taverners, fishermen, barrel-makers, salters, millers and tanners with that area.

The Medieval Parishes of New Romney and their Economic Activities

The location and economic activity in the three medieval parishes has thus been reconstructed, primarily from the evidence of *Rough's Register* and the tithe map of 1840 (Fig. 17). The parish boundaries were largely lost after the 16th century.

St Martin's and St Nicholas' parishes

Data in *Rough's Register* is not extensive for parts of the two parishes of St Martin's and St Nicholas' in the northeast of the town. As noted above St Nicholas' Church is dedicated to the patron saint of barrel-makers, boatmen, fishermen, longshoremen, mariners, merchants, travellers, pilgrims and watermen, and this must reflect the nature of trades and industries within that parish. Kiddle fishing was located along the shoreline extending northeast from the centre of town and the details of this are explored

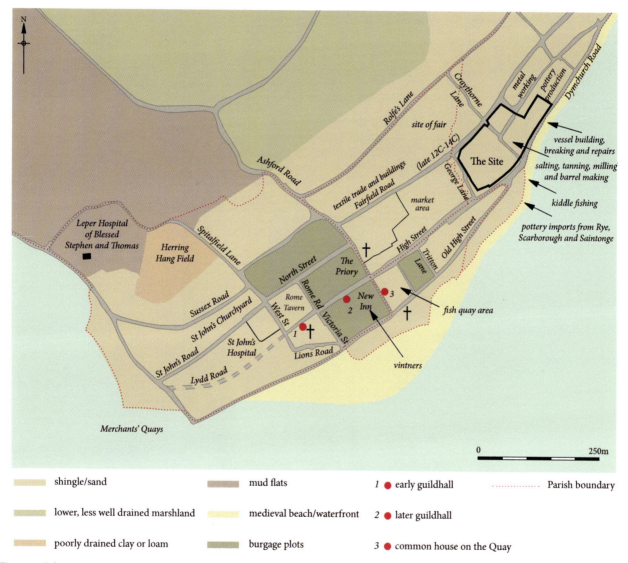

Fig. 17   Schematic reconstruction of the central area of New Romney in the 13th to 15th centuries, showing the location of guildhalls and meeting rooms, burgage plots, industries and trade (scale 1:7 500)

below in specific relation to the excavations at Southlands School. There was probably an early overland route along the shingle bank to Dymchurch by which goods, especially fish, could be distributed to Romney Marsh. The shingle bank was being reinforced or replaced by a wall by 1271; at Holewest in Dymchurch a jetty existed at some time before 1287, which was replaced by the wall (cf. Green 1988, 167; Tatton-Brown 1988, 108; Rippon 2002, figs 6.1–6.11, *Cal. Feet of Fines [Henry III]*, 377). Individuals and families known as mariners were particularly associated with St Nicholas' parish, and include for example Thomas Alayn and his wife Clemency who had a 'messuage with appurtenances', probably here meaning a house with ancillary buildings, in that parish (*Rough's Register*, 89, 160, 186–187).

The beachfront area in St Nicholas' parish

Fishing based at New Romney was of various kinds. Some took place out at sea, and the boats involved may have been based in the port rather than on the beachfront. For example, in 1354 William Baione of Hythe, captain of a fishing boat using spindle nets, abandoned his nets due to a storm and withdrew to the *haven de Romene*. His vessel was a '*Spinderelesbot*', which was a deep sea trawler. Flew (drift) nets and herring nets were also referred to in Romney's early, probably 12th-century, table of maletolts. The 'Master fishermen of each boat' paid a halfpenny a week, other crew members a farthing. Each kidelman paid one penny.

As indicated in *Rough's Register* the seasonal herring fishing off Great Yarmouth was very important to New Romney in the 12th and 13th centuries, although less so by the later 14th century. The table of maletolts measures the catch in thousands of herrings, and 'lasts' of sprats, probably containing well over 12,000 fish per last. New Romney controlled the herring fair at Great Yarmouth by appointing a bailiff to Yarmouth (*Rough's Register*, xlv–vi). Such bailiffs would have been personally involved, at a high level, in the herring fishing industry. Some are known to have held land on, or adjacent to the shore. They included Hugh Goldsmyth and J. Newene, Bailiffs to Yarmouth in the 1370s. Newene's name may be associated with the New Inn at 37 High Street (Parkin 1973, 122–123).

Another important type of fishing in New Romney was kiddle fishing, documented in the vicinity from the mid-13th century, and probably occurring much earlier (*Cal. Feet of Fines [Henry III]*, 342; *Custumals of Battle Abbey*, 42). Kiddle fishing was based on the shore, including the beachfront area, which formed the southeast boundary of the Southlands School excavation site. Fishing boats may also have been drawn up here, as they were at Brighton and Hove (Bleach and Gardiner 1999, 42). Although kiddle fishing was shore-based, the men involved might also jointly own fishing boats as for example was the case with J. Kidelman and W. Colyn, freemen of Romney, in 1357 (Daniel Rough often recorded

forenames merely by an initial). The Colyns were among the 'chief families' of Romney and Walter Colyn was involved in the salvage of boats wrecked on Dungeness. He and another man named Colyn gave evidence in other cases of wreck and salvage. W. [Walter] and T. Colyn were two of four named jurors in an inquest into a boat wrecked at Dungeness and salved by John Pondfeld and others. Daniel Rough recorded several letters dealing with the wreck, salvors, value, etc. (*Rough's Register*, 55). J. Kidelman, W. Colyn's partner, held a messuage in St Nicholas' parish on the southeast, ie shore, side of the old High Street. Immediately to the south, again, lay holdings of two men who were bailiffs to Yarmouth in the 1370s. Their holdings were not messuages, but a plot of land (*placia terre*) and a tenement, and were perhaps located right on the shoreline.

An area of New Romney frequently mentioned in various 14th-century sources is 'le kidelmanhope' in St Nicholas' parish, where kiddle fishing took place. A messuage in 'le kidelmanhope' was said in 1375 to have formerly belonged to William Spite, kidelman (*Rough's Register*, 191). Like J. Kidelman above, William Spite was quite a wealthy man, assessed for the 1334/35 Lay Subsidy among the high payers such as merchants, including vintners. One H. de Lewys is recorded as having a kiddle net in St Nicholas' parish in 1358; he was part of the urban elite and owned the Jerusalem Tavern. Other men involved in kiddle fishing may of course have been less wealthy. The kidelmanhope would have included extensive areas for repairing nets, and drying or salting fish. Nevertheless it required good access to the town and other markets, and thus to roads such as the old High Street and Dymchurch Road.

New Romney's urban records of 1454 to 1482 indicate that vintners and fishermen remained the social elite of the town, even though their trade and industry were much declined, compared, say, to that of Dover. These records comprise court books, town accounts, taxation material, including maletolts, and testamentary evidence. Men described as fishermen and vintners acted as appraisers of the value of distrained goods, ie goods seized as security or reparation. Fishing tackle, especially anchors and nets, continued to be taken as distraints at that time, and also herrings (Bowdon 2003).

Fishing-related activities such as barrel-making and salting were also based mainly in St Nicholas' parish. Thomas Salter's surname suggests that trades involving the use of salt, particularly salting fish, were based in this area. Thomas Salter was extensively involved in debt and credit involving townsmen of Romney and Dover (cf. '*Bref de Dette*', letter concerning debt, *Rough's Register*, 64, 122, 178). He had an interest in rent from the tenement of Henry *de Ripe*, ie Henry 'of the sea bank'. Henry leased four houses in St Nicholas' parish in 1359. Salter himself also had a message and appurtenances in St Nicholas' parish, which apparently abutted a property on the beach.

People surnamed Coupere (cooper) made barrels for fish and/or for wine. In 1356 R. [Roger?] Coupere and his wife had a messuage on the beach, possibly not dwellings but associated with barrel-making. One R. Coupere, possibly different from the one just mentioned, was described as a vintner, and was accused with other merchants of selling overpriced wine. One of these two R. Couperes had tenements in both St Martin's and St Nicholas' parish. One J., son of J. Coupere, made an agreement with other parties about a *messuage en le Kidelmanhoppe* in St Nicholas' parish. John Coupere was first witness to a deed appointing a messenger to London in a trade dispute between two men, one of Romney, one of London (*Rough's Register*, 176, 263). This dispute may have related to fish or wine. Involvement in the fish trade was part of the activity of the town elite, for example Daniel Rough, the town clerk, was himself a 'fishmonger'. The 21 types of fish in which he dealt, and the many places, some distant, with which he traded are listed in fragments of the town accounts. The places included London, Hertford, Dover, Bury, St Alban's, Cambridge, Newmarket, Walsingham, Wallingford, Kirkby and Uxbridge. The fish supplied by Rough to his local customers and more distant markets were sprats, porpoise, salmon, haddock, lampreys, mackerel, codling, conger eel, shrimps, herring (red and white), whiting, whelks, tench, eels, oysters, crabs, trout, 'pickerelle' (young or small pike), stockfish (dried and cured cod or other fish) and gurnards (*Rough's Register*, x). Cod and porpoise were listed in the table of maletolts, cod being counted by the hundred and porpoise singly, in contrast to the vast amount of herring and sprats indicated by this table (*Rough's Register*, 30, 34). The town accounts have eight references between 1396 and 1519 to porpoises being caught, either one or two at a time, and 'sold out of town' or given to eminent people (HMC V, 535–553).

A discussion of the fish remains recovered from various coastal sites and inland consumer sites is presented below along with a discussion of the fish remains recovered from excavations at New Romney and the possible methods of catching these (see Riddler and Armitage, Chapter 11, below). Among the fish listed by Rough cod, gurnards and eel were recovered from the excavations, along with ling, plaice and ray.

Small boats were drawn up on the Romney beach when invasions threatened (*Rough's Register*, xli). As noted, fishing boats are likely also to have been drawn up on the beach. The construction, breaking and repair of vessels which is well evidenced at New Romney also took place in this area, as the finds from the Southlands School site, particularly iron rovenails, indicate (see Goodburn, Chapter 11, below). New Romney's table of maletolts, probably of Romney's greatest period of prosperity in the 12th and 13th centuries, indicates that boats or 'ships' were constructed at the town although the exact location is not specified. By ancient prescriptive right, a halfpenny was demanded from every ship's carpenter or shipwright per week that he worked; this was the same as from carpenters of houses. Twelve pence were demanded 'From the Master ship's carpenter for a new ferry boat or ship'.

In the early 14th century, boat breaking (ie careful dismantling for the re-use of materials) was recorded at New Romney, perhaps as the port shrank and shipbuilding transferred to Smallhythe and Sandwich. William Brekebot paid 10s 8d to the Lay Subsidy of 1334/5 in New Romney as one of the 'men of the liberty of the Cinque Ports' (*Lay Subsidy* 145–146,172). The surname Brekebot refers to boat breaking, and such descriptive names are good evidence for occupational activity in this locality in this period. Ship repair, as at Smallhythe, was no doubt of great importance since boats were frequently wrecked either accidentally or on purpose on the coast around Romney, particularly at Dungeness, and men of New Romney were involved in both licensed piracy and salvage.

Maritime and related activities are thus documented at New Romney in the 14th century, particularly in the long northeast extension of St Nicholas' parish in the vicinity of the Southlands School site. This part of New Romney did not contain high-quality stone civic, ecclesiastical or mercantile medieval buildings of the type found near St Nicholas' Church and in St Lawrence's parish, nor did it contain burgage plots of the type found along the re-planned new High Street.

George Lane: milling, tanning and salting

The Southlands School site was bounded on the southwest by George Lane, which probably took its name from one Lawrence Jorge (George), who owned one or two messuages in New Romney in 1354. The vicinity of George Lane was the location of activities requiring extensive amounts of land and where medieval buildings were ephemeral, characteristic of those connected with tanning, milling, salting and the drying or mending of fishing-nets. One of Lawrence Jorge's messuages was adjacent to the Tanhous in St Martin's parish. This Tanhous was held in 1363 by a miller, John Duddyngherst. A maletolt was imposed on bark for tanning at an early period. Milling had been taking place in this area for some years, and indeed continued to do so into the 19th century. On the other side of the Tanhous in St Martin's parish from Jorge's messuage lay the messuage of John *de Ripe*, ie John 'of the sea bank' (1363). William *de Rype* had an interest in a messuage in St Martin's parish, possibly the same one, in 1374 (*Rough's Register* 30, 67, 161, 190).

The general location of Jorge's messuage(s) at the points where St Martin's and St Nicholas' parishes met can be established by the detail of property transactions, and from the reconstruction of the parishes. One messuage was in St Martin's parish, abutting land of the Madekyn family. J. Maydekyn was 'Master of La Nicholas of Romney' in 1350. This boat was used for carrying a cargo of salt, apparently to New Winchelsea (*Rough's Register*, 93, n.2).

Lawrence Jorge's activities exemplify some features of shipping at New Romney in the mid-14th century. Jorge was bailiff to a ship's master, Lucas Frensch, ship's master (*mestre de le batel Nicholas Seforde de Romene, Rough's Register*, 265). Nicholas Seforde's descendant, W. Seforde de Romene, was bailiff to Yarmouth in 1380, indicating his involvement in the herring fishing controlled by Romney. Seforde was 'head inn-keeper' in Romney, and its MP in 1384–1385 (*Rough's Register* xliv–xlv, 201, n.2, 203). Lucas Frensch, the ship's master, may also have been of Romney, but his name suggests his origins in France, and his role in cross-Channel traffic. Lawrence Jorge was also serjeant to Sir Richard de Totisham, 'an admiral in charge of seven men-of-war operating off the coasts of Normandy and Poitou', and an important royal representative in shipping goods to Calais. Lawrence Jorge organised the shipping of 21 quarters of oats, and on one occasion he accounted to Sir Richard de Totisham at the Helmes by Romney (*Le Hilmys iuxta Romene, Rough's Register*, xxix, 243, 265). Comparison with the evidence of the town accounts of the end of the century (below) suggests that Totisham would have anchored in a vessel off the coast near New Romney, with Jorge going out in a smaller boat through the silting and sandbanks obstructing the entrance to the port of Romney.

St Lawrence's Parish

The location and bounds of the parish of St Lawrence are well established from the historical sources. Trading and merchant activity were concentrated in the port area on the southwest side of the town when the port flourished in the 11th to 13th centuries. Thus St Lawrence's parish, on the port side, was the commercial quarter, where the main concentration of burgage plots ran back from the new High Street.

Economic activities or occupations at New Romney indicated in the table of maletolts include vintners, pastry cooks, glovers, cutlers, goldsmiths and coiners (*Rough's Register*, 28–35). Glover became an occupational surname associated with the town (Draper 2003, 132). Between *c.* 1070 and *c.* 1240 Jewish inhabitants of some of the larger medieval towns were involved, alongside Christians, in dealing in plate and bullion, exchanging foreign coins, money lending and goldsmithing, not least because Jews were banned from most artisanal occupations (Stacey 1995, 82–93; Hunt and Murray 1999, 36). The presence of Jews in smaller towns including the Cinque Ports is apparently little studied, although the money changing and money lending in which they were concerned would have been necessary and vital to trade in these ports (cf. Stacey 1995, 86). However, it can be noted that the existence of Jewish inhabitants is indicated at Rye and New Winchelsea from the late 12th century (Homan 1949, 29; East Sussex record office (ESRO), RYE/133/1, RYE/136/2; CCA DCc CA R69, DCc CA A171). In New Romney the residents of the town in the 1280s included one man who was apparently Jewish, or had Jewish forebears, William, son of John Moses. He was a tenant in Frencheshop in the town centre. In 1355, a house in Spitelstreet (Spitalfield Lane), in St Lawrence's parish, belonged to another John Moses (Moises). This may indicate the connection of the Jewish residents of New Romney with the commercial quarter of the town

(*Rough's Register*, 87). To judge from surname evidence, there were apparently few Jews in the town, although this is not surprising given its relatively small size. The presence of goldsmiths at New Romney is attested by the table of maletolts and a 14th-century surname (above), although the goldsmiths were not necessarily Jewish.

At this early period vintners may have been located between the commercial centre in St Lawrence's parish and the southwest part of St Nicholas' parish. This area included a stone house of *c.* 1300 with what has been suggested as an undercroft or cellar storage, at the Assembly Rooms, Church Approach (Parkin 1973, 121; Harris 1992, 5). Such undercrofts or cellars were built in great numbers in New Winchelsea from the 1290s, where the local wine trade was much more significant than at New Romney.

The meat, poultry, butter and hemp markets were held in St Lawrence's parish (*Rough's Register*, xxxvii). There were thirteen butchers and their shambles in the town in 1340 assessed for a local tax (Boys 1792, 799). Ten butchers paid the local trading tax in 1414 as opposed to the thirteen earlier, suggesting a decline in the town's trade, probably precipitated at least partly by population reduction (HMC V, 539). Several stalls are mentioned in St Lawrence's parish in an indenture of 1398; one was in Spitelstreet, which may refer either to the leper Hospital or St John's Hospital (HMC V, 534).

Hemp was produced and processed locally. It was subject to a maletolt at New Romney by the early 13th century, and there was a 'piece of land' on which hemp was grown in St Lawrence's parish in the mid- to late 14th century (*Rough's Register*, 28–29, 177). A hemp-retting pit has also been identified on the Dungeness Foreland near Lydd, dated to between AD 1000–1400 and located *c.* 2.5 miles (4km) south southwest of New Romney (Schofield and Waller 2005, 715–726). The hemp fibre, which was produced locally, was almost certainly meant for use in rope for ships' rigging. There were also two fields called Retting land in Scotney manor to the southwest of Lydd, one of 19 acres, the other of 10 acres, known in the mid- and late 15th century (All Souls College Oxford, map of the manor of Scotney in the parishes of Lydd and Broomhill, by Thomas Clerke of Stamford, 1588/89). In 1454–1455 ditches were being scoured '*apud* [at] Retyngg' lond'. Retting was also known as rotting (Middle English Dictionary, University of Michigan quod.lib.umich.edu/m/med/). In 1476/77 'tenyng', probably tugging up or clearing undergrowth, was being carried out by 'the strete at Rotyngsland'. In 1479/80 posts and rails were bought for making an enclosure there; a payment was made of 6d 'for carayge of the sayd posts and reylys from ~~Wyneway~~ [sic] Jorysgote unto Rotyngysland'. These references might suggest that this location was in disuse for hemp retting by this period (Bodleian Library Ms. DD All Souls c 323, c 321.12, c 322.15). However, hemp was apparently still grown in Lydd in the 16th century, and a ropemaker and ropewalk, where rope was laid out, also existed there at that period (Sweetinburgh 2008, 17).

The medieval haven and the early trade in wool, hides and fells in St Lawrence's parish

The northeast side of the entrance to the medieval haven of New Romney in the 11th and 12th centuries in the area where Lydd Road meets St John's Road and the western end of High Street is the probable location of quays or wharves in the 13th century. Their exact location in relation to the position of the junction of the current Lydd Road and Church Road is not yet fully established; however the plot for a quay granted in 1276 to Mathew de Horne, a merchant or trader (below), may have been here.

The size of the quayside at New Romney indicated by the street layout suggests that there would have been far fewer quays or wharves than the 79 harbour plots for merchants at New Winchelsea (Martin 1999, 44). Customs accounts of the late 13th century indicate New Winchelsea was much more important than New Romney as a trading centre by this time, when the physical evidence shows that the port of Romney was already silting up (Pelham 1932, 218–228; Eddison 2002, 137); Dover and Sandwich similarly had much more significant proportions of the wool export trade than New Romney. In the late 13th century Romney merchants such as William de Brochulle and Nicholas Barrock may have specialised in the export of wool-fells, rather than wool or hides as the other towns did. A member of the Barrock family owned land on the port side of New Romney, near the leper Hospital, which had been founded *c.* 1170 (*Rough's Register*, 272–274). The wool trade in Kent in the late 13th century was dominated by English merchants but the carrying trade by alien merchants. In contrast alien merchants were much more important in the east Coast ports, although there were hardly any operating from ports of southwest England. Smuggling by the small number of known New Romney merchants increased after duty on wool was raised from 6s 8d to £2 a sack between 1294 and 1297 (Pelham 1932, 227). The export of wool, leather and wool-fells was prohibited under Edward III (1327–1377) with the commencement of prolonged war with France. Wool-fells were a distinctive item in New Romney's exports from the 13th century and tanning a known activity there. Two vessels of Flemish merchants probably exporting goods for English merchants, including wool and leathertan were captured by Romney men in 1358 (*Rough's Register*, 139–140). Either from the

medieval period or perhaps in response to the higher duties and greater export restrictions of the mid-16th century, wool-fells and hides, as opposed to wool, may have been a major component of smuggling from the eastern (Dymchurch) side of the town. In 1593 a crown agent stated that 'not a tenth part' of the leather, grain and other prohibited wares exported from Kent and Sussex had been legally declared (Jones 2001, 16, 35).

In 1276 Mathew de Horne was granted a piece of land in the port of Romney by Edward I on which to construct a quay (*Cal. Feet of Fines [Henry III]*, 113, 118, 319). This may have been in the projected port location on the west side of St Lawrence's parish where it is envisaged that the merchant quays existed (see Fig. 17). The Horne family of Appledore were concerned with law, justice and administration on Romney Marsh and elsewhere in Kent in the 13th century (Draper 2003, 192). The Hornes rose to the status of gentry or esquire by the late 14th century (Webster 1984, 226, 229). The grant to Mathew de Horne in 1276 suggests that their local status and wealth was partly built on the merchant trade. The grant may have been made in response to the building of New Winchelsea and its merchant quays, which the Horne family is likely to have perceived as threatening its economic interests at New Romney. This family owned an early stone house *c.* 1.2 miles (2km) northeast of Appledore, now called Horne's Place. This stood on a promontory with possible water access. Appledore itself grew and flourished as a small market town on the River Rother in the 13th century. Appledore lay *c.* 7 miles (11km) inland from New Romney and had a jetty of the late 12th or 13th century which is likely to have been used 'mainly for local Appledore river trade to and from the port of Romney, but it could also have been used by sea-going coastal vessels' at this time (Burke 2004, 3).

There were changes to commercial activity in New Romney as the town's prosperity faded. Perhaps to protect its own markets, in 1397–1398 the town tried to have closed down what it deemed 'unlawful markets' locally at Brookland and Lydd, even though the one at Lydd was of early origin and had a charter (McLain 1997, 99). A probable late 12th-century fair at Brookland evidenced by finds of seal dies is not known later and was perhaps replaced by the New Romney fair (Draper 2005, 8). Hasted (1797–1801, vol. 8, 449–450) recorded only a Saturday market in the town, and the yearly fair on 21 August.

Chapter 4 The Port, Quays, Watercourses, Sea Defences and Salt Manufacture

Old and New Romney

In Domesday Book the term Romenel is used for Romney. Gardiner (1994, 329) addressed the question of the identification of Romenel with Old or New Romney, and its relationship with the port. Nowadays Old Romney is a small village approximately 2 miles (3km) west of New Romney. The terms Old and New were sometimes applied to the two separate settlements from the mid-12th century (Gardiner 1994, 339).

Was Old Romney 'the site of a Saxo-Norman port' replaced by New Romney as the estuary on which Old Romney stood silted up, as Brooks (1988) and Tatton-Brown (1989) argue? This estuary, both Tatton-Brown and Gardiner suggested, was formed by the conjunction of two watercourses close to Old Romney. One was a watercourse running from as far inland as Brenzett to New Romney, 'presumably the river known as He or Rhee' and shown on the Soil Survey map (Gardiner 1994, 329), which equates to the Rumenesea (see below). The other was 'the River Rother flowing along an earlier course'. These two watercourses, once joined, 'broadened into a wider estuary before passing to the south of New Romney' (Gardiner 1994, 329–330) and forming its haven (see Fig. 18 and Fig. 11).

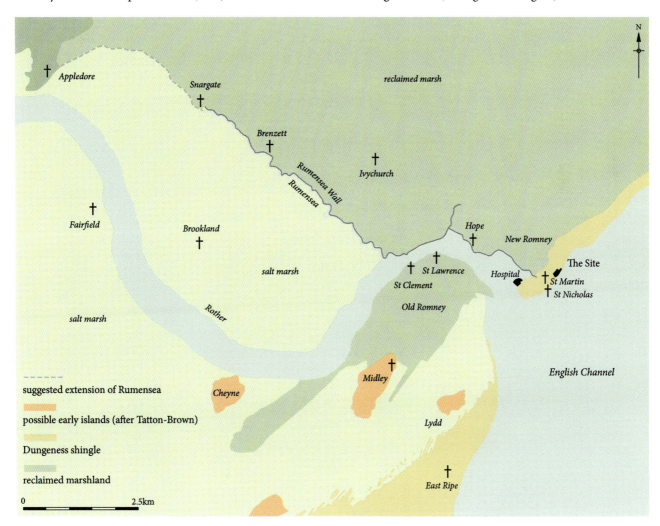

Fig. 18   Projected courses of the Rivers Rother and Rumensea from Appledore to New Romney (based on Tatton-Brown 1988 and Eddison and Draper 1997) (scale 1:80 000)

Gardiner (1994, 344–345) has made preliminary and tentative arguments that Old Romney was not the precursor of New Romney as a port, unless this occurred before the mid-11th century. He prefers the argument that Old Romney is a 'shrunken medieval village', although allows that the presence of 'up to' three parish churches at Old Romney does not fit easily with this interpretation (Gardiner 1994, 329, 344–345). Further research on this, and also on whether Old Romney had been superseded by New Romney before the late 11th century, therefore seemed appropriate (Gardiner 1994, 344–345). In fact the suggestion of up to three parish churches at Old Romney seems problematic. The standing parish church at Old Romney is dedicated to St Clement (Fig. 18, Fig. 19) (not to St Leonard, Gardiner 1994, 330, cf. 345). Field walking took place at one of the two oval ditched enclosures or moated sites at Old Romney said to be marked on the tithe map as St John's Field and otherwise known as St John's Glebe (Gardiner 1994, 330; Bradshaw 1970, 179). These two moated sites were in fact within New Romney parish as recorded on its tithe map, the parish extending right up to Old Romney. Old Romney parish and its church of St Clement lay just to the south of the two moated sites, across Five Vents Lane. Interpretation of these moated sites at St John's Field or Glebe was not easy but they may have been part of an area of isolated farmsteads (Gardiner 1994, 337, 344). The name St John's perhaps suggests that the area belonged to the Hospital of St John which itself was located in the town of New Romney. It can possibly be identified with the 7.5 acres of land on Romney Marsh belonging to the Hospital, which are recorded in 1457 (Draper 2003, 131–132).

Field walking was undertaken to investigate 'the supposed sites of St Michael and St Lawrence' immediately to the north and northeast of Old Romney (Gardiner 1994, 332). These sites were again within New Romney parish. They are marked on the New Romney tithe map only as St Michael's Church Yard and St Lawrence's (see Fig. 17). Archaeological investigation found evidence for 'masonry structures and for burials' (Gardiner 1994, 345) but their status as parish churches is dubious. *Laurenti circe* is listed in Domesday Monachorum, which is possibly of *c.* 1130 but records pre-Conquest churches. This church is one of those subordinate to Lympne and on Romney Marsh (Ward 1933). *Laurenti circe* may refer to a church at (Old) Romney, which was later replaced by the church dedicated to St Lawrence which existed at New Romney. St Lawrence's was described as a vill (a township or administrative unit) in the town in 1271 (*Cal. Feet of Fines [Henry III]*, 385).

As Gardiner (1994, 344) noted, the problems of interpreting the settlement of Old Romney as a possible Saxo-Norman port are intractable, and it is possible that before the 12th century a 'langport' or longport did stretch down the estuary between Old Romney and what became the town of New Romney, as Brooks (1988) and

Fig. 19   St Clement's Church in Old Romney

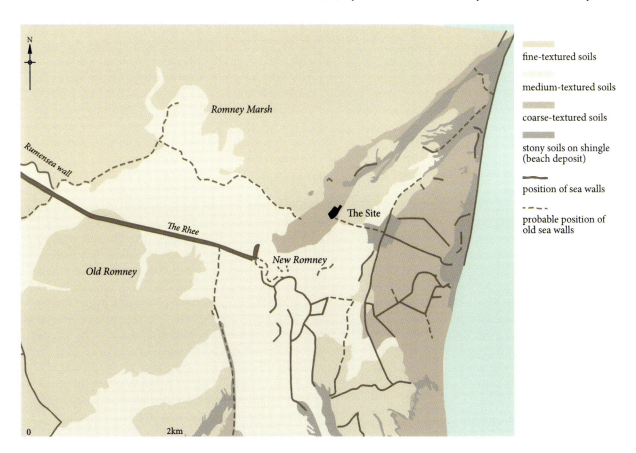

Fig. 20   Location of former sea walls (based on Green *et al.* 1966) in relation to the early 14th-century Rhee Canal and modern coastline (scale 1:50 000)

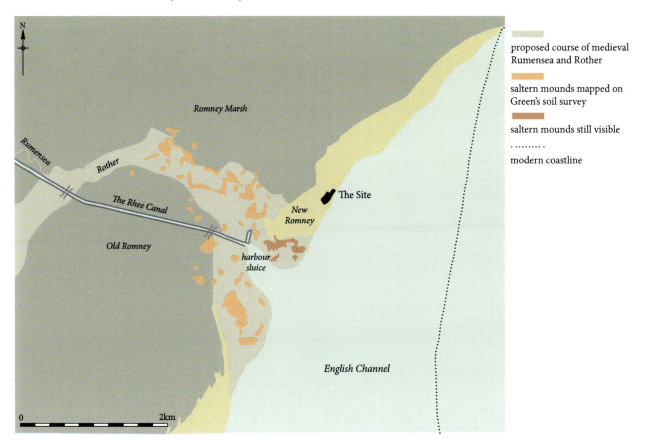

Fig. 21   Remains of medieval saltern mounds around New Romney from unpublished maps made in connection with Green *et al.* (1966) in relation to the proposed earlier courses of the Rother and Rumensea, the Rhee Canal and medieval coastline (scale 1:50 000)

Tatton-Brown (1988) suggest. From the eleventh century activity in ports (fishing and trading) tended to move down estuaries in Sussex with, for example, Shoreham replacing Steyning, and Seaford replacing Lewes. Early Romney should be seen in this light (M. Gardiner, pers. comm.) and cannot be simply identified as a conventional category of town or port. Service at sea, ie the provision of men and ships, for which Romney, along with Dover and Sandwich, received their privileges is recorded by the reign of Edward the Confessor (1042/3–1066, *Domesday Book: Kent*, D2; 5,178; 2, 2). The Domesday Book references were probably to the entire unit of holdings, rights and privileges, which made up Romenel as it had developed by that period. The first evidence for the 'urban' nature of Romney seems to be in the 11th century when minting of coins took place there (Gardiner 1994, 339). The mid-12th-century date of St Nicholas' Church, New Romney (Harris 1990, 6–7) indicates that it was New rather than Old Romney which was then the area of settlement of growing significance, with its port functions. It should also be noted that on many occasions throughout the medieval period, Romney or Romenel was not referred to as Old or New Romney, but as part of the same entity, for example in *Rough's Register* in the mid to late 14th century.

The Rumensea: a watercourse and associated wall

Allen (2002) made notable arguments about the Rumensea Wall and the watercourse of the same name. Eddison (2002) and Allen (2002, 122) have disagreed profoundly about the significance of this watercourse, its relationship to the later Rhee (see Fig. 21) and, by implication, to former courses of the Rother. The Rumenesea Wall is a sinuous, possibly Saxon, embankment which lies to the northeast of the later Rhee canal. The Rumenesea Wall ran from near Old Romney to Snargate, and possibly beyond to Appledore (see Fig. 18). It was 'probably constructed in Saxon times as the defining boundary between the reclamations on Romney Marsh proper and the extensive salt marshes which then stretched away to the southwest' (Eddison 2000, 83, quoted by Allen 2002, 124). Allen (2002, 124) made the notable suggestion that the Rumenesea Wall 'appeared to form a "bridging bank" …rooted in the high coastal barrier (New Romney) at one end and the Wealden scarp' at Appledore at the other. It was thus the earliest, and a major, sea defence in this part of the Marsh, supplemented by 'a contemporaneous coastal barrier' at New Romney and 'probably other engineered banks'. Important evidence is provided by the sea walls and probable sea walls mapped by Green, which permitted a settled and farmed landscape by, if not before, the Saxon period (Fig. 20) (Green *et al.* 1966; Allen 2002, 121, 124). At present, as argued by Allen (2002, 125) 'only circumstantial evidence dates the Rumenesea Wall to Saxon times' and further studies of the physical evidence are required to establish a more secure dating.

To the southwestern side of the Rumenesea Wall is a similarly sinuous watercourse (Allen 2002, 122). This was known as the Rumenesea, ie Rumenee, or river, as Brooks (1988, 98, fig 8.6) has clearly set out from early charter evidence and mapped. It was later known as the Yokes or New Sewer, and was adapted for the post-medieval drainage of Romney Marsh, with associated alterations to its depth and width (Allen 2002, 122; Eddison 2002, 132). Allen (2002, 122) suggested that the Rumenesea may have run westwards beyond Snargate to Appledore on an 'irregular, almost meandering course' preserved in the upper part of the later Rhee Wall or Canal; he suggested the Rumenesea Wall was apparently 'either subsumed into, or lay parallel with, the Rhee Wall' (Allen 2002, 125). Furthermore he suggested that the Rumenesea was an active tidal system prior to the construction of the Rhee Wall and could have been used for shallow draft boats of up to 10m in length bringing in beach cobbles, Ashdown sandstone boulders and flints for church construction on parts of the Marsh near this tidal watercourse (Allen 2002, 123). This church construction referred to was presumably during the 11th to 13th centuries.

The Rumenesea may therefore have been an early exit of the tidal Rother running from the Appledore area to its estuary near Old Romney. The 'geomorphological evidence for the scale of the waterway' was that it could have been about 30m wide at Old Romney reducing to 10m wide at Snargate (Allen 2002, 123). However, current geomorphological research suggests that the main channel of the Rother in the period during which the port of Romenal originated and flourished ran as a wide course southeast from the Snargate area, around Brookland then south towards Cheyne Court (see Fig. 11, Fig. 18). It is likely but not certain that this channel then continued northeast to Old Romney then New Romney and provided the route for the Rother to the English Channel at Romney (Long *et al.* 2007, 201–202), perhaps joined by the much smaller Rumensea to form the haven of Romney as Gardiner (1994) and Tatton-Brown (1988) suggested.

The estuary and haven at Romney

The deeds of the leper Hospital of New Romney in the early 13th century suggest that at that period the entrance to the haven was close to the hospital. There was a tidal flow against a wall, which was built on the west side or up against part of that hospital in Spitalfield Lane. This location appears to be confirmed by the town accounts and includes the site of what is marked by Tatton-Brown (1988, fig. 9.1) as the 'harbour sluice' (1409–1413)' (Fig. 21). Eddison (2002, fig. 9.6) suggested that the entrance to this haven from the sea was perhaps just under a third of a mile (0.5km) wide.

Recent work by Martin and Martin (2004) on New Winchelsea and an examination of the evidence about salt making at New Romney indicates the nature of the haven and the river estuary or tidal inlet. This suggests that at New Romney in the late 12th and early 13th centuries there may have been a navigable channel in the estuary forming the haven, with mud flats or salt marsh alongside (Fig. 21). Although New Winchelsea differed from New

Romney in that it was newly established in the 1280s and was sited on a river estuary rather than having both a river estuary (tidal inlet) and a beachfront, it suffered similar significant problems of access within a short period. The main anchorage at New Winchelsea was the Brede river estuary, which was quite wide, mostly 'tidal mud flats and salt marsh…overflowed only at high tides', in comparison 'the primary navigable channel was perhaps quite narrow' (Martin and Martin 2004, 36). Within a short time at New Winchelsea significant problems of access occurred. By 1344/5, 33 of 79 documented merchant quay plots laid out along the estuary had been deserted as waterborne access became problematic and those remaining were grouped where that access may still have been viable. Some of these harbour plots did have private wharves and quays but there was also a nearby common quay belonging to the town (Martin and Martin 2004, 36–38, fig. 4.2). The evidence for salt making (below) at New Romney suggests the possibility that the wide estuary of the Rother (indicated on Fig. 21) had become a similar narrow channel with tidal mud flats or salt marshes on either side.

The nature of the Romney haven and navigable channel in the 12th to 14th centuries is linked to its apparent obstruction by silt and/or sand, and to the suggested extension of the Rhee canal from Old to New Romney in *c.* 1258 in an effort to remove that obstruction. There is a record in the *Calendar of Patent Rolls* of 1258 which Tatton-Brown (1988) and later Eddison (2002) have taken to describe as an 'extension' of a canal (the Rhee) from Old Romney to the port of New Romney soon after 1258, the first part of the Rhee having been constructed sometime after 1190. The model of the building of the Rhee canal from Appledore to New Romney in the late 12th and 13th centuries by Eddison (2002, 131) depends strongly on two points: that Romney Marsh was (only) exposed to storm activity from the 13th century and that there was a shingle barrier across Rye Bay which was not finally broken asunder until 1287–1288. However, the absence of documentary sources for earlier storm activity does not mean that it did not occur, and the most recent geomorphological research demonstrates that in the Rye Bay area the tides penetrated through the shingle barrier about AD 700–800 rather than in the so-called period of stormy activity in the 13th century (Long *et al.* 2007, 203). This accords with the evidence of the early existence of Old Winchelsea and Rye (Gardiner 2000). Some aspects of Eddison's model of the building of the Rhee, which bear on the haven or port of Romney may therefore need re-examination. There is no documentary evidence of the building of what was described as the first two stages of the Rhee, although the interpretation of the landscape evidence and maps is important. This may indicate that there were two preliminary stages in the construction of the Rhee by *c.* 1190 (Eddison 2002, 129, 135, 136). It can also be noted that the 1258 Patent Roll entry on which the model depends is complex, referring for example both to the need to remove obstructions in the old course of the river of Newenden on which the port of Rumenal was founded as well as the making of a new course.

Salt making at New Romney and the maintenance of the 'harbour sluice'

Salt making is known at or near New Romney from the time of Edward the Confessor. In 1086 seven salt houses at a value of 8s 9d were recorded under one of the four manors in or linked to Romney, that of Langport (*Domesday Book: Kent*, 2:43). Physical evidence suggests that salt production at New Romney was of considerable importance, with concentrations in two areas: one to the west of the town and the other southwest beyond the exit of the haven (Fig. 21). This is compatible with the historical evidence of salt making near the projected location of quays near the intersection of Lydd Road and St John's Road by the 13th century. Caldecot, perhaps another saltcote, was *c.* 1 mile (1.5km) to the southwest of the harbour sluice, (Tatton-Brown 1988, fig. 9.1). Sandy hummocks or mounds near Lydd road, to the west of St John's Hospital, have been identified as possible remnants of salt making (J. Eddison, pers. comm.). The location of the saltern mounds has been mapped using information based on Green's preliminary sketches for the Soil Survey, which recorded these mounds (Green *et al.* 1966). The sketches record the mounds extensively to the northwest of the town within the area inside the haven mapped by Eddison (2002) and Tatton-Brown (1988, fig. 9.1). Here the location of the mounds is shown in relation to the proposed maximum extent of the tidal estuary of the Rother as defined above (see Fig. 18) as well as the courses of the Rumensea and of the Rhee canal and its extension to the harbour sluice, constructed in the early 15th century. Clearly there are inherent problems with mapping the mounds in relation to the estuary; partly as the process of silting and canalisation changed the appearance of this area over time and also as salt manufacture was taking place apparently from the 11th century, if not earlier, and on into the 15th century.

In the late 13th century the Brethren of the Leper Hospital of St John are recorded as owing half a seam of salt as rent to the Archbishop of Canterbury, in Archbishop Pecham's survey of the Bailiwick of Aldington of 1283–85 (*Pecham's Survey*, 242). Other individuals owed salt rents from holdings on the north or northwest side of New Romney, including Philip Holingbrok, a townsman of New Romney, who owed two seams, and Elias Croche, possibly from a merchant family with a holding in St Lawrence's parish, who similarly owed two seams (*Rough's Register*, 66–67, 182). A seam of any commodity was a load capable of being carried by a beast of burden or a person, so variable in volume (Middle English Dictionary, University of Michigan). Other individuals owing salt were the heirs of Robert Pere who owed 1.5 seams, 1 bushel, Nicholas Barrock, a 13th-century merchant, and his associates who owed 6.5 seams, and the heirs of John Barrock who owed 2 seams, 1.5 bushels. The rector of Hope All Saints parish, north of New Romney, also owed 2 seams of salt. Eight other people or groups including some 'of Romney' were also listed as owing salt rents, mostly similar amounts to the above, but cannot be

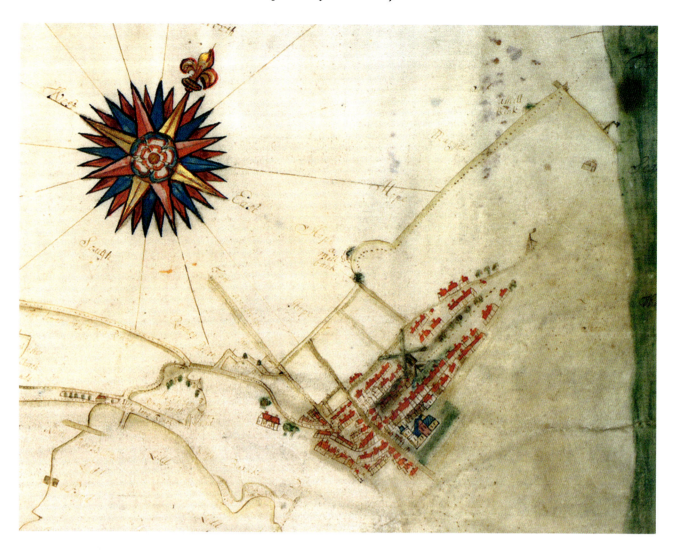

Fig. 22   Detail from map of the liberty of New Romney 1683 (reproduced by kind permission of the East Kent Archives Office)

further identified. Only one group, the heirs of Roger Blund, were due to pay an amount substantially larger, 14.5 seams.

In total in 1283–1285 the Archbishop was due rents of salt of 47.5 seams and 14.5 bushels, approximately 50 seams. In 1468 one seam of white salt was paid for the rent of a salt-pit by John Hamon, possibly 'opposite High Mill'. If an equivalent rate was paid earlier, it indicates that the Archbishop was receiving rents from approximately 50 salt-pits (HMC V, 545).

Some evidence of salt making between the late 14th to the mid-15th centuries comes from the town accounts, which survive in a series from the 1380s. These accounts also suggest that at a period of extensive work to keep the haven open, salt making was taking place close by, at a 'saltcote' owned by the town. This suggests that salt making took place alongside the harbour channel, which was dug out in an attempt to keep it open for vessels. Some details are as follows: in 1410 carpenters and labourers were paid 10s for drawing timber to the [harbour] sluice near Geffes Saltcote; in 1412 William Thwoyt and assistants were paid £5 4s 2 ½d for 'digging & walling, in making the wall around Jeffes Saltcote, and for digging opposite the Qwenehalle [location unknown]

and other days' work… about the Sluice' (HMC V, 538). There were extensive works at this time on the sluice, again presumably the harbour sluice. In 1445 John Colkyn labourer was paid 10s, a large amount maybe representing 25–30 days' work, for 'digging in the channel, near Saltcote' (HMC V, 542). In 1457 John Portere paid 5s rent to town for the saltcote. Clearly this saltcote belonged to the town and so was presumably in or near the harbour as in the previous references (HMC V, 544).

References to the harbour sluice in the 15th century are as follows. In 1438 John Legge paid 2s for pasture called 'the Horssho' (HMC V, 542). A feature which appears to be the 'Horssho', ie horseshoe, was mapped by Tatton-Brown (1988, fig. 9.1) as the 'Harbour Sluice (1409–1413)' but unfortunately no references for this were given. As mapped by Tatton-Brown this harbour sluice was immediately south of the lands of the leper Hospital of the Blessed Stephen and Thomas. It appears that until 1413 the town was endeavouring to keep open the entrance of the channel into the haven. However, by 1438 that sluice was, as noted, being used for pasture and, like the Rhee, was clearly no longer functioning. In 1454 2s rent was paid for the Rhee land between the walls of the silted-up Rhee canal near the port, from the Horssho to Longbrigge, near

Cotehelle, possibly saltcotehill (HMC V, 543). Another reference in the town accounts (1458) is to pasture rented out by the town between Islesbridge and this 'horseshoe' or former harbour sluice (HMC V, 544). Islesbridge was apparently the location of another sluice at the end of the Rhee extension (Tatton-Brown 1988, fig. 9.1; Eddison 2002, fig. 9.6).

A wooden bridge had been made or repaired over the Rother at Ille in 1388. This was Isles bridge between Old Romney and New Romney on the south side of the haven and suggests that the Rother outlet into the haven was narrow enough to be bridged by then. Men were paid for 'groynynge' this bridge in 1389. At this time, efforts were being made to prevent the obstruction of the haven by ballast from vessels. In 1391 a Margate man was bound over not to throw sand, etc, into the harbour of Romney and in 1396 a man of Reading in Tenterden parish, which lay on the Rother a little east of Smallhythe, was forbidden to throw ballast or sand in the haven. A series of efforts to renew the harbour were begun, with for example £4 16s 6d paid in 1401 for 'making and digging the new harbour' [*novum portum*] (HMC V, 533–536).

Between the late 1380s and the 1430s the town paid for work on the sluices at Snargate on the Rhee, and the harbour entrance, including paying £100 for the expertise of a 'Hollander', and for John Rone to come from Flanders to attend to the sluice. After the harbour sluice ceased to exist, perhaps by 1413, it should probably be envisaged that what remained of the harbour lay only to the east of that point. The harbour entrance/exit channel, the *cursum aque maris*, had been increasingly diverted from that area to the northeast past St Nicholas' Church and ultimately towards the Helmes, or sand dunes to the north and east of the town, in the later 14th century (below). In 1452 the house belonging to Romney at Snargate associated with the operation of the sluice there was finally sold (HMC V, 533–543).

The end of the haven

In 1468–1471, attention was paid to setting booms apparently across the entrance to the harbour (HMC V, 545). This may have been for a similar purpose as at Rye in 1636 when 'booms, buoys and light had to be set up to guide shipping around the "great bar" of sand which, according to Rye's "best experienced seamen" in 1638 had risen "not less than four feet" within the preceding four years' (Hipkin 1995a, 146). In 1493 booms were carried and laid at the New Romney haven (HMC V, 548).

In 1469 the town 'paid men for scrutiny of the Helmes, for carrying water off the marsh'. This suggests that the watercourse running through the haven or port was draining out via the Helmes area by that time. However, it indicates concern about even that watercourse and again in 1488 a survey of the common watercourse of the Helmes was made (HMC V, 545, 548).

Final efforts to preserve a haven of some kind were made at the end of the 15th and at the start of the 16th centuries. In 1497 the enormous sum of £60 was paid for mending the haven. In 1514 Robert Dunney was paid 2s to view the haven and in 1517 work began on the 'old haven' and there was a voluntary levy 'for provyng of the dykes of the haven' (HMC V, 549–550, 552). Dunney came from a Smallhythe shipbuilding family with land next to the River Rother where shipbuilding had taken place until the mid-16th century (James *et al.* 2005, 17, 25, 36, 40, 50, 57). Nevertheless action was ultimately unsuccessful. In 1518/19 the course of water known as the 'Havene stremes' was leased out for a small sum, and probably consisted of channels running through a sandy silted bay to the east of the town, as a map of New Romney in 1683 (formerly held in the Town Hall) shows (see Fig. 22). It is clear from the map that the harbour and water-access is long gone and the settlement has become virtually land-locked.

Chapter 5 Ship Service, Piracy, Local and Continental Trade

From the 1230s royal instructions to individuals and towns including the Cinque Ports were enrolled on the Patent Rolls and Close Rolls. In the 13th century these instructions or mandates indicate the use of the haven at New Romney, the relative importance of towns belonging to the Cinque Port confederation, the nature and size of their vessels, and the use made of the Ports' ship service by Henry III (ruled 1216–1272).

Merchants and Pirates

In the 1230s the Ports' ship service was mainly used for the protection of merchants, including that against piratical actions. Several instances are recorded where ships from Romney were part of a number called upon from the Cinque Ports to provide defence or protection for the King's Men on their voyages.

In May 1234 the king required ship service from the Cinque Ports and on this occasion asked 'the barons of the port of Hastinges to have at Portesmuth ten good ships of their service due to the king fitted out and furnished with good mariners and other necessaries, to be in the said port by Sunday before Ascension, to cross with the king's people whom he is about to send to Brittany'. Five ships each were requested from Hythe and Romney, the full number each provided at this time (*CPR 1232–1247, 18 [Henry III]*, 44), although the king did not always require the 'whole service' of the Cinque Ports, ie all the vessels they could be called upon to provide. On 10 February 1235 he made a 'request' to the barons of Winchelsea and of Rye to let Stephen Aylard and William Beufiz have from each port 'two good ships well fitted out (attilatas) to go on the king's service, whither they are enjoined'. This was presumably a request rather than an instruction because these men were not royal, and the Ports might have resented a demand to transport them. The request made the point that these two men were on the king's service (*CPR 1232–1247, 19 [Henry III]*, 92). The king also wished other ports, and not just the Cinque Ports, to 'go on the king's service with the said Stephen and William'. These ports, less likely to be willing to do so, were instructed in no uncertain terms:

'by their fealty as they love their life and limbs and the king's honour and their own, to fit out a good sound ship and to furnish it with good people, at least 40 men,

and with arms and victuals sufficient for 40 days, at their own cost… and to go with the first favourable wind to the port of Winchelsee ready and furnished'.

Dover, Hythe, Sandwich and Romney were each to provide one ship in this way. The men of Dunwich, an important Suffolk port, were ordered to provide two ships, and 'the good men of Southampton' one ship.

War, Transport and Ceremony

Specific requests were made to the Cinque Ports at the time of the Saintonge War with France (1241–1242), and the subsequent years of fighting over 'English possessions' there until 1259, for 'all the good galleys' that they could provide so that 'they can grieve the king's enemies by sea and land so long as the war lasts with France' (*CPR 1232–1247, 18 [Henry III]*, 64.). This was addressed to Winchelsea, Dover, Hastings, Rye, Sandwich and Hythe; Romney's omission may indicate it did not have suitable galleys to provide or may merely be an oversight. The request probably goes beyond what was required by ship service and on similar occasions the king specifically stated that he would arrange payment for the crews of the ships (eg, *CPR 1232–1247, 26 [Henry III]*, 303; *CPR 1232–1247, 19 [Henry III]*, 125, in reference to Winchelsea).

Some of the king's mandates indicate the size of the vessels, for example that of March 28 1242 'to have ready the whole service due of ships from their port at Portesmue (Portsmouth) on Palm Sunday to go on the king's service, as well as the other ships arrested in their port against the king's passage capable of carrying sixteen horses or more on the same day' (*CPR 1232–1247, 26 [Henry III]*, 293). The latter requirement may only have applied to these 'other ships' detained in port because of the king's anticipated need.

The centrality of New Romney to the organisation of the confederation in the 13th century, which is also evident in local records, is clear in a mandate of May 18, 1242 addressed to the barons of Romenal (Draper 2003, 21):

'The king is sending to the sea coast R. Bishop of Chichester, the chancellor and B. de Crioyl, constable of Dover, to provide by the counsel of them and the other barons of the ports for defence of the said coasts; and he therefore commands them in no way to omit to send 12 men of their town, on Monday after Ascension Day, to meet the chancellor and constable at Sypewaye, with the bailiffs of their town, there to make provision for such defence' (*CPR 1232–1247, 26 [Henry III]*, 305).

Sypewaye was the Shepway court of the Cinque Ports, the other court of this period being the Brodhull, then held at Dymchurch.

In 1260 the Cinque Ports of Dover, Hythe, Hastings and Romney were summoned to send all suitable ships (naves) to Wytsaund (Wissant), for the transport of the king. In the same year they were commanded to send small boats (batellae) decorated with flags, and with horns and trumpets, to play on the Thames at Westminster for the entertainment of the king and others, reflecting the Ports' ceremonial role which was applied to all the five head ports, Dover, Sandwich, Romney, Hythe and Hastings, as well as Winchelsea (*CClR 1259–1261, 44 [Henry III]*, 211, 250).

Piracy and privateering

By the late 14th century *Rough's Register* records the mariners of Romney practising skumerie (licensed piracy) and from 1410 Henry IV was keen to control what was effectively 'an unofficial war raging in the Channel between English privateers and their continental counterparts'. The activities of the privateers Sir John Prendergast and William Long of Rye interrupted maritime commerce and damaged relations with Flanders. Henry, Prince of Wales, was appointed Lord Warden of the Cinque Ports and captain of Calais. A crackdown on attacks on Flemish shipping by men of the Cinque Ports ensued, such as imprisoning at Romney one William Worthe, 'a Winchelsea shipowner who engaged in illegal privateering'. This provoked local resentment at Romney, New Winchelsea, Sandwich and Rye, where the privateer William Long was elected as MP and took up smuggling (Mercer 2005, 56–57). The agreement between New Romney and Lydd over the ransoms of Frenchmen, and Romney's seeking of Prendergast's 'friendship' in this period, were manifestations of resistance to the changes being imposed (HMC V, 538–539). In 1411 the Lord Warden as Admiral punished the vicar and a fisherman of Lydd for sheltering and supplying a group of pirates under Prendergast's command (Murray 1935b, 9). From 1415, the energies of the Cinque Port pirates and privateers were redirected to protecting the coast and supplying Calais, Harfleur and Guisnes. Richard Clitherow of Sandwich, forebear, presumably father, of Richard Clitherow of Romney, was prominent in organising supplies to Harfleur (Mercer 2005, 60–62; Draper 2003, 143). However in 1441 the Court of Chancery and Admiralty held in Dover was still dealing with the 'felonies of the pirate Prendergast' (Murray 1935b, 133).

New Romney's Vessels and their Role in Local and Continental Trade

The vessels which New Romney and the Cinque Ports used for their ship service were those which otherwise they used for their normal maritime activities: trade and fishing. The maletolts, the customary tax on commodities bought or sold there, covered grain, animals, fish, tallow, oil, wax, pitch from the Baltic, hides and pelts, lambswool, woven cloth including carpets or tapestry, silk and Aylsham (Norfolk worsted) cloth, salt, hemp, sea coals, firewood, building and baking materials, iron (probably both Spanish and Wealden), and timber from Ireland; the latter as much of the old 'wild wood' forest had gone in England by AD 1250. As discussed above, the table of maletolts which lists these is undated, but undoubtedly originates before the early 13th century, although it probably also included goods traded up till the mid-14th century when the table was recorded by Daniel Rough. It does not distinguish between imports and exports (*Rough's Register*, xviii–xxi, 2, 19, 28–33). Grain was supplied by water to the London market from New Romney in the late 13th century (Milne 2003, 97).

Cross-channel and coastal trade

Documents of the 13th to the 15th centuries provide evidence of cross-Channel and coastal trade and those who participated in it. A late 13th-century source suggests the (earlier) presence of French residents in New Romney presumably in connection with trade and/or fishing. A large-scale manorial survey made in 1283–1285 of Archbishop Pecham's holdings in and around the town was analysed to distinguish the town centre quarters from those outside. In New Romney the various quarters were usually called hopes and this survey records the name of an early town centre hope, Frencheshop (*Pecham's Survey*, 232).

In the 14th century many alien (non English) merchants and shipmen carried goods to and from Romney. Nieuport, Sluys, Bruges, Amiens, Boulogne, Calais and Dunkirk were the 'most frequently mentioned' as destinations of alien or Romney merchants and shippers. For example S. Walop, a Romney freeman, delivered victuals (corn, suet, sacks and tubs) to C. Mistlelyn of Nieuport which the latter should have taken on to Calais but had 'long detained' (1356). *Rough's Register* makes it clear that pressure was exerted through the town authority on behalf of its freemen to recover debts or materials from traders or shippers in other towns across the Channel, as for example in a formal letter (*bref de chattel detinue*) to Sluys concerning 26,000 laths, 60 spars, 50 bowls and skillets, and corn flour shipped by S. Walop and detained at Sluys by M. de Frode. As one would expect, there are also references to the accommodation of mariners or traders from across the Channel in the homes, or possibly hostels, of New Romney townsfolk: for example a 'letter of process' was sent to the Burghmaster and officers of Bruges in 1370 on behalf of P. le Gay concerning the debts and lodging expenses of one G. Aman for the last time he stayed with P. le Gay in Romney (*Rough's Register*, xlvi–ix, 96, 97, 181).

Shipwrecks

The town of Romney claimed a quarter of the value of all wrecks between Dungeness and Hythe as recorded in the table of maletolts. *Rough's Register* gives several examples of wrecking, including a Flemish ship (*une Nef de Flandres*) laden to go to Normandy which was wrecked at Lydd in 1357, and a merchant ship from La Rochelle wrecked at Romney in 1361 (*Rough's Register*, lviii, 102–103). In 1374 J. Rose, master of the town barge or balenger, captured certain Frenchmen and was issued with safe conducts for them under the common (communal) seal (*Rough's Register*, 189). Captured goods being transported in Flemish vessels in 1357–1358 included sea-coal, corn, timber, yarn, iron, wood, wool, cloth and 'leathertan', bark for tanning (*Rough's Register*, 128, 137–142, 145–146). In 1360 six named merchants of Genoa had three carracks and one cog laden with goods at Bruges. These vessels then crossed the English Channel and although officially under the protection and safe conduct of Edward III, these ships were 'boarded at sea' by 'some evildoers' of Kent and Sussex after being 'wrecked' on a sandbank 'at Dyngenassh (Dungeness) by Romeneye'. Although the merchants and mariners 'came to land alive', the evildoers carried off their goods and merchandise which were said to have been washed ashore. It is possible that the vessels had been heading for Sandwich where Genoese merchants used carracks to import goods (Mate 2006, 86). Deep draught vessels such as carracks could operate out of Sandwich but not Romney. However vessels such as cogs could enter the Romney harbour, and the cog seems to have been from Romney. The cog's name was recorded as *Seinte Domenyk de Romeria*, probably for Romenia, ie Romney (*CPR 1358–1361*, 482–483, 516).

The town barge, or balenger

The town or chamberlains' accounts of New Romney reveal aspects of coastal and cross-channel trade in the late 14th and early 15th centuries that were carried out in the town's balenger. This may have been the same vessel as the 'common ship', which is also mentioned in the accounts, which give extensive information about the town barge and other vessels which has been very briefly summarised here (Boys 1792, 800). In 1354–1355 various named barons (freemen) of Romney negotiated with the king at Sandwich over his purchase of a barge, which he had ordered them to make for use between Plymouth and Cherbourg. A fleet was being assembled with boats also being commissioned from Sandwich (*Rough's Register*, 89–91, 160). It is possible that the barge was built at New Romney although little other suggestion of vessels being built, as opposed to broken or repaired there, has been found in the historical sources after the 13th century

(below). The town obtained its own replacement barge at the end of the 14th century from Smallhythe, then an important shipbuilding centre.

The town barge is mentioned in 1374 when John atte Wode, captain of the town barge, was arrested for refusing to give up goods taken from Italian merchants and resisting capture at the Camber by Rye (*Rough's Register*, 55). J. atte Wode, probably the same man, was described as a ship's master and also a vintner and was master of a vessel involved in skumerie or licensed piracy. The town of Romney issued a letter of process to Rye on his behalf about two anchors, two capstans, and a ship's yard and rigging (*Rough's Register*, 55, 84, 155–157, 189n).

The town barge is mentioned in the town accounts as being extensively repaired in 1381. Various materials were purchased for it including four 'waynscot bords' and a buoy and rope. The sum of 4d was paid to the lads of the barge (*garciones bargie*) for transporting the jurats, the town governors, from the barge to land in the boat belonging to the barge in this year. The sails of the barge were carried into the churchyard of St Nicholas to dry and certain mariners were given 4d worth of beer to do so (Boys 1792, 801–802, 804). Despite these repairs, the balenger or 'barge' was broken up shortly before 1385, and a townsman, William Holynbroke, paid twelve Spanish silver coins for part of it. A replacement barge was obtained in 1396–1400 from Smallhythe at a cost of £53 6s 8d and new equipment for it included a dyole (dial) and a kettle. The new barge sailed to Sandwich with firewood, to Newcastle, Scotland, and to La Rochelle to fetch wine. The common ship brought wine from Sandwich and from Bordeaux, escorted wool to Flanders, and fetched wood from Gerounde (Gironde). A 'boat' was bought for the common ship in 1403, presumably because it could no longer enter the haven or reach the common quay. New sails were brought from London for it in 1405 (HMC V, 533–536). The role of the barge or common ship in transporting the jurats, perhaps partly a ceremonial role, continued in 1428 when one John Mokayt was arrested and brought before the same jurats for expressing the wish that 'they had all been burned in the common ship' (HMC V, 541). The town also owned a common crayer, mentioned in 1381 when its old ropes were sold (Boys 1792, 800).

Ship service in 14th- and 15th-century New Romney

The members of the Cinque Port confederation continued to have a special relationship with the monarch in the 14th and 15th centuries. Despite the decay of their havens, as at Romney, they still provided transport for the king and his forces across the Channel and to Ireland and suppressed piracy by their own skumerie. Their strategic importance was great and the monarchs of the 15th century recognised this in the major role and royal rewards given to the Lord Warden of the Cinque Ports. During the Wars of the Roses, the Cinque Ports had to balance the obligations to the monarch against the possibility that the king might be ousted, as Richard II was by Henry Bolingbroke in 1399. The Lord Warden in that year, John Beaufort, supported Richard II by organising the defence of the southern coasts when he realised that Bolingbroke was likely to make an attempt to land there in the summer of that year. Bolingbroke and his forces did land at various places partly to gauge what support and opposition he would have locally, including in the Cinque Ports. Meanwhile the Cinque Ports took a cautious and pragmatic approach given the uncertainty about what might happen. The town of Romney garnered information about what was occurring by sending riders to Sandwich, London and along the coast routes. Some Portsmen supported Bolingbroke's 'invasion' but others temporised. Eventually Bolingbroke landed in the East Riding of Yorkshire at Ravenspur and usurped the throne as the Lancastrian Henry IV. The economic difficulties of the Ports and of Romney's harbour, as well as the frequent French raids, particularly on Rye and New Winchelsea, had contributed to lack of support for Richard II by the confederation. Between 1461 and 1470 the Cinque Ports and east Kent supported the earl of Warwick, the 'kingmaker', and the Romney jurats' accounts show the town paying the expenses of local men, including John Cheyne, gentleman, 'employed on the voyage of the earl of Warwick' in 1469–1470 (Mercer 2005, 46–54,;HMC V, 545).

In the late 15th century, the town accounts of New Romney record co-operative action between the townsmen and those of the ports of the confederation and elsewhere in Kent in providing vessels and equipment for ship service. For example in 1492, the Trinity of Folkestone, the Thomas of Newhethe and the Anthony of Snodeland as well as the James of Romene are all mentioned (HMC V, 548). Snodland was on the River Medway, as was New Hythe (Newhethe) near East Malling. The Thomas of New Hythe is noted in the correspondence of the Cely family of wool merchants as exporting Cotswold wool-fells from New Hythe to Calais in 1481, an indication of the declining importance of Cinque Ports like New Romney in such export activity and the lack of harbour facilities and vessels for doing so (Sinclair Williams 1973, 52).

The Warren House and Maytham Wharf vessels

The remains of a substantial oak built vessel with some elm and fir elements were found at 'the Warren', near New Romney to the north (see Fig. 16), probably in the base of a former water channel. The remains of the ship are recorded as measuring 7.32m in width by 15.85m in length and the depth of its hold was 2.44m; however, the ratio of these dimensions are unrealistic and it therefore

ANCIENT VESSEL DISCOVERED IN THE CHANNEL OF THE ROTHER IN THE BEGINNING OF JULY, 1822.

Fig. 23   Remains of an early post-medieval vessel found in one of the former stream channels of the River Rother at Maytham Wharf

appears likely that they were inaccurate or that parts of the ship were missing. The vessel was clinker built and trunnelled and some goat skulls, animal and possibly human bone as well some 'copper coins' were recovered from her (Urban 1834). John Reeley, school master at the Lydd National School between 1817 and 1848 reported in 1833 that the timbers of the vessel were sold at auction. Its size and construction materials suggest a post-medieval (*c.* 16th century) date and its width suggests a Low Countries origin (D. Goodburn, pers. comm.). This vessel appears to be similar to one found under the bank of a stream or sewer, in the East Maytham level near Maytham Wharf (TQ278 868) (*sic*) in Kent (Fenwick 1978, 258). This vessel was clinker built, was 19.1m in length and 4.57m wide, and built of oak (Fig. 23). From its hold and cabin pottery, a sword hilt, two iron locks, a brick, a cooking stove, glazed tiles, an hour glass, a pewter plate, a sounding lead, human remains and a few other finds were recovered. This boat too was thought to have been 16th-century in date and possibly of Dutch origin (Fenwick 1978, 258–260). The two vessels are clearly distinct finds (Tyler 2004, 9–10). Though both found on or near the river Rother, the 'Warren' boat was near a channel on the mouth of the river whereas the Maytham Wharf vessel was located significantly inland, some 20km west of the 'Warren' find. Both boats appear to represent sea-going coastal trading vessels of northern European, probably Low Countries, origin.

Chapter 6 The Town Centre and Corporate Activities, Local Government and Associated Buildings

The medieval town centre included a large part of St Lawrence's parish and a smaller area of St Nicholas' parish, close to the church of that name. Commercial and market activities were concentrated in this area. Corporate functions and buildings were also concentrated in this west-central part of the town. The buildings consisted of an early and a late guildhall, a communal meeting house of the jurats, and other nearby corporate establishments. There was also a town or communal quay known from the end of the 14th century, located on the southeast corner of this commercial area, the fish quay area. The communal quay was associated with the loading of firewood and the landing of fish, rather than merchant activity. This section considers these buildings and the activities there in order to interpret the nature of town government in this Cinque Port. The town government consisted primarily of the jurats, twelve men elected annually by the barons or freemen (commoners or commonalty) of the town to govern it (Salisbury 1887, 26). The Archbishop's bailiff was also influential, and mostly managed to prevent the development of greater self-government at New Romney by way of a mayor.

The Meeting Places of the Town Governors: the Guildhall and the Common House of the Jurats

An early guildhall at New Romney stood on the northwest side of St Lawrence's Church on land belonging to the town (see Fig. 17.1). This may have been the common house referred to in an early but undated custumal of the town, recording its customs from time out of mind (copied into the start of *Rough's Register*, lxvi, 1–2). It was probably the meeting place of the Halimott (hall-moot) which witnessed a town deed in *c*. 1200 (*Rough's Register*, lii, 1–2; MCM Romney deed 38). However, by about 1234 this early guildhall had apparently been demolished since 'the site was given by the Barons to the Hospital of Eastbridge, Canterbury' (*Rough's Register*, xxxvi–xxxvii). The jurats, bailiff and sub-bailiff met in St Nicholas' Church by 1357, making legal records there and sealing them under the common seal (*Rough's Register*, 135). There are few surviving civic records for New Romney between 1234 and 1357, and it is not possible to say for certain whether the jurats met in

the church from the time the guildhall was sold.

By the late 14th century, the meeting arrangements are made clear in the town or chamberlains' accounts (material is cited by the year of commencement of the account and quotations are generally translations). In 1395 the town paid rent for 'the chamber for the Jurats, and forms in the same'. The chamber was in a central part of the town within the bailiwick of the Archbishop of Canterbury in Romney, a bailiwick whose income the town had leased from the Archbishop in that year for nearly £16 (HMC V, 535). This seems only to have been a temporary arrangement and in the early 15th century (1404) the jurats were again 'holding session' in St Nicholas' Church (HMC V, 536). However, by 1407 John Hacche, vicar of Romene, made a 'free gift' of 3s 4d 'that the Jurats shall not in future hold their session in his church, while Divine Service is being celebrated' (HMC V, 537) and for a few years the jurats are recorded as renting both a meeting chamber and a store room. In 1408, the town paid rent to William Clidrowe for 'rent of the house in which the Jurats hold sessions', in 1410 the sum of 13s 4d was paid 'for rent of the common house' and 4s 11d was paid for 'counters, coals, rushes and wine, drunk at various times at the session of the Jurats and others coming amongst them'; wine, ale and beer were of course drunk extensively rather than water. Within a few years a decision had been made to buy a place for the jurats to meet. In 1413 the jurats acquired 'Colbrondes tenement' for £16 as a common house for their meetings. Furnishing, equipment and materials were bought for it; and various repairs carried out (HMC V, 537–538).

The exact location of this meeting house has not been established and from 1483 onwards this common house was not apparently considered suitable for entertaining the town's influential visitors such as the Archbishop of Canterbury, Lord Arundel, the Warden of the Cinque Ports, or George Cheney from an important Kentish gentry family; instead they were entertained at the house of Richard Randislow, a jurat, chamberlain and vintner which was near the High Street and market place (EKAO NR/JB2). Until the early 16th century, the jurats entertained important visitors or drank together and discussed important matters in the homes of the town's elite. Towards the end of the 15th century, it appears that it was decided that a new meeting place for the town was required. In 1495 the beams of the common house were taken down, a court hall is mentioned for the first time in 1517/18 and the next record in the accounts is of the jurats holding their meeting in 1553 'in the Guyledehalle' (Guildhall) (HMC V, 549, 553), which may have been on the site of the current Town Hall in the High Street (HMC V, 545, 547, 548, 553). (see Fig. 17.2).

The common house on the quay of St Nicholas

The common house is mentioned in the town accounts between 1399 and 1495 and it is clear that this term was generally used to refer to the common house used for meetings of the jurats. It should be distinguished from what was sometimes called the common house on the quay or strand (see Fig. 17.3). Either could be called the common house because they were the communal property of the town but they can be distinguished in the town accounts.

In 1398 the town paid the then large sum of £5 6s 8d to John Tymberden for purchase of a house on the 'quay of St Nicholas', presumably near the church of that name (HMC V, 535). His surname suggests that this quay may have been used for the shipping of timber and firewood grown and felled in one of the nearby Wealden dens, firewood being a 14th-century export

Fig. 24   Wall remnant with a blocked stone doorway and window behind the Assembly Hall in Church Approach

of New Romney. In 1352 Sir Richard de Totisham at New Romney 'freighted a certain ship whereof Lypyn Monfort is master, with 18 thousand [*sic*] of firewood to be conveyed (with the aid of God) and delivered at Calais within the week, for 4d. a thousand', (*Rough's Register*, 249). This practice was well known along the local reaches of the river Rother in the 14th and 15th centuries at Bodiam, Maytham, Newenden, Reading, and most remarkably at Smallhythe (James *et al.* 2005, 23–24). This house was known in the following years as the common house on the quay, and was let out. There are several instances of monies received for rent of the property, for example in 1403 the town received 5s for occupation of the 'Common House at the Keye' and the next year 3s for 'the hire of the house of the community upon the Keye'. In 1413 the town arranged for the 'mending the Common House upon the Keye' (HMC V, 536, 539). There are records too in 1437 and 1439 of rent received for this house, described in the former year as the rent of the 'house upon the Strond' but in the latter year as that of the 'Keyhous'. In 1448 the town received 6s 8d in part payment of a larger sum for the sale of the Cayhouse (quayhouse), possibly suggesting that quay itself was no longer in active use, although of course the landing of vessels on the strand might still have been occurring (HMC V, 541–542).

A closer identification of the location of the common house on the quay may be possible. The New Romney corporation owned the 'hall, or brother-hood house', built and used in the late 18th century for the brotherhood court of the Cinque Ports (Hasted 1797–1801, vol. 8, 449). This hall is now known as the Assembly Rooms, and lies in Church Approach just northwest of St Nicholas' Church. It is likely that this was built on land owned earlier by the corporation, and that therefore the common house on the quay in St Nicholas' parish, in active use 1398 to 1448, was in this area (see Fig. 17.3). The messuage called the 'Kayhouse' was located in St Nicholas' parish in an indenture of 1398 (HMC V, 534). Possibly it is linked to the wall remnant with a blocked stone doorway and window behind the Assembly Rooms (Fig. 24), dated to the 13th century and tentatively suggested as part of a possible merchant house with undercroft (Parkin 1973, 121).

There may be parallels with the common quay at New Winchelsea although the latter was rather different from New Romney in being newly established in the 1280s and in being sited on a river estuary rather than having both a river estuary (tidal inlet) and a beachfront. Late references associate the common quay of New Winchelsea (called Town Dock in the 16th century) with the landing of fish. There was also a town storehouse on the strand (Martin and Martin 2004, 36–38, fig. 4.2). At New Romney the common quay was in a similar central position, and it was associated with the landing of fish and a nearby store room (above). This quay at New Romney may have been along the line of the shingle bank and have functioned at high tide as a quay with the strand being used for the vessels at low tide.

Fishermen, Ripiers, Vintners and Jurats; Occupations, Social Status and Town Government in Medieval New Romney

In medieval New Romney wealth was clearly linked to the social status of individuals and families, and in particular to membership of the jurat body. The table of maletolts and the 1334/35 Lay Subsidy indicate that the wealthy occupations in the town between the 12th and 14th centuries were those of master fisherman, vintner, carpenter (ship or house), merchant, goldsmith and coiner (irrelevant after the late 12th century when minting was concentrated in large towns, in Kent's case Canterbury). There is a small amount of evidence for the 13th and 14th centuries concerning the occupations of those involved in town government. For example, John Spite, mayor in *c.* 1270, belonged to a family known subsequently for kiddle fishing, whilst in the early 14th century (1309), the mayor was from a merchant family, the Colebrands, of whom Hugh Colbrond (Colebrand) also had an interest in a tavern within the liberty of Romney; the jurats in 1309 also included a man from a merchant family (*Rough's Register*, 104). In the second half of the 14th century men involved in kiddle fishing, possibly the wine trade, and perhaps goldsmithing, participated in town government or offices such as bailiff to Yarmouth (above). In the 15th century wealth continued to lead to membership of the political and governing elite of the town, and men known as vintner were prominent among the jurats and town officers, although historical or archaeological evidence of an extensive wine trade in New Romney at that time is limited. The town court books of 1454–1482 suggest that the term vintner was a label of status as well as of occupation. In this locality surnames were closely related to an individual's occupation until the early 14th century after which they still indicate sometimes-earlier family activity (EKAO NR/JB2). In these court books a dozen men who were described purely as vintners were also jurats and the high social status of some of these vintners, such as John Cheyne, is known, although seven men described as vintners were not jurats. These men also had extensive involvement in a variety of town offices such as chamberlain, common clerk, custodian of the common seal, or porter, an office concerned with the control of the fish market. Some of the jurats also had other official roles in the town such as churchwarden or foreman of one of the various wards. Besides these dozen men, there were seven other vintners who also took part in various trades, suggesting that they needed or chose to make money in an additional way. These were two butchers, two millers, and three ripiers. This appears a significant change from the 14th century when those involved in maritime activity and town offices were kiddle fishermen, and thus can be taken to reflect a change in the economy of the town. These vintners who participated in other trades were usually but not always also jurats.

In the 15th century some local inhabitants participated in the major changes in landholding precipitated by a move by lords from direct management of their land to leasing them out. Across Romney Marsh, Canterbury Cathedral Priory leased out fourteen properties, mainly rural manors, and All Souls College also leased out the lands with which it was endowed at its foundation in 1438–1442. These lands were six pieces of rural property, plus the rectory of Romney, including the alien priory there. The mid- to late 15th century agrarian depression made this land on Romney Marsh available to lease at low rents for local inhabitants. Much of the land they leased was used for sheep grazing to supply the Wealden cloth industry, which was at the height of its prosperity. This extensive use of land for grazing was in contrast to the mixed agricultural economy of the late 14th century, and was partly a response to population decline. The lessees were typically called husbandmen and their social origins had been in the higher echelons of local peasant, not urban, society (Draper 1998, 113, 117–119). Despite the rural origins of their families, these lessees included a number of men dwelling in the parishes of New Romney and Lydd, forming over 50% of the lessees whose parishes are known from testamentary sources. A comparison was made between these lessees living in urban Marsh parishes and the townsmen who appear in the New Romney court books at the same period, specifically their names, roles and activities. Some of these lessees, or men from their families, appear among the appraisers and pledges of distrained goods in New Romney, but not as jurats or officers of New Romney at this period, although this does not apply to the men who leased the 'Priory' buildings in the town from All Souls College, ie the former Pontigny property. The lessees or their relatives instead frequently held the office of scot collector, which was much more relevant to the maintenance of rural parts of the Marsh. The lessees seldom overlapped by name or family with the jurats or officers. It is clear that although a number of these lessees did live in New Romney or Lydd parishes their interests were largely agrarian. A preliminary examination of their wills suggest that they were of roughly similar prosperity to all but the wealthy vintners (Bowdon 2003). However, these lessees did not form part of New Romney's governing elite, which was dominated by families rooted in urban trading occupations. The position at Lydd in the medieval and early-modern periods has been examined by Coatts (2005, 16). Here the medieval economy was heavily based on fishing, and fishermen were important among the freemen of the town. Between *c.* 1500 and *c.* 1700 the wealth of Lydd's ruling elite was based on sheep and cattle grazing, with some of the richer freemen owning sheep as well as fishing equipment.

The fish market on the strand

There was a fish market on the strand, which was regulated by town officers known as porters and measurers. This has been identified as the fish quay area (see Fig. 17). The fish market is mentioned by name in the town accounts between 1414 and 1427 but undoubtedly took place earlier and later (HMC V, 548). Herring from eight boats operating out of New Romney were assessed for a local tax in 1340, which raised £4 13s 3½d for the town compared with over £5 from the butchers (Boys 1792, 799). The quay where the fish was landed may have been named 'heaper' in the 14th century (*Rough's Register*, 36). This name referred to the rent charged by the town on each fisherman, or possibly specifically each ripier, for the right to place his 'heap' of fish upon the ground by the waterside (HMC V, 494). In 1391 one man was fined for buying 100 mackerel at Widiness, presumably on Dungeness, for later sale in the market. Another was fined for buying 200 mackerel at the 'Keye' before sunrise for the same purpose (HMC V, 536). This may have been the quay near St Nicholas and the common house on the strand. The town authorities tried hard to ensure all 'fish and herrings' landed were brought to market and offered for sale there simultaneously (HMC V, 535.). They also tried to prevent, or at least fined, townsmen for catching fish elsewhere and trying to sell it at New Romney. Men were 'paid to search incoming vessels for fish being sold ahead of others' and in 1452 for herrings which were forfeit for being sold at night. The illicit trade in fish therefore took place at night and away from the quay and the strand at New Romney where fish should have been landed and taken to market. In 1459 two men were 'arrested for buying 1300 herrings before sunrise at Fowleness before the market from Robert Hou' (HMC V, 543). Richard Stuppeney, a townsman of New Romney, in 1484 paid 12d 'for fish forfeited at Fouleness'. This was not Foulness in Essex but a place local to New Romney, perhaps on Dungeness.

The ripiers who bought fish to transport for sale in London and elsewhere were permitted to carry out their activity on payment of large maletolts in the mid-14th century. The fish was transported swiftly by horseback. This form of distribution is known at New Romney when in 1340 the local tax raised from ripiers amounted to £1 5s 9½d (Boys 1792, 799). In 1448 maletolts totalling £1 3s 6d were paid by 'strange (non-local) ripiers upon the Stronde'. This indicates that non-Romney men acted as ripiers, although a significant number of townsmen were described in the town accounts and wills as ripiers in the second half of the 15th century and owned the necessary horses. The ripiers included men from Harrietsham and Woodchurch, as well as London, suggesting that fish was transported via those places and probably also sold *en route* in the central Kent towns of Maidstone, Ashford, Tonbridge and Sevenoaks (HMC V, 542)

In addition to fish being sold fresh, they were preserved on a large scale at New Romney. Fish were soaked in brine and then hung up to be smoked at the Herring Hang Field, as they are nowadays at Dungeness. On the tithe map this field (field 291) is *c.* 4.5 acres, suggesting the size of the medieval operation. It was a triangular field north of Sussex Road, one of the roads leading from the projected port location to the town centre, in a poorly drained area, bounded on two sides by Spitalfield Lane leading to the leper Hospital of *c.* 1170, and by the precincts of this Hospital to the west (Fig. 17).

The corporate activities of the jurats of New Romney

The activities of the jurats and the town officers were based in the common meeting house, as established above. The officers were a bailiff and sub-bailiff appointed by the Archbishop of Canterbury. In the 13th century, at least, the bailiff of Romney, as well as those of Hythe and Lydd, were appointed in this way. Although the greater Cinque Ports such as Sandwich, Dover and Old Winchelsea elected mayors at an early period, others including Romney did not do so until the end of the 13th century and in fact New Romney remained subject to the Archbishop's bailiff throughout the Middle Ages (Murray 1935b, 5, 10). Electing a mayor was a desirable marker of urban independence or status, and Romney aimed at contesting the Archbishop's overlordship of the town by doing so. One John Spite was described as 'mayor' in a Romney deed of *c.* 1270 (MCM Romney deed 40). Spite was named as the first witness to the deed, a position usually accorded in local deeds of this period to officials such as bailiff or serjeant. Subsequently royal records show there was an attempt by the burgesses or freemen of Romney to establish the right to elect a mayor and jurats: and in 1309 'the king 'heard that the barons of Romeneye elected a mayor, William Colebrond, and twelve jurats… as they used to do in the time of the king's ancestors, as they say' (*Cal. Chancery Warrants*, 294). The Archbishop opposed this in Chancery and the king ordered the mayor and jurats not to act this way until the matter was resolved. The Archbishop seems to have prevailed in the issue of the mayor, for there is no mention in *Rough's Register* of a mayor in the 14th century, merely of the archbishop's bailiff. Jurats are known from mid-14th century when Rough's record begins (above), but a mayor is not mentioned in the printed town accounts until 1484 when there was a largely unsuccessful attempt at creating one, with gentry support, in the reign of Richard III, under conditions of local as well as national political strife. This mayor was however swiftly deposed by a writ under the privy seal (HMC V, 547, 553). After 1563 the charter of the town was changed and it did routinely have a mayor, reflecting the oligarchic concentration of urban power more generally in English towns and particularly the Cinque Ports (Hipkin 1995b; Gibson and Harvey 2000, 211).

A most important function of the jurats was to account in the common house to the commonalty of the town for its finances, and those who had expended money on the town's behalf over the year claimed it on the day of accounting. This was done on the Day of Annunciation (25 March) and was a public occasion with the common horn being blown in the town. There was a common clerk to record the town accounts, which survive sporadically in writing in the 1340s and in a series from 1383, and this common clerk inscribed other material into the town account books as the jurats saw fit. He was also paid half a mark (3s 4d) in 1385 for 'writing out the watches upon sea-coast', that is making lists or rotas to distribute to groups of people liable to be on watch at different points. The jurats and chamberlains' accounts were recorded in Latin until 1519/20 and increasingly thereafter in English (Salisbury 1887, 20). Many administrative functions were carried out in writing in this locality in the medieval period, and many people could read if not also write, reflecting both the location of the town and its relative prosperity. About half of those known as leasing property on Romney Marsh in the later 15th century could write in either English or Latin (Draper 2007a).

Yearly meetings to hear accounts between lords, serjeants, bailiffs or lessees was a remarkable feature on Romney Marsh from the late, or perhaps even the early, 13th century. These accounts were very frequently simultaneously recorded in writing because of the preponderance of strong ecclesiastical lords on the Romney Marsh and the early literate traditions in the Cinque Ports such as New Romney, Hastings and Hythe (Draper 2003, 205–206, 236; Butcher 2003). There was also a growing involvement in the production of accounts by lay people from the mid-15th century (Du Boulay 1966, 271–274; Draper 2003, 120–122). This no doubt is the reason for the finds of counters at New Romney whose purchase, along with red wax, paper and a green cloth for the accounting table, is attested in the New Romney town accounts (HMC V, 541). Other town business was conducted in meetings on days such as the Feast of St John, and the common clerk or others sometimes made notes at these in the account books of matters they considered especially important. Sometimes these notes were made in French, reflecting a fashion tied to status at the time, for example some of the ordinances of 1412 (below).

The jurats also exercised limited judicial functions in their meetings, for instance fines for the drawing of blood, and they attempted to control standards of conduct, in one example forbidding dice or chequer board to an apprentice. They also arranged for new charters to defend their privileges. A major activity of the jurats was to assess and collect the maletolts in the various wards of the town from Romney and non-Romney traders. They also admitted men to the freedom of the town if they had been born in Romney, and increasingly applied a degree of pressure to join the franchise. Many men from other towns whose favour they sought were also admitted (HMC V, 540, 542, 543, 552).

Weaponry at the common house

In 1456, 24s 6d was laid out on 'bows and arrows for Common House' and two guns with six chambers were brought for the town in that year. In 1451 a beacon had been set up in St Nicholas' campanile and in 1475 a penny was paid to a man to bring the gun from the harbour to the common house. As with the watches on the coast in 1385, special action was taken when the New Romney townsfolk judged it prudent or were instructed to do so. In 1490 to 1491 the town had five guns and two 'vorlokkes' mended, and purchased 'gunstonys'. A man rode to Deal on the town's behalf to see one Master Joseph about

'armour and artillery'. These were the years in which raids were made on Brittany and Normandy, and commissions of array against invasion and for the defence of Calais were made; Henry VII was on the brink of war with France. In 1512–1513 a messenger from Rye was given a small sum for bringing 'a warning from Rye of three ships of the King of France'. In the same year a proclamation was received that all Frenchmen should wear a white cross on the left shoulder, a marker ultimately derived from the Knights Templar and an identification of foreigners that was particularly relevant to a town like New Romney. The following year a letter was received from Lord Howard for 'watching the bekons for Scottes and Frenchmen' (HMC V, 543–550).

Taverns and boarding houses

The town accounts give the names of inns known in the 15th and 16th centuries, the Rome, the Hoope, and the Crown. These inns are in addition to those revealed by *Rough's Register* in the 14th century, including the New Inn in the central High Street (see Fig. 17), the tavern of John Knobett in St Lawrence' parish and the Jerusalem Tavern in St Nicholas' parish (HMC V, 543–550). The Jerusalem and Rome taverns presumably took their names from the destinations of pilgrims travelling from New Romney, and perhaps served as meeting points and boarding houses or hostels for those gathering to make journeys (Webb 2004, 47). The Rome tavern gave its name to Rome Road, a cross-street leading into the High Street, which still exists.

Taverns, lodging-houses and brewing were significant sources of income in towns, particularly after the plague epidemics and demographic changes of the second half of the 14th century. This was partly because there were higher disposable incomes, particularly among wage labourers. Services such as accommodation and refreshment typically began to be provided more 'professionally', ie outside the homes of the suppliers, with a greater capital investment and dependence on loans. Under contemporary legal conditions this meant that men rather than women controlled these services, particularly production, although to a lesser extent retailing. The introduction of beer preserved with hops rather than ale reflects these changes. In the 13th and early 14th centuries ale production is widely known from manorial sources and in rural areas as a small-scale occupation and income for women. In the city of Exeter, all the hostellers brewed ale regularly as an accompaniment to their main occupation in the late 14th century. Hopped beer was imported into coastal towns of southeast England by the 1430s and subsequently produced there, initially by alien brewers. Beer kept better than ale and so could be brewed on a large scale, thus most beer makers in 15th century towns were men, and women were servants in the brewhouse or retailers in the ale-trade. Negative images of 'corrupt tradeswomen', women acting as brewsters, have been depicted in artefacts such as misericords and texts such as Piers Plowman (Mate 1999, 38–45). Ale and beer production, and the provision of accommodation, were thus important trades and have been subjected to large-scale analysis in the countryside and some medieval towns. Although New Romney has not been examined in this way, it presents an opportunity to examine practice, change and attitudes to these trades from an episode recorded in the town accounts.

In 1412 to 1413 a clash left traces in the town account book between the bailiff and jurats on one hand and the taverners, supported by certain clerics, on the other. Some ordinances or mandates were inserted after the account for 1412, dealing with the usual urban concerns about cleanliness: dunghills, swine and dogs; in addition the bailiffs and jurats ordered that all priests and those who visit taverns should be in their houses 'where they ought to spend the night' by 9pm on pain of a penalty of 6s 8d, and that 'no taverner shall maintain such delinquents'. A record was then made in the account book that Dame (*domina*) Beatrix Prendergast had exposed for sale a tun of wine in a tavern called Rome, 'contrary to the tenor of the mandates before stated' (probably, given the involvement of the clerics and the dates, the ordinances of 1412–1413). However a chaplain stood surety on her behalf of ten marks (£6 13s 4d) (HMC V, 533–535, 538–539). This record was then struck out. The precise nature of the clash between Beatrix and the jurats of the town is impossible to judge, but evidently it centred on what the jurats perceived as unsuitable behaviour at the taverns between women, other residents, clerics, pilgrims or travellers, and even pirates. Prendergast was a rare surname in this locality and Beatrix was presumably related to John Prendergast the privateer, noted above.

The evidence of the maletolts in New Romney demonstrate that hostels or boarding houses run by women were superseded by inns or taverns, run by men,

between 1384 and 1414. The earliest recorded maletolts were paid by six women and one man. Subsequently men only were named as paying the maletolts on hostels. In 1414 hostellers (*hospites*) no longer appeared as a category among those who paid maletolts, although (male) taverners or vintners did (HMC V, 533–535, 539). This might perhaps partly account for the clash of 1412–1413, since the occupation of providing accommodation (hostelry) which had afforded women a small income, the maletolts on hostels being low, was taken over by much richer men. As the discord suggests, the men who formed the town government were apparently also trying to control or even clean up the women's activities at the time the hostels disappear from the record. These men were of course sometimes innkeepers. Peter Newene (New Inn) was one of the wardens or chamberlains of the town in 1422 (HMC V, 539). A beermaker, a man, also appears in the town accounts for the first time in 1413 (HMC V, 539). Large quantities of beer seem to have been required in the town, not only for craftsmen and labourers but also to be drunk by the jurats on the odd occasion instead of wine. A record inserted into the town accounts in 1432 of a noteworthy house with a great kettle suggests beer production required more investment than ale brewing. The beerhouses of the late 15th century in New Romney apparently also sold wine, and thus were in some ways equivalent to taverns (HMC V, 542, 547). There were therefore several changes between the late 14th and late 15th centuries: a switch from ale to beer, and a move from hostels (where accommodation as well as ale was supplied) to taverns, and greater and more profitable control by men of the traditionally female activities of brewing and accommodation. These suggest that economic and occupational transformations partly triggered the incident recorded above.

Chapter 7 Hospitals, Welfare and Dramatic Traditions

The two hospitals of the town were small, early institutions which fulfilled important roles in New Romney. As well as supporting the sick or needy, they provided commemorative services for the townspeople. Their functions were shaped over the centuries to suit the needs and wishes of people living in the town. The leper Hospital, or Hospital of the Blessed Stephen and Thomas, became a means by which merchant families consolidated their rise to gentry status by patronage and subsequently developed into the base for a group of men associated with the Archbishop's interests in and around the town, but this Hospital ceased to be operational by the early 16th century. The other Hospital, that of St John, attracted support and donations from the townsfolk, particularly the jurats, and was a focus for their burials and collective memorialisation. It thus avoided dissolution in the mid-16th century and continued to provide a service to the town in supporting the poor as an almshouse.

The Leper Hospital or the Hospital of the Blessed Stephen and Thomas, New Romney

The early Hospital

The leper Hospital was a noteworthy early building in New Romney, occupying an important site on the northwestern edge of the town (see Fig. 17). The phases of its development contribute to an understanding of the economic, social and cultural history of New Romney. The Hospital can be located by the name of Spitalfield Lane, and its site has been the subject of various excavations (Murray 1935a; Rigold 1964). These identified remains comprise the chapel, associated burials and a probable domestic hall of timber construction (see Chapter 1). The remains uncovered appear to predate the c. 1363 refounding of the hospital as a chantry by John Fraunccys (Rigold 1964, 47-69), although Murray (1935a, 210) thought the plain and patterned stained glass found dated to the second half of the 14th century.

The leper Hospital was in existence by c. 1170 to 1180 as confirmed by four charters conveying various lands (Butcher 1980, 18). It appears to have been located close to the medieval route between Old Romney and New Romney which apparently followed the Wallingham Sewer (Gardiner 1994, 331, fig. 2, 337, 341, 343). Leper hospitals were usually founded just outside the central urban area but close to roads or bridges where the inmates could beg for alms from travellers. Those at Canterbury and Rochester were established early, shortly after the Conquest, but the rest, including that of Rye, were mainly built in the 12th and early 13th centuries (Sweetinburgh 2004b, 44–45; Draper *et al.* forthcoming; Martin and Martin 2004, 91–93).

The information in the earliest charters is that one Stephen was the chaplain at the Hospital of the Blessed Stephen and Thomas of Romney, his name reflecting the first dedication of the Hospital. The dedication to Thomas (which was to Thomas Becket rather than the apostle) may have been added after he was martyred in 1170. Thomas Becket had strong connections with Romney, and his attempt to flee from England via Romney in 1164 has already been noted. One Adam of Charing was on the ship in which Thomas attempted to flee and Adam is 'represented as the leader of those who prudently counselled abandoning the attempt' (Rigold 1964, 48). Adam de Charing provided the first Hospital endowment.

In the period c. 1170 to c. 1180, the Hospital of the Blessed Stephen and Thomas at New Romney had a chapel, a chaplain and inmates who were infirm or lepers. The earliest surviving charter conveyed lands from William son of Wulfi to Adam de Cherringes (Charing in Kent). Adam de Charing subsequently conveyed these lands to the Hospital together with rents and income from offerings. Some of these were in the manor of Aldington, of which part was at New Romney. The others conveyed land in Langport manor, also at Romney, 40 acres and rents at Snargate and an estate, which had belonged to Geoffrey Turcople (Butcher 1980, 18). Adam is stated on one of the charters to have died in 1209. Other charters of the early 13th century indicate the Hospital's location and also grants of property, which are connected with the economic development of New Romney. Its lands as acquired by the early 13th century can be mapped from estate maps of Magdalen College Oxford and onto the tithe map of 1840, confirming the details below.

The new grants included half the rights (income) of a mill and a half-acre between a road and the house of William Bavec. The boundaries of the lands mentioned included the house of Eilnod the weaver, and a road leading to the Black Wall. The Hospital was also given land outside the wall on the west side of the Hospital insofar as that wall could be held against the tidal action of the sea (Butcher 1980, 19). The Hospital seems to have lain very close to the entrance of the haven at this time (cf. Tatton-Brown 1988, fig. 9.1). Spitalfield Lane, which abuts the precincts of the Hospital, runs partly on the remnants of that wall as is evident on the ground, the soil survey map (Green *et al.* 1966) and on the tithe map (see Fig. 13, Fig. 14). There is further detail in a confirmation of all the lands on which the Hospital stood about a saltpan and its appurtenances, which had been an early possession. The saltpan, with an access road to it, apparently lay within five acres sited between the river He and the land of Thomas the priest's son (Butcher 1980, 19). The saltpan was therefore also close to the haven, into which ran the river He, Rhee, Ee or Rumensea (Gardiner 1994, 329–330; Allen 2002, 122). The Hospital had a chapel, where Stephen the priest had served, and by the early 13th century there was 'a messuage of the chaplain'. In sum the historical sources indicate that in the 13th century there were roads, walls and houses near this Hospital, a chapel, the house of the chaplain, and accommodation for up to thirteen or fifteen inmates (Butcher 1980, 20).

In the early 13th century grants of property to the Hospital included one by Adam of Charing's grandson, and another 'from the lady Alda de Laggeport (Langport, a manorial and hundred name at Romney), daughter of William Crispin', whilst grants of smaller pieces of property to the Hospital by local Marsh inhabitants began to be recorded in deeds from *c.* 1220–1240, often in return for commemorative services (MCM Romney deeds 53, 38). This continued until the end of the 13th century. Besides deeds there is an acknowledgement in the form of an indenture by Richard le Barber of Romenal that he was bound to the brothers and sisters of the Hospital concerning a rent from a plot of ground.

Robert son of Elvin of Lide (Lydd) in *c.* 1260–1270 gave the brothers and sisters of the hospital a messuage in the parish of St Lawrence (MCM Romney deed 39). The messuage lay next to the hospital's own site with one end abutting the highway from the 'bridge of Romenal' to the churchyard of St John, and the other to the tenement of the Hospital, either Spitalfield Lane or the route on the northeast side of the haven (Fig. 3, Fig. 14). There is little documentary evidence about the Hospital in the last decades of the 13th and first two decades of the 14th centuries, although it was investigated in 1298 by a commission of Archbishop Winchelsey for maladministration (Butcher 1980, 20; Rigold 1964, 49–50).

The Hospital between 1322 and 1363

In the early 14th century, members of the Cobham and Alard families were 'patrons' of the Hospital. These included William Alard (1313), Reginald Cobham, chivaler, and his sister Agnes, who was married to Gervase Alard, son of William Alard of Snargate (Draper 2003, 116, 246; MCM Romney deeds 55, 56). It appears that William Alard and his son Gervase were establishing the patronage of a chantry at the Hospital of the Blessed Stephen and

Thomas at New Romney, which paralleled those of Stephen and Robert Alard at the church of St Thomas, New Winchelsea (Martin and Martin 2004, 79–80).

From the 1320s the property of this Hospital of Romney was being leased out by its then patrons, Gervase and Agnes Alard (Butcher 1980, 25). Leases of the lands of the Hospital survive from 1322, 1339 and 1340, and give an indication of the extent of lands owned by the Hospital (MCM Romney deeds 36, 34, 50). In the lease of 1322 the Hospital leased all its houses and rents, 80 acres of arable land and 20 acres of pasture for a term of five years to Nicholas Gobylonde, a local man. However, the Hospital remained closely concerned with the management of its property and with the spiritual and material provisions for the inmates. The lessee was to provide a chaplain 'from Michaelmas next onwards', and a specified corrody (allowance) for each inmate including wheat, cash and firewood. The Hospital provided Gobylonde with animals, fodder (or seed corn) and farm implements to stock the land which were to be returned at the end of the five-year term. Gobylonde was to pay the expenses of walls and watercourses, and give up the land at the end of the five years sown with certain acreages of crops specified in detail. This consisted of 30 acres of wheat, 10 of winter barley, 18 of oats, 6 of beans, and 16 of peas and vetches .

The leases of 1339 and 1340 were again made to local men, Richard de Harnhelle of Ruckinge (1339) and Robert ate Smethe and Alan Cok of Fairfield (1340). In the lease of 1339, the Hospital's property around Romney was rented out: two houses, together with 73 acres of which 62 acres were said to be on the south side of the watercourse of Romene and 11 acres on the north. In the lease of 1340, the Hospital's property at Snargate was leased: 30 acres land in Snargate parish in a certain land called Snawerland with its walls, pastures and vorlandis; on Romney Marsh, vorlandis or forlandes were the land immediately next to embankment walls. Snawerland (Snorland) lay between Fairfield and Snargate Churches (Eddison and Draper 1997, fig. 6).

The provisions of the leases of 1339 and 1340 suggest an increasingly 'hands-off' approach of the patrons of the Hospital to the supervision of its leased-out land. That is to say, there were longer terms of years for the lease, less concern with detailed management, and no specific provisions for inmates. This may have occurred as part of general change in the middle decades of the 14th century in which institutions or individuals such as manorial lords became less concerned in close agricultural management of their property. It also appears that the Hospital ceased to function as a place where the lepers or the infirm were cared for at this time, although its chapel exercised chantry functions for the Cobham and Alard families, with masses celebrated in the chapel and two processional candles always provided there. There is insufficient detail to reconstruct the buildings of the Hospital at this time but the overall impression is of agricultural and commercial usage of its lands, as the leases also indicate. This was the situation when Gervase and Agnes Alard, acting as patrons of the Hospital, or chantry, conveyed apparently all the lands and property of the 'chantry of the Chapel of the Hospital' to its chaplain in 1352 (MCM Romney deed 56). One John Fraunceys was a witness to this grant, and the other witnesses were of knightly or gentry status, marking a change in the social standing of those associated with this Hospital compared with the townspeople such as a tanner and a barber mentioned in the mid to later 13th-century deeds.

The 're-founded' Hospital

In 1363 the Hospital was 're-founded' as a chantry by John Fraunceys, who lived in St Lawrence's parish. The Hospital was said to be lying abandoned and desolate with its sumptuous buildings falling into decay, and its hospital activities had ceased. With the re-foundation two chaplains were to celebrate masses for the souls of founders and benefactors in perpetuity. This acknowledged that chantry functions were already one of the reasons for its existence (MCM Romney deeds 29, 30, 61, 31, 29). One of the chaplains was to be master or warden, appointed by the patron, initially John Fraunceys. The other chaplain was to be appointed by that warden or master (Butcher 1980, 21). There was already a warden, *custodi*, by 1313 (MCM Romney deed 55). The refoundation and the patronage would shape the special character of the Hospital of the Blessed Stephen and Thomas for the rest of its existence.

In the 1370s, parts of the Hospital's property were again leased out to provide an income, this time in the name of the chaplain who now formally held all its endowments. For example, on 20 September 1378 Richard Scherwynde, chaplain and Master of the Hospital, made a ten-year lease of 5.75 acres and certain pasture to William Keene of Snargate for £1 6s annually (MCM Romney deed 33). John Fraunceys, patron of the Hospital, was among the witnesses to the lease. On the same day Master Scherwynde similarly leased 10 acres of pasture in Snargate to Adam Milet of Snargate, for 14s 4d annually (MCM Romney deed 52).

Nicholas Chamberleyn was Master of the Hospital in 1386, followed by Adam de Cokermouth, the vicar of Hollington near Hastings. Cokermouth complained to the Archbishop of Canterbury that the patron, John Salerne of New Winchelsea, had appropriated to his own use some offerings belonging to the Hospital and 20 acres of its land, putting Adam's income at risk. John Salerne was part of the merchant and governing elite of New Winchelsea and Rye, being mayor of Rye in 1386. An earlier John Salerne was appointed the lay rector of St Clement, Old Romney in 1322. In the late 14th or early 15th century John Salerne presented John Harard as Master. Harard was followed as Master by Robert Hemynborugh, who was presented by the son-in-law of the re-founder John Fraunceys. Hemynborugh leased 11 acres of the Hospital lands to Thomas Elys of Snargate for twelve years at 22s a year, lands which had previously been held by John Coupere (MCM Romney deeds 25, 28, 35; *CClR 1385–1389*, 290; *CPR 1321–1324*, 4, *[Edward 11]*, 84).

As re-founder of the Hospital, John Fraunceys was clearly a wealthy man and perhaps had urban connections beyond the Marsh. His widow and subsequently his daughters exercised patronage over the mastership of the Hospital during the late 14th and 15th centuries when it was a desirable post. This patronage formed part of the further rise in status of members of the Fraunceys family via marriage into merchant and then gentry families. One woman, apparently granddaughter of John Fraunceys, acquired sufficient wealth and status to be the founder of chantries herself, in Canterbury Cathedral and at Bexhill near Hastings (Draper 2003, 143–145). For several decades after Fraunceys' re-foundation, the Hospital of the Blessed Stephen and Thomas became a focus of the activities of a distinctive group of men from New Romney and Lydd. They worked as a network by supporting each other as feoffees, agents and intermediaries in each other's land and legal transactions, and buttressing the bid for the mastership of the Hospital by one Andrew Aylwyn, priest of Lydd, one of the group. This network was crucial to the post-Black Death changes in the land market in New Romney and more widely across Romney Marsh. Its members bought up land, and in time arranged for its acquisition by Archbishop Chichele. The network worked through personal contacts, and its members confirmed their activities in extensive amounts of legal documentation, most of which was produced locally and some kept at the chapel of the Hospital along with its books, chalices and other ornaments (MCM Romney deeds 1, 23). The men of the network were of higher social status than many of the townsfolk, including the jurats, who were more strongly connected with the other hospital in New Romney, St John's. The network included among its most exalted members Richard Clitherow of Romney, sometimes its Member of Parliament. Richard was the descendant, presumably the son, of William Clitherow, gentleman. William Clitherow was son-in-law of John Fraunceys, the re-founder of the Hospital, and was briefly made bailiff of Romney in 1414 by Archbishop Chichele. William was also nephew of one John Clitherow. John rose in a clerical career, becoming a chancery clerk by 1396, rector of Dymchurch on Romney Marsh in 1409, then subsequently dean of Shoreham, rector of Crayford and finally Bishop of Bangor. Bishop John Clitherow apparently had knowledge of the re-foundation of the Hospital of Romney, and of his nephew William Clitherow's links by marriage with John Fraunceys, the re-founder, since in 1380 he was among the archbishops and bishops who granted an indulgence to the Hospital (Draper 1998, 113–116; Draper 2003, 80, 138–143). The indulgence to the Hospital was 'of 40 days to all persons contributing to the repair, amendment and establishment of the Chapel of S. Stephen and S. Thomas the martyr at Romene' (MCM Romney deed 2). Similar indulgences were granted in 1391 and 1451, as they had been in the 1360s (Butcher 1980, 24, n.40; MCM Romney deeds 1, 14, 18, 32). In his will of 1435 Bishop John Clitherow bequeathed his books (religious texts) to various clerics identified as *magister* or *dominus* and a horse and

100 shillings to William Clitherow. The Bishop also bequeathed one of his best horses and his black robe furred with beaver to his brother, Richard Clitherow of Romney, esquire (*Reg. Chich.* IV, 532–534).

There are thirteen more documents of 1457 to 1471 concerned with the patronage, advowson and grants of the Mastership to this Hospital (MCM Romney deeds 3–12, 20–21, 24, 27). Nevertheless by this time the situation of the Hospital was changing, perhaps partly because its vital role as a base for those involved in Chichele's land acquisitions was over. By around 1485 the Hospital or chantry was said to be dilapidated. Its property had been appropriated after the death of John Fraunceys' granddaughter in the mid-15th century firstly to Bishop William Waynflete and then *c.* 1471 to his college at Oxford, Magdalen (MCM Romney deeds 3–6, 8–13, 15, 20, 21, 27, 32). In the late 15th century Magdalen College appointed lessees of, or receivers for, the rents of the Hospital estates; in 1484–1485 and 1490–1491 this was a local man, William Doble (Butcher 1980, 24). Doble was perhaps chosen because he could keep simple written accounts in English and could manage Magdalen's rents and property locally for it (Draper 2007a, 226, 235). Subsequently the management of estates on Romney Marsh by Oxbridge colleges became increasingly remote from the Marsh, with lessees being non-local men and paying their rents in London. It is unlikely that Magdalen College maintained any spiritual connection with the former Hospital into the 16th century by way of paying a chaplain, but it kept a fine series of maps of the hospital estates, not least because it did not want to lose track of their whereabouts once the local connections were lost. Magdalen College's map of the Hospital lands at New Romney of 1614 shows what appears to be the former chapel of the Hospital, possibly merely a conventional depiction (Eddison and Green 1988, frontispiece). The 1683 map of the liberty of New Romney shows only a few stones at the site of the Hospital.

Butcher (1980, 25–26) suggested that the stages and adaptations in the history of this Hospital posed a challenge to the archaeological interpretations and chronologies of Murray (1935a) and Rigold (1964). The excavated features and finds assemblages uncovered appear to cover 13th- and 14th-century components and therefore include both the period prior to, and that following, the re-founding of the Hospital.

St John's Hospital

The Hospital of St John at New Romney was founded before 1283 or 1285 at which time a salt rent is recorded as due from the Hospital to the Archbishop of Canterbury (*Pecham's Survey*, 242). The churchyard of St John is mentioned in a deed of *c.* 1260–1270 (MCM Romney deed 39). These references push back the earliest known date of existence of St John's Hospital, as recorded for example by the Victoria County History, by over a century. As noted above the record of the salt rent occurs at the end of Archbishop Pecham's survey of the Bailiwick of Aldington

of 1283–1285, where the Brethren of the Hospital are recorded as owing half a seam of salt to the Archbishop. Part of Aldington bailiwick lay at New Romney, and analysis of the manors and manorial subdivisions in this survey demonstrated that other people owing salt rents had holdings on the north or northwest side of New Romney. The record emphasises the importance of salt making in the 13th century in this part of town where St John's Hospital lay.

St John's Hospital: location and identification

The location and remains of St John's Hospital can be identified from buildings, the tithe map of 1840, street names and the reconstruction of the parish boundaries of medieval New Romney. The Hospital lay in St Lawrence's parish. Its precincts appear to be marked by the building formerly known as Old Stone Cottages in West Street and the remnants of an old wall and gate or doorway in St John's Road (Fig. 25) (Old Stone Cottages comprises the building known as 3 Old Stone Cottages and also Plantagenet House, formerly known as 4 Old Stone Cottages, and recently re-named). Across St John's Road to the northwest lay the Hospital's associated churchyard, marked St John's Churchyard on the tithe map. This churchyard was where the medieval parishioners of St Lawrence's parish were buried, since St Lawrence's Church was on a small site with inadequate burial space (*Rough's Register*, xxxvi). In 1464, John Bukherst, a jurat who lived in Butchery ward in St Lawrence's parish, left money to that church and his 'body to be buried in the churchyard of St John the Baptist at Romene' (HMC V, 544).

The building known as Old Stone Cottages, now comprising 3 Old Stone Cottages and Plantagenet House, is one of the ancient houses of New Romney and was surveyed by David and Barbara Martin in 2004. They concluded that 'almost certainly the well-constructed main range of the house dates from the first half of the 14th century'. It has a grand first-floor chamber with a low ground floor room. There was a fireplace on the first floor. The house is single-aisled and, even more important, neither the parlour nor the parlour chamber were accessible from the hall. It was thus 'not typical of a medieval house having standard parlour accommodation'. The building subsequently underwent notable alterations including the replacement of its southern end by a crosswing in *c.* 1400 and the insertion of a chimney in the late 15th or early 16th century. The 14th-century main range of Old Stone Cottages may have been preceded by an earlier building of which there are slight remains. There is also a blocked doorway into the adjacent house to the north, 5 West Street, to the north of which Southlands Hospital adjoins.

Old Stone Cottages can best be identified as the Master's dwelling of St John's Hospital, or possibly as a communal hall of that Hospital, although it appears small for that purpose (information from David Martin; cf. Harris 1992, 5; Teichman-Derville 1929, 190; SMR TR02 SE4, KCC, as above). The documentary sources

Fig. 25   Wall remnant and doorway of St John's Hospital, on the south side of St John's Road

do not make clear whether St John's Hospital followed either of the common building layouts for a medieval hospital: a complex of adjacent and adjoining buildings or a communal infirmary hall with an attached eastern chapel (Martin and Martin 2004, 91). The part of the Hospital now represented by Old Stone Cottages lies within a block formed by Lydd Road, West Street and St John's Road. The rest of the St John's Hospital buildings, including the chapel, probably lay under where 5 West Street and Southlands Hospital now are, within the block and precincts identified.

St John's Hospital is recorded as having 7.5 acres on Romney Marsh proper in 1457 (Butcher 1992), which would probably have included its site and precincts plus its churchyard in New Romney, which together amounted to *c.* 2.5 acres. This consisted of St John's Churchyard which had an area of 1 acre, 3 rods, 23 perches, and the hospital precincts as outlined above had at least another 0.5 acre (New Romney Tithe apportionment and map). The precincts presumably included the inmates' accommodation, and possibly the Spitil grounds known in 1519/1520 (below), although the latter may have been in a separate location near Old Romney (above). The location of the other *c.* 5 acres making up the 7.5 acres are not known, but the salt rents owed in the 13th century suggest they lay to the west of the Hospital and churchyard towards Lydd Road, where early salt pans are thought to have been situated.

St John's Road and Lydd Road both lead from the projected port location and quays of the 13th century past the hospital location and into the town centre. Lydd Road, on the south side of the block in which lies St John's Hospital (3 Old Stone Cottages and Plantagenet House) leads directly into the High Street as newly laid out in the

early 13th century. St John's Hospital lay in St Lawrence's parish, where a 'Saltshoppe' is recorded in 1398 (HMC V, 534). A lane called Shoptownelane, apparently near the market dyke and thus near the High Street, is recorded in 1492–1493 (HMC V, 548). One or both represent places where salt, an important asset among the Hospital's early endowments, were sold.

The inmates of St John's Hospital between the late 13th century and the mid-15th century

St John's belonged to the category of hospital frequently set up in the late 12th and 13th centuries for the sick and feeble. These people were the lay brothers and sisters known here between 1283 and the mid-15th century. They do not appear to have followed any kind of monastic-type rule but were under the direction of the Master of the hospital. As at other hospitals, they may have worked in the hospital's brewhouse or bakehouse, in its garden or on its other lands. The inmates may also have collected alms from passing travellers including pilgrims, and the importance of getting funds is indicated in the appointment of a proctor for three years for the house or Hospital of St John in 1362 (*Rough's Register*, 157). The proctor would have solicited alms in the locality and offered indulgences and possibly prayers by the inmates for the souls of those who gave (Sweetinburgh 2004b, 44). In 1424–1425 two young men local to Romney Marsh, John Huchon and John Redyng, were licensed in just this way to collect alms throughout the cities and dioceses of Canterbury, Rochester and Chichester for various hospitals. They were to carry a 'cedule [list] written in Englisshe' setting out the 'indulgence and pardons' on offer to potential almsgivers (Draper 2003, 258) and the alms given to St John's Hospital enabled the inmates to be given a weekly corrody or allowance, here apparently 6d or 8d a week. In 1413–1414 the town received a large bequest (£11 6s 8d) from a townsman to allow a corrody of 26s, probably representing 6d a week, to be paid to a female resident in St John's House. Hospitals frequently did not cater for the very poor but rather those with these kind of arrangements (HMC V, 536, 539).

The names of Masters or priors of St John's Hospital are listed between the 1370s and 1495 (VCH Kent: II, 225; *Rough's Register*, 181 n). The Hospital was under the control of the corporation, like the Hospitals of St John and of St Bartholomew at New Winchelsea and that of St John at Sandwich (Martin and Martin 2004, 90, 93; *Rough's Register*, 157, 193; VCH Kent II, 226.). Thus at New Romney it was to twelve jurats of the town that John Wygynton formally resigned the Mastership of St John's in 1399 or 1400. It also appears the town should have paid the Master of St John's Hospital £10 yearly, but sometimes did not do so promptly and its debt to the Master was recorded as a receipt in the town accounts until paid. For example, in 1396 it was found that £10 was due to the Hospital of St John. However, in 1401 £10 was 'received' by the town from what was then described as St John's House. In the same year the town paid 13s 4d in part payment of a debt of £10 to John Halegood, Master of that house. In 1407 the town repaid an 'old' debt of £3 18s to Thomas Rokysle, Master of the Hospital, so that nothing further was then due to him. A few years later, Rokysle supplied the town community with a large quantity of wine, which was 'drunk in the tavern of Knobett' where the jurats socialised (HMC V, 535-39.) The town took some other financial responsibility for St John's Hospital. In 1408 the town paid the maletolt due on the Spitlemelle or hospital mill. It had also paid the maletolt of 7s 6d due from the hospital in 1340. One of the wards of the town was named Hospital ward, and in 1408 Robert Curthose and Thomas Mellere (miller) owed maletolts in that ward. Thomas paid 8d on what was described as another mill in that ward, 'Loverotismelle' or Loverote's Mill (Boys 1792, 800; HMC V, 537).

Changes at St John's Hospital from the mid-15th century

In the 1430s to 1450s change is evident at St John's House, with some of its lands in Lydd disposed of, although it is not clear if it ceased to function as a hospital then. In 1434 Stephen Pocock, Master of St John's House, rented or sold 8.5 acres in Lydd, which belonged to St John's brothers and sisters, to Richard Glover, chapman and bailiff of Lydd (HMC V, 537; Draper 2003, 132, 139). In the mid-15th century, those in charge of the hospital began to be referred to on occasion as Prior rather than Master. In 1458 Simon Maket was 'admitted to the rule and governance of the Hospital of St. John at Romene by the name of Prior …taking for his wages and soap for washing the vestments of the said hospital, yearly 20s'. This was considerably cheaper for the town than making a payment of £10 a year to a Master. In the same year, John Porter took over as seneschal or steward of the Hospital and was paid 15s to supervise and lease out the land and tenements, and collect and account for the rents (HMC V, 544). In the 1450s to 1470s bequests continued to be made by townsmen to the fabric, works and memorial masses of St John's chapel, described as a 'church' (Scott Robertson 1880, 246). The continued close connections between the town government and the Hospital are reflected in the admission in 1473 to the town's freedom of a cleric or priest, *dompnus* Robert Bernyngham, the Prior of the house of St John the Baptist (HMC V, 545). (These references to Prior and St John the Baptist, to whom the former cell of Pontigny in Ashford Road, New Romney is sometimes said to have been dedicated, should not be taken to refer to that cell, since in 1414–1415 it had been taken into the king's hands, like the possessions of all alien priories in England and by 1438–1442 its lands granted to All Souls College Oxford).

The records of the end of the 15th century indicate that the Hospital had changed and perhaps was no longer functioning. Its buildings and land were being rented out by the town, and this fits well with the evidence

Fig. 26   Southlands Hospital, now cottages or almshouses for the elderly

Fig. 27   Plaque commemorating the gift of Southlands Hospital by John Southland and later renovations

and chronology of changes to the building represented by 3 Old Stone Cottages/Plantagenet House at this time which are outlined above. In 1511 leave had been given to Richard Richarde of Old Romney 'to make a way to his barn near the churchyard of St. John the Baptist', suggesting a change from urban to rural in the character of this quarter of the town, and possibly that the churchyard was in less use due to the demographic decline which had occurred in the town. The last reference to the Hospital in New Romney's chamberlains' accounts is in 1519/20 when the town paid 8d for a bill sent to the bailiff concerning the Spitill grounds (HMC V, 550, 555). Thereafter the accounts are incomplete so it is possible some unrecorded activity continued over the next decades until the formal dissolution of hospitals along with monasteries.

St John's Hospital becomes Southlands Hospital

As suggested above the building known as 3 Old Stone Cottages/Plantagenet House may be identified as part of the buildings of St John's Hospital in West Street. Part of the site or precincts, it is argued, subsequently became the location of Southlands Hospital, nowadays cottages or almshouses for the elderly (Fig. 26). A plaque on the wall of the almshouses commemorates its gift to the town in 1610 by John Southland of Romney, gentleman (Fig. 27) (HMC V, 550, 555). However, there is an earlier record of the acquisition of 'an estate in a parcel of marshland' by William Southlande, a jurat of Romney, in 1584 (Birmingham City archives, MS. 3415/77). The estate which William Southlande acquired was in St Lawrence's parish, and so is likely to have been what formed Southlands Hospital. Southlands Hospital lay immediately adjacent to the surviving buildings of the old St John's Hospital (these being probably just the Master's dwelling), and within its precincts where the other Hospital buildings had lain (above). It thus appears that the town community preserved the memory and practice of charitable functions in that street and block of New Romney. This transformation of the form and functions of an urban medieval hospital in the mid- or later 16th century is paralleled by similar events in the Cinque Ports of Sandwich and Hythe and, temporarily, at New Winchelsea, as well as at Canterbury and Rochester (Sweetinburgh 2004b, 44; Martin and Martin 2004, 91). Such transformations were generally presented as new foundations attributable to a particular person and year, as at 'Southlands Hospital' in 1610. However, they typically took place over years or decades as plans were made and property acquired for the foundation's endowment (Draper 2007b).

Southlands Hospital becomes Southlands School

In the early 17th century, the town of New Romney controlled Southlands Hospital as it had St John's Hospital, in accordance with the will of John Southland. In 1611 Richard Baker, MA, was appointed as governor of Southlands Hospital by Thomas Dodd, bailiff of Romney Marsh, by this period the bailiff of New Romney and that of Romney Marsh being apparently one and the same (HMC V, 547). Baker's university qualification may indicate that he also acted as a teacher at Southlands Hospital (cf. Thomson 1983, 349). John Southland provided for the education of local children in his will as well as for the hospital (EKAO NR/Z/8). Southlands Hospital may have replaced the former leper Hospital of the Blessed Stephen and Thomas as the focus of schooling and literate practice after the

property of the leper hospital was acquired by Magdalen College at the end of the 15th century. Teaching is likely to have been carried out at Southlands Hospital from the later 16th century when provisions were being made by William Southland for the re-foundation of the medieval hospital. This is suggested particularly by the concentration of wills with arrangements for schooling at New Romney in 1579 to 1583. In the 1560s the townsfolk lamented the lack of a good schoolmaster who remained unappointed despite them being willing to contribute £4 a year out of the town's purse (HMC V, 553). Between the late 16th and early 17th centuries, schooling across Kent moved from being based around individual teachers in many towns and villages, as it had been in the medieval period, to being based in school buildings or 'new' school foundations (Draper 2007b, 75–91). By the 19th century the schooling funded originally by John Southland in his will had moved from its location at the former Hospital to Southlands School, the building which formerly stood on the excavation site in northeast New Romney.

The Passion Plays at New Romney, Communal and Dramatic Traditions in the 15th and 16th Centuries

Evidence from the town accounts suggests a wider link with the location of communal dramatic and literate traditions of the town in the Southlands Hospital quarter (HMC V, 533–547). From at least 1441 New Romney's passion play was staged at Crokhille (Crockley Green) just to the south of Southlands Hospital, and probably also involved a procession to Crokhille. The route of such a procession, which would have passed all three parish churches before making its way to Crokhille, has been reconstructed here (Fig. 28). Players, minstrels or entertainers from many other places, mostly coastal, gave performances in this location at New Romney between 1387 and 1517/18.

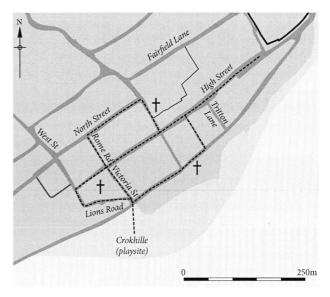

Fig. 28   Projected route of the procession through New Romney (scale 1:7 500)

The places from which players came included members of the Cinque Port confederation, New Winchelsea, Rye, Hythe, and Folkestone; minstrels also came from Sandwich. Players from small local places on or near Romney Marsh such as Ruckinge and Brookland, and Appledore and Wittersham on the river Rother, also 'show[ed] their play upon the Crokhil'. Other players came from Chart in east Kent, Bethersden and Halden in the Weald, and Herne on the north Kent coast. The minstrels of the 'lord of Scerburgh' (Scarborough) appeared in 1445, presumably when fishermen and traders from that place were plying their trade at New Romney, as evidenced by the finds of Scarborough Ware from the excavations at Southlands School. Coastal contacts via fishing and trade thus appear important to the performance of plays and other entertainments

Small payments by the town to minstrels are recorded between 1422 and 1519/20, when the accounts become incomplete. The payments were mainly made to minstrels of the royal and noble households, perhaps as these lords and ladies travelled via New Romney. These payments occurred particularly in the tricky dynastic years of the early 1480s. New Romney promoted its connections with the monarch, whoever it might be, not least because it valued the town's participation as a Cinque Port in coronation ceremonies. Several payments were also made to the minstrels of the Lord Warden of the Cinque Ports whom the town was keen to entertain in order to seek his favour.

The passion play performances also offered opportunities to New Romney and Lydd to discuss joint arrangements over vessels sailing to France for commercial purposes or, more likely, ship service. The players of Lydd made two visits with their May (play) to New Romney in 1422 and 19s ½d was paid to men of Lydd in expenses (HMC V, 540). These players and the townsmen of New Romney took the opportunity to 'converse' about two voyages to Le Crotoy. Lydd provided a boat towards New Romney's ship service and undoubtedly the need to converse was linked to that service and to current political events. 1422 was the year of the death in France of Henry V of England and in which the infant Henry VI succeeded him; within two months, he also became king of France on the death of Charles VI. Humphrey, Duke of Gloucester, was uncle and Protector of the infant Henry VI and his interests in England. In 1423 Gloucester married Jacqueline, countess of Hainault and Holland, who had fled to England in 1421 from her husband John of Brabant. This put her, with Gloucester's support, in conflict with the heir of the Brabant lands, Philip of Burgundy. Gloucester's expedition to Hainault was opposed by Henry Beaufort, Bishop and Chancellor, who exported large amounts of wool to the Low Countries from his considerable estates in England, and manipulated control of the wool staple and customs collection (Thomson 1983, 101, 138, 184, 186). It is no wonder that the men of Lydd and New Romney decided to take the occasion of the play in 1422 to discuss how to proceed in the face of these political and regional economic interests. In fact they decided to make the two voyages to

Le Crotoy, which cost New Romney £15 15s in expenses. In 1441 there is a further record of a requirement for similar ship service and 4d was given to a messenger 'bringing a letter of the Lord Duke of Gloucester to have men at Crotay' (HMC V, 542).

The town government and religious change

Under the prevailing conditions of religious reformation in the early 16th century there was discussion, if not conflict, over the performance of the passion play and other traditional religious practices at New Romney. In the background was resentment by the jurats about various visiting preachers with Protestant inclinations at St Nicholas' church in 1512 to 1518, whose expenses the jurats had to pay, and also mistrust of the parish priest himself. This mistrust culminated in 1516 with 'drinkings of the Combarons in the dwelling-house of John Hyxe on the matter of the said Richard Pever, the Vicar', costing 5s. The jurats then had the vicar watched 'for his demerits' and he was in fact imprisoned for a time (HMC V, 549–550). The jurats were enthusiastic about long-established religious institutions and orders, as is demonstrated by their dependence on the Austin friars of Rye rather than the local parish priest for spiritual services in the later 15th century. John Bukherst, jurat, also left money to the prior of the friars of Rye, since the Franciscan friary of New Romney no longer existed after 1331 (HMC V, 544, 548; Little 1939, 151–152).

On 14 December 1516 the jurats and commons 'chose Wardens, to have the play of Christ's Passion, as from olden time they were wont to have it'. However on 26 May 1517 a serjeant of the Lord Warden of the Cinque Ports 'brought a mandate to the Barons of New Romene here, that they ought not to play the play of the Passion of Christ until they had the King's leave' (this note was not recorded in the original town account book but in a later volume put together from fragments, partly of an Assembly Book and partly another book of accounts (HMC V, 552, 553)). Despite the Lord Warden's mandate, the play was apparently prepared or performed in that year, since the players received their expenses from the town amounting to nearly £4 in the accounting year 25 March 1517 to 25 March 1518 (HMC V, 550).

By summer 1516 the jurats and players had clearly been aware that their play might be forbidden. *Le Playboke* (play book) was delivered at that time to Henry Robyn, probably the Common Clerk, 'to keep such book to the use of the town' until it was required again. Henry Robyn subsequently delivered it 'into the hands of Robert May, Common Clerk there, safely and securely to be kept to the use and behoof of the said town' (HMC V, 552). On 9 July 1517 the play book was 'then and there' sent for from Robert May and delivered into the hands of William Bukherst, a descendant of the jurat John Bukherst who was a supporter of traditional religious practices (HMC V, 553). These moves and the care taken to record them in the town book demonstrated that at least some of the jurats anticipated being able to perform the play again in future, as in fact occurred. There is no record of the play's performance again until Queen Mary's reign, although it should be noted that the town accounts as printed are incomplete between 1521/22 and Elizabeth's reign (1558–1602). The New Romney play is notably absent from the record of miracle plays performed at Rye until 1560, although players of some kind visited in 1526 and 1540. Interpretation is complicated by the record in the town accounts of New Romney and Rye of all kinds of visiting players and entertainers including secular ones such as minstrels, sword-players and the Lord Warden's players (Mayhew 1987, 57–59, 292). When conditions were right during the reigns of Mary and Philip (1553 to 1558) New Romney's passion play was again performed: in 1555 the players committed themselves by a bond or recognisance to learn their parts and many of them signed the bond in person. Clement Stuppeney, who took part as one of the tormentors of Christ at his crucifixion, was from a family which had supported the play's performance in 1516 to 1518 (Draper 2003, 276; HMC V, 553). The passion play was still being performed in 1568, with the play book as well as the individual players' parts written out by the common or town clerk (HMC V, 553).

A bronze crucifix found in road works in the High Street (Teichman-Derville 1936, 248–249) is of particular interest in relation to the procession. It measures 17.8cm by 10.2cm, probably represents part of a processional cross and may be a continental import, the loss of which may be related to the Reformation changes acted out in the Anglican Church in England. Processions which included religious plays ceased to be performed in nearby southeastern towns in the 1520s and 1530s (see below). Its loss or even purposeful burial in one of the principal streets of the town suggest an evocative link with the procession route, of which the High Street undoubtedly would have been part. The last time a passion play is documented to have been performed in New Romney was in 1568, the same year in which the High Street was paved. After this date it would therefore have been more difficult to bury things in the High Street and this year thus appears a good candidate for the year in which the cross was buried.

In the period when New Romney's own passion play was under threat, the jurats had given monetary support in 1517–1518 for miracle plays from other local places such as Rye, New Winchelsea and Appledore (HMC V, 550). The Lord Warden of the Cinque Ports, who required that New Romney stopped performing the play in 1517, was the conduit of royal instructions to the Ports. The town of New Romney, like all the other Ports, was keen to have the favour of the Lord Warden, sending him on occasion gifts such as curlews, capon, a conger eel and wine, and entertaining him at the Crown Inn (HMC V, 548–550). In the late 15th and early 16th centuries, the Lord Wardens were usually chosen from a major Kentish gentry family and for their loyalty to the Crown, and thus their views on religious reform are likely to have chimed with those of the king. Although many Kentish

gentry were moderate and uncommitted to Protestantism until the 1560s and 70s, they were largely more open to the new religious practices than other social groups in the county. Kentish townsfolk, in contrast, were much more concerned to continue older religious traditions, for example at Canterbury and Faversham, where the hot Protestant John Bale complained in 1561 that the townspeople 'mocked their Protestant preachers with blasphemies and false reports'. The mayor and aldermen of Canterbury 'encouraged Catholic practices and had countenanced the unruly celebration of May Day and saints' days with "superstitious" bonfires, processions and "filthy songs of bawdry" '. Similar was found in 1569 at other towns, Ashford, Wye and Dover, and also at New Romney (Eales 2000, 296; Zell 2000, 201, 233–241). The local economy at New Romney was partly supported by traditional practices such as pilgrimage and support for hospitals and chantries, and value was also placed on the customary performance of its miracle play and procession. The town government however was strongly influenced by the Lord Warden and had been prepared to respond to his orders about the play in 1517 while making arrangements to preserve their written copy of it, an action which facilitated its later revival.

Gibson and Harvey (2000, 203, 214) assumed that play performance at New Romney had been continuous between 1428 and 1568 but there is no evidence for this. They took it as almost certain that by the 1530s and 1540s Kent had a greater proportion of committed Protestants than any other part of England except London, and so viewed what they thought was New Romney's continuous play performance as exceptional rather than part of a wider pattern in Kent. In this they failed to engage with the strong evidence of urban support, when feasible, for traditional religious practices, and with the variation between townsfolk and gentry in their enthusiasm for the new religion. Gibson and Harvey (2000, 217–220) also speculated that the performances between 1555 and 1568 were evidence for a wealthy civic oligarchy at New Romney, although many players in fact came from nearby villages, and that the motivation for performing the play was profit from spectators, 'prestige and self-esteem'. The apparently large numbers of spectators may equally have been attracted by a revival of a traditional religious and communal practice, on which large amounts were spent (Salisbury 1887, 29).

In reviewing the ongoing performance of miracle plays nationwide during the Reformation, Palliser (1987, 103) and Haigh (1987, 206–207) made distinctions between continued Catholic traditions in northern England as against their loss then revival in southeast England, specifically Sussex. Palliser noted that Chester, Wakefield, York and Boston maintained performances of their medieval miracle plays until the 1570s. However Chelmsford in Essex did so too and, as Palliser remarked, this latter exception does not fit easily with his distinction between northern and southeastern practices of popular religion such as miracle plays. The evidence of play performances at New Romney needs to be considered in relation to the suggested distinctions between northern and southeastern Catholic traditions. It is not certain whether the New Romney and other local plays continued to be performed after 1521 because of the gap in the town accounts. However, it is notable that the last references to the plays were by 1518 when 18d were given as a reward to the players of New Winchelsea and Rye (HMC V, 550). Gibson and Harvey (2000, 214) recorded that the players of Hythe, Folkestone and nearby Elham, Lydd and Brookland disappeared between 1532 and 1535. This suggests that dramatic performances had no part at, as did those of Rye (see Chapter 6), New Romney or nearby places in continued catholic traditions after 1520, nor in the 'flourishing faith' and 'continual embellishment' of early Tudor religion suggested by another Catholic-revisionist historian reviewing the local impact of the Tudor Reformation (Hutton 1987, 115–116). Rather local political considerations were greater until religious conditions temporarily changed in Mary's reign, at which point New Romney revived its passion play for some years. However, after 1568 the performance of New Romney's play ceased, undoubtedly under the final pressure nationally and in Kent to conform to the Protestant religion. The great majority of the Kentish gentry, influential in the governance of the Cinque Ports, conformed to Protestantism by the 1580s and in the following decades almost all of the rest of the Kentish population did so (Zell 2000, 240–241; Eales 2000, 296). By 1598, the site of the passion play was used by the town in a new way. It consisted of 'the common lands of the mayor, jurats and commonalty of the said town, usually called the Bowlinge Greene' accounting for the change of place name from Crokhille to Crockley Green.

Urban Decline in the 15th to 17th Centuries

At the time of the Armada, the small town of Lydd was considered by contemporaries to have overtaken its head port New Romney in wealth. A Privy Council letter dated 6 May 1588 and sent to Sir Thomas Scott, Thomas Randolphe, Thomas Fludde and Charles Scott, assessors, directed that Lydd 'should be taxed to the charge of shipping by ability and not according to any former composition', ie agreement between the two towns. This

was because they are given to understand that Lydd 'is presentlie in farre better estate than yt was in olde tyme or Newe Romney is'. The money collected was to be sent up to William Southland, jurat of New Romney, who had hired a ship as required (EKAO NR/CPw/56). It should be noted that although the haven of New Romney silted up between 1415 and 1450, and there was contraction of the numbers of wards and people within the town in that period, some people remained reasonably wealthy in the late medieval and early-modern periods. This is suggested by the town accounts and the buildings themselves, many of which are late medieval properties, although refronted in the late 17th or 18th centuries. Thus, for example, the High Cross of the town market was repaired in 1499, the High Street was paved in 1568, and Hasted noted in 1799 that there were about 'one hundred houses' in New Romney 'which are mostly modern, neatly built of bricks, and sashed' (HMC V, 533–549; Hasted 1797–1801, vol. 8, 449).

The men who had performed the New Romney passion play in the 1550s and 1560s were mainly townsmen of New Romney or Lydd; they sometimes leased pasture land outside the towns and were typically called yeomen. A century earlier some, at least, of the townsmen who performed the plays had been fishermen or coastal traders (Draper 2003, 272–277). This change reflects the wider ones in New Romney's economy over the period. From the 15th to the 17th century New Romney's remaining role as a port and beach market was profoundly affected by wider events. The end of the 15th century saw the journeys of Vasco da Gama to India, the 'discovery' of the New World by Columbus, and Cabot's trip to North America. This was rapidly followed by increasing numbers of commercial ventures, which served to expand the horizons of Europeans. In the establishment of groups of merchant adventurers, trading companies, and organisations of pirates and privateers lay the foundations of modern capitalism. Indeed the associated opportunities for religious and social dissenters had by the 17th century substantially altered social and political conditions (Killock and Meddens 2005). But there were no new opportunities for New Romney since its port facilities had already declined, it had reverted to a beach market facility at best, and it was located away from the centres of capital and political influence. As a result, these changes confirmed New Romney's loss of status and the end of the Cinque Ports as contributors to England as a naval power.

Chapter 8 The Archaeology of the Southlands School Site

As established above (see Chapter 3) there is little information in historical sources to indicate in which parish the area of the site originally lay and this part of town may have belonged to either St Martin's or St Nicholas' parish (see Fig. 15).

It is known that kiddle fishing was located along the shoreline extending northeast from the centre of town and an area of New Romney frequently mentioned in various 14th-century sources is 'le kidelmanhope' in St Nicholas' parish, where kiddle fishing took place. Kiddle fishing involved nets and was shore-based, and is likely to have taken place on the beachfront area, directly to the southeast of the boundary of the Southlands School excavation site. Fishing boats may have been drawn up here, onto the beach, as they were at Brighton and Hove (Bleach and Gardiner 1999, 42). Whether the area immediately to the southeast of the site relates directly to that alluded to in the records, or not, has not been established, but such an area would also have included extensive areas for repairing nets, and drying or salting fish and it seems likely, especially given the evidence recovered from the excavations, that this extensive area would have included the beachfront adjacent to the site.

The kiddle-fishing area would have required good access to the town and other markets, and thus to roads such as the old High Street and Dymchurch Road and there was probably an early overland route along the shingle bank to Dymchurch by which goods, especially fish, could be distributed to Romney Marsh. This shingle bank was reinforced or replaced by a wall by 1271 (see the medieval parishes of New Romney, Chapter 3), probably in response to the documented violent storm activity around this time, evidence for which was revealed on the site.

Smaller fishing boats are likely to have been drawn up on the shore in the vicinity, though larger, sea-going, vessels would have used the harbour facilities to the southwest. Chapter 11 provides a discussion of vessels used and the types of fishing employed as demonstrated through the finds evidence from the site.

New Romney's table of maletolts, probably of Romney's greatest period of prosperity in the 12th and 13th centuries, indicates that boats or 'ships' were constructed at the town although the exact location is not specified. However, by the early 14th century, boat breaking (ie careful dismantling for the re-use of

materials) was recorded at New Romney, perhaps as the port shrank and shipbuilding transferred to Smallhythe and Sandwich. Construction, breaking and repair of vessels are all suggested by finds from the Southlands School site, particularly iron rovenails (see Goodburn, Chapter 11, below).

The southwest of the Southlands School site was bounded by George Lane, which probably took its name from one Lawrence Jorge (George), who owned one or two messuages in New Romney in 1354. As described above (see Chapter 3) the vicinity of George Lane was the location of activities requiring extensive amounts of land and where medieval buildings were ephemeral, characteristic of those connected with tanning, milling, salting, and the drying or mending of fishing-nets.

Above all, however, the archaeological remains found at the Southlands School site tell a moving story of a community at odds with its environment. Recurrent storms and flooding caused the loss of property and lives. During the 13th century the people of New Romney repeatedly had to rebuild their storm-damaged town. At the Southlands School site there is evidence that the documented severe storm of 1287 resulted in destruction of buildings and property and consequently much-reduced activity in the following centuries. The excavations, located to the northeast of town along the strand, reflect the development of that area for shore-based fishing activities, boat building, breaking and repair but also provide evidence for the storms that ravaged the coastline in the later 13th century.

In the following the archaeological sequence uncovered has been subdivided into nine phases based on the site's stratigraphy and dating of the archaeological features from associated cultural remains. Of these, Phases 2–7 represent a very short, yet intense, period of the site's history when this area of the south coast was subject to frequent storms. This has resulted in the mixing and redeposition of much material and precise dating from recovered finds is difficult. Where pertinent, and in particular for dating, finds evidence has been integrated into this narrative. Details of the finds assemblages retrieved are presented in the following three chapters. The stratigraphic sequence presented here draws on work undertaken by PCA as well as Wessex Archaeology and Archaeology South-East as outlined in Chapter 1.

Phase 1: The Early Medieval Topography; a Shingle Bank and Foreshore

The earliest phase of activity identified on the site consisted of wind- and water-deposited layers of natural shingle and sands, which were found underlying the whole of Area B, wherever sufficient depth was attained in the excavations. The lowest strata were formed of pebbles and shingle. Although generally found to be between 0.3m and 0.7m in thickness towards the northeast of the area of investigation this deposit was found to be in excess of 1.50m thick. The strata underlying this material were formed of pebbles and shingle, found in 21 of the foundation and drainage trenches. The surface of these deposits lay at levels up to 4.42m OD along the Dymchurch Road (southeast) and Fairfield Road (northwest) boundaries of the site, falling to a lowest level of 3.07m between these two boundaries, demonstrating that the shingle had been laid down in ridges running parallel to, and backwards from, the beach which would have been close by to the southeast. The shingle ridge banks are the result of the drifting of the gravel by sea action. Overlying these deposits the upper part of this natural sequence consisted of layers of sand, the surface of which was found at levels of 6m OD and above in drainage pit D61, to the south of Area A, falling to c. 3.80m OD in the southwest. Although generally found to be between 0.3m and 0.7m in thickness towards the northeast of the area of investigation this deposit was found to be in excess of 1.50m thick. These shingles and sands were naturally deposited and produced no dating evidence, on the basis of subsequent activity the upper surface of these deposits was apparently laid down in the early medieval period (see Phase 2, below). No evidence for earlier activity was recovered, in any form, from the excavations at Southlands School, although the beach front area may have been used during the Saxon period, the location of the shore at this time was not established. Modern Dymchurch Road runs along a raised bank with the land on the southeast side of the road dropping significantly down to a level plain at c. 3m–3.2m OD (Fig. 29), this modern topography apparently reflecting the early medieval foreshore and beach.

Fig. 29   The raised bank on the southeast side of Dymchurch Road; Southlands School site lies to the west of the image

Phase 2: 13th-Century Activity on the Foreshore

The earliest human activity on the site was represented by deposits found on the south side of Area A. As these were found at the formation level of the access road that was being built they were subsequently preserved *in situ*. Layers of thin clay and sandy material were uncovered which were burnt in places, and flecks of charcoal were abundant. These deposits were found at a level of c. 6m OD sloping down to the southeastern limit of the development area along Dymchurch Road. A single isolated stakehole was found cutting the clay and sandy layers, which have been interpreted as accumulations on a sloping foreshore, dropping down to the level of the beach and sea on the south side of the road. Small quantities of cultural material were associated with these layers, consisting of pottery fragments post-dating 1250, thus a mid-13th-century deposition date is likely. However, other than attesting to human presence on the foreshore during this period, the remains tell us little of the nature of that activity. The sloping foreshore leading down to the beach and the shingle bank, along which Dymchurch Road now runs, can still be seen in the modern topography of the town and to the southeast of the site, beyond Dymchurch Road, the ground slopes sharply away to the former seafront (Fig. 29).

Phase 3: Storm Deposits

Overlying these layers was a deep layer of coarse sand, up to 0.5 m thick, apparently laid down by water in a high-energy depositional environment, suggesting that it was deposited during a particularly severe storm (context [150]). Ceramics recovered from the sand date to between 1150 and 1350, with a probable deposition date of between 1250 and 1300. A single silver Long Cross penny (small find <26>), dated to Henry III (1247–1272) was also recovered from this layer. Considering the projected deposition date and the stratigraphic position of this part of the sequence, a severe storm documented for the winter of 1252–1253 (Brooks 1988), may have been responsible for the laying down of this sand.

The evaluation at Southlands School, Dymchurch Road (NCR 02) to the northwest by PCA exposed sandy deposits in the deeper sections of three evaluation trenches; these layers were also attributed to a storm event (Wragg 2002). These were initially interpreted as being the result of the great storm of 1287, on the basis of the overlying archaeology being predominantly dated to the late 13th century by ceramics including Rye wares and Saintonge imports (C. Jarrett, pers. comm.). However, given the limited investigation here it is possible that some of these layers, at least, may have been earlier.

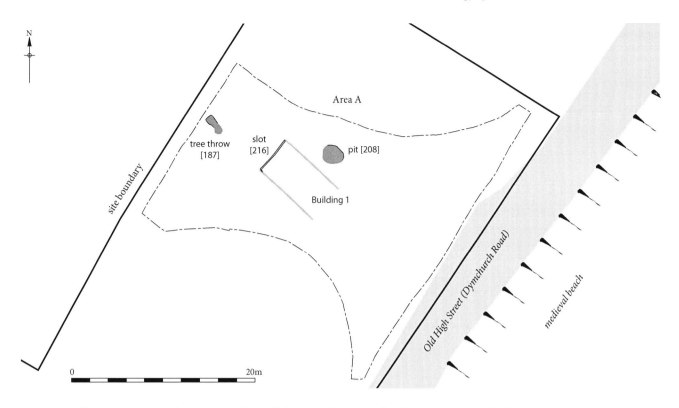

Fig. 30   Building 1 shown in relation to the Old High Street as shown on the tithe map of 1840 (scale 1:400)

Phase 4: Building Construction on the Beach Front

A series of features were identified in Area A, cutting into the top of the storm-deposited sand. On the northeast side of the excavations, a single cut [216] *c.* 4m long and 80mm wide, was found on a northeast by southwest orientation, running parallel to the projected former beachfront. This apparently represents a foundation for a beam slot, with the suggestion of a right-angled return running to the southeast from its southwestern end (Fig. 30). It is likely that the linear feature represents the truncated fragment of a structure (Building 1), facing the sea and either on the beach or facing on to it. The artefact assemblage and archaeological remains did not assist in defining the type of activities undertaken here, although given their location, focussed on the beach and sea, a link with these seems probable. To the northwest of the foundation remains was a tree-throw hollow, the fill of which included pot sherds with a broad 1150–1400 date range, and a small copper-alloy key <33>. To the east of the beam slot was a pit, also containing pottery fragments, which dated between 1150 and 1350. There was no evidence for any superstructure and given the limited remains excavated it is not possible to determine the form of this building with any certainty, although the beam slot suggests a building constructed of timber, clay or wattle and daub. The wall return to the southwest and the pit to the north suggest an approximate width of 4m for the building.

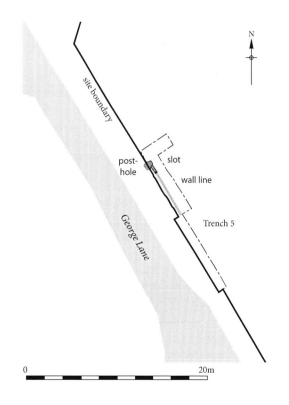

Fig. 31   Phase 4 activity in Trench 5 shown in relation to George Lane as shown on the tithe map of 1840 (scale 1:400)

Any such building constructed on or near the beach during the second half of the 13th century would have been vulnerable in an exposed seafront location. The very fragmentary nature of the surviving archaeology is a testament to the fragility of such buildings on the margin of land and water, especially during a period when frequent storms, some of which were very severe, are documented along this stretch of coast. To the southeast, towards the sea front, any remains of this building would have been removed by the storm that destroyed Building 2 (Phase 6, below), if not by earlier storm events. Although there was no evidence found to indicate that this building was destroyed during such an event, it clearly fell out of use, either due to damage or falling into disrepair, as indicated by the deposits covering the remains (Phase 5, below).

Further structural features assigned to Phase 4 were uncovered in Trench 5 along the southwestern site boundary (Fig. 31). Two postholes and the fragment of a beam slot foundation, 2.2m in length and 0.22m wide, running parallel to the present site limit were uncovered here. Associated pottery dated to between 1150 and 1350. These features appear to have formed part of a medieval fence or wall line, though could conceivably be the fragmentary remains of a timber-framed building. The alignment with the site boundary along George Lane, antecedents to which are present on the earliest Ordnance Survey map, the 1840 tithe map (Fig. 13) and the 1683 map in the town hall of New Romney (Fig. 22), indicate the longevity of this boundary, which probably dates to the mid-13th-century period of use of this sector of the town.

Phase 5: Abandonment and Accumulation of Dumped Material

Dumped waste and silt deposits, containing lenses of charcoal and ash including occasional pockets of more cessy material, were found overlying the fragmentary remains in Area A suggesting that once the building fell out of use the area was peripheral to settlement, being used for deposition of refuse. However, given the dating evidence and rebuilding of the structure described below, this plot of land is not likely to have remained unoccupied for long. The associated cultural material dates to *c.* 1250–1450, with a 13th-century deposition date being indicated. Some residual 10th–11th-century Saxo-Norman pottery was also recovered as well as a cut early 13th-century Short Cross penny <34>. The latter was minted between 1229 and 1232 in London (moneyer Ledulf, see coin catalogue, Chapter 10). The Short Cross coinage was recalled and replaced in 1247, this coin is therefore likely to have been originally lost between 1229 and 1247, and redeposited here, given the presence of a Long Cross penny dated to after 1247 in an earlier (Phase 3) deposit.

A single, incomplete, robust iron fish hook, of a type considered suitable for line fishing in open water rather than off the beach or for coastal fishing, was recovered from a layer of silty clay in Trench 5, Area B. Fish hooks of medieval date have turned up at other sites excavated in New Romney, such as at Prospect House, in Fairfield Road, adjacent to Southlands School (Willson 2003). Further afield they are known from Great Yarmouth in Norfolk (Rogerson 1976), from medieval Dover (Riddler 2006b, 289–290), from Meols on the Wirral and from sites along the Thames and they are also known to have been manufactured in King's Lynn (J. Cowgill, pers. comm.). A discussion of medieval fishing implements and practices in relation to the finds recovered from Southlands School excavation and the later evaluation (NCR 02, Wragg 2002) is provided below (see Riddler, Chapter 11).

Phase 6: Further Building Construction on the Beach Front

Following the storm damage, building and subsequent abandonment of the beachfront area in the vicinity of site there are indications of intensification in occupation of the beachfront and its immediate hinterland. Evidence of a substantial building was found in Area A, overlying the footprint of Building 1 and extending somewhat beyond it, apparently representing a replacement for that building, rebuilt on a more substantial scale. This was demonstrably in use for some time, as it had been re-floored at least twice during its lifetime. The main room of the building, aligned northeast to southwest, perpendicular to the beachfront, was *c.* 7m in width and at least 11m long. It was truncated to the east by storm activity, but probably extended almost to the line of the Old High Street (Fig. 32). A small rectangular lean-to had been added on to the northwest corner of the building, on the side facing away from the sea (Fig. 32, Fig. 33). The building had trench-built foundations [167] filled with a layer of crushed greensand, gravel and mortar, capped with a layer of large rounded cobbles, measuring up to 0.3m across, set in mortar. This foundation appears to have served as a dry-course for a timber-framed construction.

The large, main room of the building contained the remains of two floors, the lower of which comprised creamy grey mortar, up to 80mm thick, similar in composition to the mortar in the layer capping the foundation base. The upper deposit was a layer of dark brown sandy clay [142] 50mm thick, which may represent an earthen floor in its own right or a levelling deposit for no longer extant raised wooden flooring. A single silver Short Cross penny <16> dating to 1180–1182 and minted in Northampton (see coin catalogue Chapter 10), was recovered from the sandy clay deposit. This coin was relatively little-worn, which would suggest likely deposition before the partial recoinage of the Short Cross coinage in 1205, however given the recovery of a Long Cross penny from underlying Phase 3 deposits, the upper floor layer must have been laid down after 1247 at the earliest. In addition a copper-alloy buckle fragment (<37>),

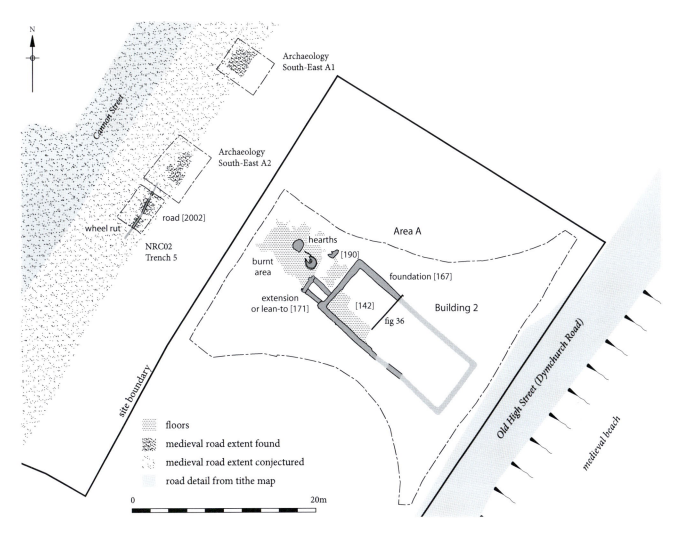

Fig. 32 Building 2 shown in relation to the Old High Street as shown on the tithe map of 1840 and an adjacent road to the north, a medieval precursor to Cannon Street, as identified during evaluations by Pre-Construct Archaeology and excavations by Archaeology South-East (scale 1:400)

as well as locally made early medieval shelly-sandy ware (EM3) and Rye ware jug sherds, including one example decorated with pairs of incised diagonal lines, banded by horizontal lines, were recovered (see Chapter 9, below). It is considered that in the Romney Marsh region early

Fig. 33 Building 2, during excavation, from the northwest

medieval shelly-sandy wares were made until *c.* 1300 (Cotter 2002, 60). The dating of Rye ware indicates that it was being made by 1250, even possibly as early as 1225 and that its production continued until *c.* 1400/1450.

The extension or small lean-to [171] was of a similar construction to the rest of the building and measured 2m x 2.3m, but appeared to be a later addition to the main structure, as the foundations were not bonded or anchored into the base of the walls of the main part of the house. Externally two floors were identified, the lower floor comprised a layer of rounded pebbles [190], which was overlain by an off-white mortar floor. No datable cultural material was associated with this part of the building.

To the northeast of the extension were the remains of a further floor made of mortar, sand and chalk. The nature of these deposits suggests an internal surface and it thus seems likely that this area was in some way roofed, although clearly the elements of the structure associated with these floors was not as substantial as the rest of the building, indicating a further, more flimsy, addition to the back of the building and extension, with the roof supported either on posts or timber walls resting

Fig. 34   The building and foreshore at New Romney, reconstruction by Jake Lunt-Davies

on ground beams, the remains of which did not survive. Beyond the building to the northwest was an area of intense burning, and the remains of three hearths. The associated deposits produced sherds of early medieval shelly-sandy ware including a flared bowl with two bands of curvilinear combed lines, one on top of the rim and one on the inside of the neck of the vessel. Some Rye ware was present including a jug with two bands of horizontal incised zigzag lines as well as a sherd of a Ashford/Wealden pasty ware comprising a jug with a circular point ('daisy') stamp. The latter has been dated *c.* 1200/25-1400. A single un-diagnostic iron nail was also found in association with this hearth complex.

The gravel, mortar and cobble foundation is likely to have supported the base plate of a timber-framed two-storey house. In layout and size the building is somewhat similar to that of a medieval house excavated at 28–34 Watergate Street in Chester (Grenville 1997, 187), which can serve as a workable parallel. The latter had internal measurements of *c.* 7m by 18m, was partially open fronted, and had a yard and detached kitchen to the rear. The re-flooring of the Southlands School structure demonstrates that it had some longevity although the available evidence unfortunately does not assist in establishing whether it was in use seasonally or permanently. The lack of evidence for internal divisions suggests an open hall, at least at ground level within

Fig. 35   The road identified in evaluation Trench 5, looking west

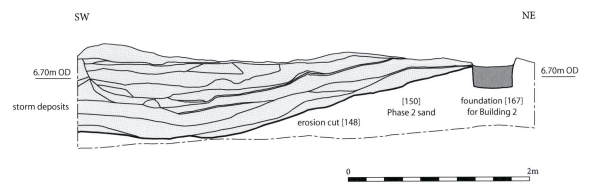

SW   NE

6.70m OD   6.70m OD

storm deposits

[150]
Phase 2 sand

foundation [167]
for Building 2

erosion cut [148]

0   2m

Fig. 36   Section through Building 2 showing storm damage (scale 1:40)

Fig. 37   Building 2, during excavation, showing storm damage in section, looking northwest

the excavated area, although there may have been subdivisions towards the front of the building in that part of the structure that was subsequently lost to the sea. The lack of slag and industrial waste in the space to the rear of the property at the Southlands School site around the hearths located there suggests that, as was the case with the Chester house, this represents a kitchen area. However, archival information indicates that one of the processes carried out in the town was the smoking of fish in order to preserve it, and the physical evidence uncovered here may point to its occurrence here near where the fish was landed, as well as close to the harbour at Herring Hang field (see Chapter 6, Fig. 17).

The building is likely to have been weather-boarded to protect the walls from the elements, and the relatively limited quantities of roofing tile found from the excavations suggest it had a thatched roof. It did not have a stone- or brick-built chimney, but the recovery of fragments of ceramic 'ventilators' from later (Phase 7) destruction layers suggests the building had ceramic chimney or ventilation pots set into the roof to help in drawing out smoke (see Jarrett, below).

The remains of the house were located some 25m from the modern bank supporting Dymchurch Road,

on its southeast side, and the surviving wall extended to approximately 7m from the projected line of Dymchurch Road. The ground beyond would have dropped some 3m onto the beach. The surrounding area was perhaps most comparable with that of the present Dungeness foreland, comprising shingle ridges filled in with sand, with a sparse and intermittent gorse, grasses and moss cover. The building probably had a workshop or working area at the front end, facing the sea and fronting onto Dymchurch Road. Almost certainly the property would have been associated either directly with fishing or with a trade dealing with the maintenance, repair or making of things relevant to boats or fishing, or alternatively to the commerce coming in over the strand. The cultural material found with the remains unfortunately does not help in narrowing down the nature of the activities carried out on the premises any further. However, pottery manufacture and iron-working are both indicated very close by (see below, Stevenson and Hunter 2005, 10).

Along the northwestern perimeter of the site in Trenches 2 and 3 were make-up layers which, in Trench 2, were overlain by a metalled surface. The pottery which came from these layers consisted of Ashford/Wealden or Rye sandy ware. In addition there was a fragment of lead waste.

The archaeological evaluation at the Southlands School, Dymchurch Road (NCR 02) site carried out by PCA to the northeast of the main excavations revealed a metalled surface along the eastern margin of the site in Trench 5, parallel to Cannon Street, which may represent a former medieval road. A wheel rut and posthole were found cutting this surface (Fig. 35) (Wragg 2002). This road appears to be a medieval precursor to Cannon Street, either more substantial and significantly wider than the road depicted on the tithe map of 1840, or located further south. The line of this road appears to join up with the medieval 'lost lane' proposed by Willson (2003), based on the location of property boundaries and excavated evidence for buildings between Fairfield Road and the High Street to the west of George Lane (see Fig. 40). A kink in George Lane may reflect the crossing point of this former lane, as might the similar kink in Craythorne Lane at its junction with Cannon Street.

Subsequent excavations by Archaeology South-East identified further sections of this medieval road surface (Stevenson and Hunter 2005, 24–26) and uncovered numerous pit features and importantly the truncated remains of a pottery kiln and a small assemblage of ceramic wasters in sand and shell tempered wares. This ceramic production evidence represents the first

substantiated material confirming pottery production in New Romney (Stevenson and Hunter 2005, 10; Barber 2005, 28–29). Further indications of limited iron-working were also uncovered, comprising metal-working slag. Evidence for fishing was found in the form of a group of spade-end fish hooks and lead net weights (Barber 2005, 34–36), as well as for the consumption of considerable quantities of marine molluscs, dominated by oyster but additionally including common cockle, mussel and common whelk (Dunkin 2005, 43–45). The fish assemblage bears out the reality of coastal as well as deep sea fishing with the remains including plaice, sole, turbot, cod, ling, whiting, conger eel, gurnard, mackerel, sea bream and ray although surprisingly little herring. The ling and cod are particularly large specimens in excess of a metre in length, with some being nearer 1.5 metres; these in particular are indicative of the exploitation of deep waters (Jaques 2005, 47–50). A discussion of the fish remains recovered from the Southlands School site is provided below (see Armitage, Chapter 11), here remains included cod, ling, gurnard, conger eel, thornback ray and plaice. This can be compared with medieval fish remains from a sample of other southeast Kent sites as presented by Riddler (see Chapter 11, below).

Fig. 38   The impact of the storm, reconstruction by Jake Lunt-Davies

Phase 7: Storm Damage and Attempts at Consolidation

The surviving remains of the building were severely truncated to the southeast on the side facing the beachfront, demonstrating the calamitous impact of a serious storm event. The whole eastern end of the structure was ripped away and undercut by water-action; the profile of the deposits on which the building was founded was visible here and the truncation cut was filled with coarse, water-sorted and deposited material. The force of the storm is evinced by the destruction of the front of Building 2 and the massive cut [148], 1m deep and over 4m wide, left by the storm (Fig. 36, Fig. 37).

It is possible that as much as 7m of the length of the building was lost, based on the assumption that its frontage extended as far as Dymchurch Road (old High Street). The surrounding area and the hearths to the rear were sealed by a layer of coarse sand and gravel, further indicating the seriousness of the episode. The finds assemblage associated with these deposits comprised an uncommon group, which, as demonstrated below, shows both the relative prosperity of the inhabitants of the site and also the unexpected nature and ferocity of the storm which affected them. Clearly a gale of the magnitude indicated here, accompanied by a surge tide as demonstrated by the deposition of thick layers of sand and gravel at levels above 6m OD, would have been a significant threat to the survival of people and livestock. There would not have been many places for individuals to retreat to in the face of the onslaught unleashed by the weather, with nowhere else offering higher ground in the vicinity, except perhaps for the stone-built churches and hospitals. The former would have been a natural refuge as they would have offered both physical and spiritual protection in this time of need.

In spite of the destruction wreaked by the storm, determined attempts were made to stabilise the slope of the beach, with midden material and sandy silt being used to plug the erosion gaps. These stabilisation deposits produced 500 sherds of pottery, the largest single group of material found at the site. This group contains a high frequency of sherds from fabric types which were generally diminishing in popularity up to that point, such as East Sussex shell and flint-tempered coarse sandy ware (fabric EM33) dated to *c.* 1075–1250 and particularly non-local fine sandy with flint and sparse shell (fabric EM29) which has a date range of 1125/50–1250. The generally early dates for this material perhaps indicate that the storm damaged and eroded earlier deposits and cast up this pottery.

The principal pottery type present was shell and sand-tempered ware comprising just over half of the assemblage (251 sherds) with jar-shapes dominating but bowls, dishes, ventilators and jugs all being present. Rye ware was also common mainly as jug sherds, frequently with white-slip painted designs. Baluster, rounded and shouldered jugs were also found, as well as jars, a dish, probable louvers and a pipkin handle. Other locally produced wares included Ashford/Wealden or Rye sandy ware, most frequent in the form of jug sherds and with a possible cylindrical vessel present. Amongst the other local wares there are bowls or dishes, a cauldron, jars and jugs including a jug sherd painted in a white slip with a horizontal arc and dot design in Rye/Wealden pink-buff ware with flint shell or chalk, which was produced between 1250 and 1450. Occasional sherds in other Ashford/Wealden fabrics were also present.

Pottery imported to the site was principally Scarborough type ware (seven sherds) in the form of green-glazed jugs with incised line decoration or with a clear (honey-coloured) glaze with scale decoration and green-glazed ribs or pellets as well as 'red-slip' painted ribs and a single Kingston-type ware green-glazed jug sherd with evidence of applied decoration. Grey sandy wares from Northern France or Flanders were found including sixteen sherds from a single jug, fragments of the rim of which were identified in Phase 5 deposits, demonstrating that the midden deposits used to repair the damage to the beachfront were sourced in the immediate vicinity. Other imported vessels include Saintonge wares (nine sherds), green-glazed jugs and the pouring spout of a probable sgraffito jug with a band of red slip. There is also a single sherd of a Rouen polychrome jug with raised circles surrounded by brown glaze and a single sherd of Flemish Highly decorated ware clear-glazed, with multiple horizontal bands in a rouletted square (see Jarrett, Chapter 9, below).

In addition to the pottery a small number of rovenails came from these deposits. These derive from the building or breaking of medium-sized clinker built vessels (see Goodburn, Chapter 11), indicating that these activities were being carried out in the immediate vicinity.

Numerous varied personal finds are further indicators of the nature of life on the foreshore. The group includes four copper-alloy strap ends, a lead token and a lead cloth seal. In addition there are a lead weighted sheep/goat phalange for the game of knuckle bones, a fragment of copper-alloy sheeting, a rim fragment of a copper-alloy vessel and a lead plug for repairing holed ceramic vessels, as well as five lead fishing net weights and a fragment of an iron fish hook, two copper-alloy buckles, two mounts, two copper-alloy brooches and one silver one.

The associated coinage from these deposits is listed below (see coin catalogue, Chapter 10) but includes: <36>, a Short Cross cut halfpenny dated 1205–1207, minted at Northampton; a second Short Cross cut half penny (<38>) dated to 1207–c.1210 and minted at Canterbury and a third Short Cross cut halfpenny (<32>) dated to *c.* 1229–1232 and minted in London. The Short Cross coinage was recalled and replaced in 1247 so all three coins are likely to have been deposited before that date. There was also an imitation Short Cross, cut halfpenny (<35>). Its style somewhat resembles that of coins struck following the 1205 reform, so it is likely to date to the first half of the 13th century. A single Long Cross cut halfpenny (<456>) dated 1248–1250, minted at Canterbury was also recovered. This coinage was withdrawn and replaced in 1279–1280 and it is virtually certain that this coin was deposited before this date. Also recovered were an Edward I farthing (<1>) which dates to *c.* 1279–1280, with the coin showing little wear, and a single Edward I penny, which dates to 1282–1289, from the London mint. Both of the latter coins, given their condition and weight, were probably deposited within a decade or two of issue.

The animal bone assemblage from these same deposits comprises food debris including beef/veal, mutton/lamb, pork, goose, chicken bones, and a variety of fish bone (cod, plaice and conger eel) as well as a single bone element of an adult cat.

What is crystal clear from the cultural material present is that as a group it comprises an uncommon, indeed odd assemblage of items, which would not normally be readily discarded, further confirming the catastrophic nature of the events that resulted in their deposition. The power of the storm is demonstrated by its uncovering of earlier buried archaeology and its suddenness comes to the fore in the group of small finds which poignantly include many personal items not normally found in any great numbers in archaeological contexts. It also confirms the existence of a thriving community up to the moment in time when the group of artefacts was buried together. Indeed it demonstrates the richness of the activities associated with the beach front up to the time this particular storm struck.

The storm's sheer ferocity combined with a deposition date of around the fourth quarter of the 13th-century for the assemblage as a whole is consistent with the storm damage being the result of the historically documented 1287 episode (see Chapter 2, above). In particular the coin evidence supports such an interpretation although it includes a significant portion of earlier material, reflecting the effect the storm had on archaeology predating Building 2.

Similar storm-deposited sands attributed to this calamitous event were revealed during the evaluation at Southlands School, Dymchurch Road (NCR 02). As outlined above (Chapter 1, Historical and archaeological background) similar, storm-deposited sands have been encountered at numerous sites throughout New Romney.

Fig. 39   Fire pit and flue in evaluation Trench 1

Phase 8: After the Storm, a Decline in Activity

Activity immediately following the storm event recorded on the site appears (unsurprisingly) to be significantly reduced, in spite of the attempts to consolidate the 'beach', and the next clear phase of activity is dated to the late-medieval/early post-medieval period. Archaeological evidence in Area A suggests the focus of the subsequent activity shifts to the northwest, somewhat further back from the beach. As established above (see Chapter 2), as a result of the storms by the 14th century the beachfront had migrated to the southwest and access to the strand alongside the area of site had diminished to a watercourse known as the 'havene stremes'.

Along the western and southwestern perimeter of the site contemporary archaeological remains were identified in Trenches 5, 2 and 3. In Area A, a silty clay earthen floor was found with what appeared to be evidence of burning. Immediately to the west of this was a layer of chalk, possibly representing a make-up dump for another floor. On the west side of the chalk deposit a large pit measuring *c.* 4m across contained burnt material in its base. A row of large posts crossed the excavation area immediately west of the floor and make-up layer remnants, on a northnortheast by southsouthwestern orientation, possibly representing a fence or palisade line. Slightly further west was another substantial pit, one of the fills of which produced a fragmentary iron fish hook.

A number of structural elements were identified in Trench 5, including what appeared to be a shallow construction trench with chalk remnants running parallel to the southwestern site boundary; adjoining this feature on its northeast side was a cut, which may represent a robbed-out wall fragment. Further east still a third *c.* 0.3m wide foundation element ran again on the same alignment. This comprised a mix of chalk, mortar and occasional medieval tile fragments and it may have served to support a timber base plate.

To the northwest in Trench 2 was a heavily truncated foundation element surviving to 0.75m in width by 1.10m in length with both faces having been damaged by modern foundations. It was constructed of stone cobbles and gravel. Immediately east of the wall stub were two, probably associated, postholes. These structural elements almost certainly belonged to a late medieval/post-medieval building (Building 3) facing on to Fairfield Road. Further north along the same boundary, in Trench 3 a rubbish pit containing medieval pottery was located. Considerable amounts of residual earlier medieval pottery were found with these contexts, demonstrating continued disturbance of medieval remains in to the late medieval and post-medieval periods.

To the northeast of Area A, in Trench 1 of the Southlands School, Dymchurch Road (NCR 02) evaluation area, a fire pit and flue-type feature were exposed. In the centre of the fire pit, near the flue was the base of an oval unfrogged brick built structure (Wragg 2002),

Fig. 40   Detail of the tithe map of 1840 in the vicinity of the site, in relation to areas of excavation, showing conjectured route of
the lost medieval lane (scale 1: 2000)

thought to have served as a type of furnace associated
with metalworking (Fig. 39). Under the circumstances of
this phase of fieldwork the remains were left *in situ* and
on subsequent excavation by Archaeology South-East the
feature was thought to represent a hearth (Stevenson and
Hunter 2005, 11). A large pit or ditch was located just to
the southwest of the furnace, in Trench 2.

Phase 9: Later Post-Medieval Developments

The post-medieval deposits found demonstrate that the area
at the northeast of the site was put to horticultural use as
indicated by extensive dumps of charcoal-rich soils with a
high humic content found across much of Area A.
Occasional pits, postholes and post pits cut these layers.
Some of these may be associated with the post-mill, which
is known to have stood in this part of the site until its final
demolition in 1914.

In the 14th century five windmills are known to have
been present in New Romney. The windmill at the north
end of town is referred to in many early documents, it
served for the milling of corn, and a decision to rebuild it
was recorded in 1794. It was at this time in very bad repair

with its main post being decayed (Teichman-Derville
1929, 165–166). Limited evidence for the presence of this
windmill and its predecessors comprising a post pit in the
approximate position at the Southlands School site suggests
that the post-mill had little impact on the deposits on
which it was founded. The feature would have originally
have been cut from a medieval surface, the fill of the post
pit cut included pottery of 19th-century date, probably
derived from the demolition of the mill, which is known to
have been carried out in 1914. This windmill was perfectly
sited on one of the highest locations fronted by the exposed
lower-lying meadowland to the east. The wind would have
been unimpeded by any prominent landscape features
on this side of the town. If the location of the windmill as
shown on the tithe map is correct then most of the remains
of this would have lain outside the excavation area at
Southlands School.

Along the southeastern site boundary a metalled surface
was found in Trench 5. This may be part of a post-medieval
road or yard, perhaps part of George Lane. Several brick
wall foundation elements were found in Trenches 1 and 2
as was a single course of a chalk and ragstone foundation in
Trench 3. These were all part of late 18th- and 19th-century
structures, which once stood facing on to Fairfield Road.

Chapter 9 The Ceramics: Pottery Consumption and Trade

Chris Jarrett

The Southlands School site produced the single largest group of pottery to have been excavated in New Romney and it can be used to characterize the medieval assemblages from the area and inform on supply, manufacture and trade. The pottery types have been classified according to the Canterbury Archaeological Trust coding system for Kent medieval and post-medieval ceramics (Cotter 1997a; Cotter 2006).

A total of 3,744 sherds of pottery were recovered falling into two broad groups by date, one dating mainly to the 13th century and the other to the post-medieval period. Their condition was largely fragmentary, but profiles of vessels could be reconstructed. This report concentrates on the medieval material, which adds to our understanding of the town as a market for local pottery types and aids in its dating by reference to the stratigraphic relationships of the deposits it derives from. The imported wares are also important as an indicator of the trade and contact this Cinque Port had with the continent.

The Medieval Pottery

Local wares

Shell-tempered

The medieval shell-tempered wares have been divided into two groups, those with little or no sand (EM 2), represented here by a single sherd, and fabric with moderate sand (EM3), which is the principal pottery type for the medieval period. Medieval Shell-tempered wares are common throughout Kent and the southeast and production ceases at different times in different areas. It is believed that in the Romney Marsh region the shell-tempered wares continued to be made until *c.* 1300, using local clays containing contemporary marine (rather than fossil) shell, with fairly sparse occurrences of brackish water gastropods (Cotter 2002, 60). The shell occurs in variable amounts, from sparse to abundant. Evidence for local production of this ware comes from a truncated medieval pottery kiln found on the adjacent Southlands School excavation on Dymchurch Road (site code: NRC02) and associated with the kiln is a small number of wasters in a sand and shell-tempered fabric (Barber 2005, 28–29).

The forms are mostly jar-shapes (Fig. 41.1– Fig. 41.6), in a range of sizes, usually rounded or globular in profile with a saggy or convex base. The shapes of the rims are variable, with one example, dating to the late 11th or 12th century, being everted with a thickened rounded end (Fig. 41.1). Within the site stratigraphy typological changes can be observed in vessel form over the ware's period of use. During the 13th century more upright rims with external rounded thickenings (Fig. 41.2) or hooked rims (Fig. 41.3) and bevelled rims Fig. 41.4) are gradually superseded by flat topped rims with squared or rounded profiles (Fig. 41.5– Fig. 41.6). The jars when decorated can have either vertical or diagonal applied strips and are often pinched. Applied horizontal strips with finger pinching also occur, sometimes on the shoulders of vessels. Some examples have a raised horizontal strip, which was finger-decorated or thumbed (Fig. 41.6). Other decoration comprises incised lines on the necks of the vessels and in the late 13th century, horizontal rilling applied on the wheel on the shoulders of vessels. Jar sherds with pierced bodies (made before firing the vessel) are dated to after *c.* 1290, and one vessel found was sooted. The jar-shaped vessels are wheel-thrown or of composite manufacture, where the body and base were formed by hand and the rim added with a slow wheel. Jar-shaped vessels would be used for a range of functions. Certainly many of the shell-tempered wares were sooted and contained food residues, indicating they were used as cooking pots. Occasionally the presence of lime scale indicates they were used for boiling water. Many of these closed-shaped vessels were probably used for storage, especially where residues are not present on the pot.

The bowl- and dish-shaped vessels on the site mostly have a flared profile. A small rounded example was present as was a spouted bowl (Fig. 41.7). The rims of these vessels are mostly flat-topped with a squared profile (Fig. 41.8), but rounded and bevelled examples, with the rim folded under, also occur. Decoration is restricted to the tops of rims and the insides of vessels and comprises incised and combed curvilinear lines (Fig. 41.9). Some of these vessels were used for cooking or heating water, as indicated by the presence of external sooting, internal carbonised deposits or lime scale. Some vessels were not sooted and therefore perhaps used for serving food or storage.

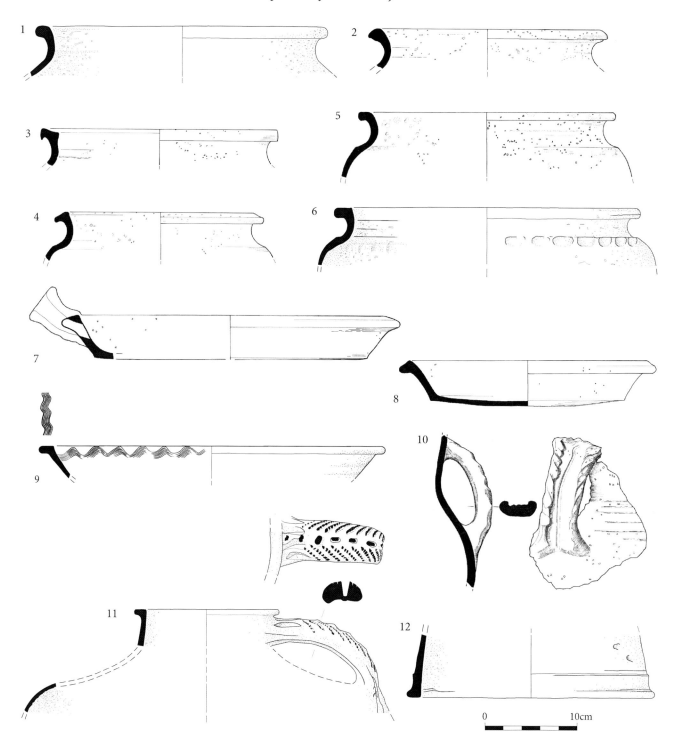

Fig. 41   Medieval pottery, local shell-tempered (scale 1:4)

The jugs (Fig. 41.10– Fig. 41.11) in the shelly sandy ware appear to be of a rounded type, but are fragmentary. One late 13th-century example has a clubbed rim, whilst handles on mid- to late 13th-century examples are of a strap type with the edges curved up and thumbed. Additional ornamentation on the strap handles can be seen, as on an early to mid-13th-century example with a central line of point stabbing, whilst another handle from the *c.* 1287 storm deposits has an incised line (Fig. 41.10). Other decoration consists of a thumbed base, and shoulders with widely spaced, light ridges. The Phase 8

(post *c.* 1287) and later jugs have thickened, but narrow flat-topped rims and two examples have a cordon on the neck, formed by pinching the exterior and using a finger to push from inside. Body decoration consists again of widely spaced ridges on the neck, occasionally with applied thumbed vertical strip decoration. In this phase handles consist of the strap type with thumbed edges, as well as broad oval profile handles which first appear here at this date and are decorated with complex stabbing, either using knife slashes, pointed tools or combs (Fig. 41.11). The jugs appeared to be handmade and wheel finished. Two

Fig. 42   Ventilator in early medieval shell-tempered with moderate sand ware

examples demonstrate how the handles were attached to the vessels: one instance shows how the lower handle was attached, possibly by a small cut out in the body through which the handle was mortised; on another example a finger had been used internally to push the neck on to the handle on the rim. There appears to have been no attempt at additional finishing to disguise how the handles were added to the jug body.

Possible curfews were represented by four sherds, one with a circular piercing and another part of the dome of a vessel, both with internal sooting. These inverted dish-shaped vessels with a handle on the top were placed over embers to keep them alight enabling restarting of fires.

Roof furniture in the form of ventilators (in EM3) was common (Fig. 41.12, Fig. 42), represented by eighteen sherds, in the form of open cylindrical vessels. The 'rims' have a variety of finishes, usually a flattened top, but external and internal thickening and occasional collared or clubbed types are also found. One or more circular piercings are present in the middle of the vessel. When decorated, the ventilators usually have applied pinched strips, often vertical but occasionally with a horizontal strip below the rim, or diagonal examples, while one has vertical knife notches on the rim. These have often been called chimney pots but ventilators would appear to be a more appropriate term as they rarely show internal signs of sooting. The ventilators from this excavation conform to Dunning's 'Sussex type chimney pots'. However, ventilators are commonly found in excavations along the southeast coast, representing something of a local phenomenon, particularly in Hampshire and Sussex where they are often found amongst the wasters on pottery production sites (Dunning 1961). Ventilators would be used on the roofs of buildings which did not have chimneys, set into the thatch to allow smoke from a central fire to escape readily.

Shell and flint-tempered sandy wares

Fabric EM28, ?Kentish sandy ware with moderate shell and sparse flint-temper, has a pinkish-brown colour with

grey or darker surfaces and contains abundant ill-sorted multi-coloured quartz of up to 3mm, abundant ill-sorted angular quartz up to 3mm and sparse iron-ore inclusions. Cotter (2006, 166) makes a comparison with the ?Ashford/Wealden fabrics M40A and M40B, besides the later PM2 fabrics common in Folkestone and Dover to suggest the source for this pottery type. It is rare on the site (five sherds, mainly in Phase 2). Only jar-shaped vessels could be recognised and the only rim is thickened and rounded externally (Fig. 43.1). It has a date range of 1175/1200–1225.

The non-local fine sandy ware with flint and sparse shell (fabric EM29) has a grey core with pinkish brown surfaces, ill-sorted multicoloured quartz up to 3mm in size and moderate, sub-angular multi-coloured quartz, but with a predominance of reddish brown flint up to 3mm. The shell inclusions in this fabric occur as very sparse flecks up to 2mm across. A suggested common source for this pottery type may be at Ashford, or between there and the coast (Cotter 2006, 163). Bowls or dishes are present either with flat tops (Fig. 43.2), or with a thickened rounded exterior. There is a ventilator with applied vertical strips. The most common forms are jars with a rounded profile, the rims being clubbed or rounded, sometimes with a bevel or flat top (Fig. 43.3) and convex bases. One vessel is decorated with a notched applied vertical strip and is dated to 1125/50–1250.

?East Sussex-shell and flint-tempered coarse ware (fabric EM33), dated *c.* 1075–1250, has a mid-grey core with pinkish-brown surfaces, abundant sub-angular grey quartz of up to 0.3mm, sparse sub-angular multi-coloured flint up to 3mm and sparse shell flecks, but there are also moderate ill-sorted angular ?grog inclusions of up to 3.5mm in size. The distribution of this ware appears to be coastal, between Dover and New Romney (Cotter 2006, 160) indicating production within this area. Four sherds are present and include fragments of a probable jar and dish that appear to be of composite manufacture. It has a production date range of *c.* 1075–1250.

Wealden sandy wares

Wealden pink-buff sandy ware with flint, chalk and iron oxide (M10F) and ?Rye-Romney Marsh Wealden buff-brown sandy ware (M10R) are related to the Ashford/Wealden or Rye sandy wares (M40). The M10F ware when comprising bowls or dishes, is exclusively represented by base sherds with an internal clear glaze that appears yellow and is frequently externally sooted. The jars in this fabric recorded from the excavation are rounded in shape and can be collared (Fig. 43.4) in profile or with a flat top with a glaze just inside the rim. Except for rilling on the shoulder of one example, no other decoration is found on these vessels. The jug sherds include rounded forms and have rim types that are either collared or flat-topped with a rounded profile. Decoration consists of rilling on the neck and shoulder or as combed wavy incised horizontal lines. These are green-glazed and sometimes splashed or coarse in appearance. The Rye/Romney Marsh variant (M10R) is present with three sherds from the convex bases of a bowl or dish with an internal glaze and a jar. The dating of these wares in Kent is uncertain and although thought to be after *c.* 1350, their presence here can only be used to demonstrate a production date of after *c.* 1250.

Rye wares

Pottery kilns have been found in Rye at St Bartholomew's Hospital, Spital Field. The products of this industry are difficult to distinguish by fabric as the potters were using several different sources of clay (Vidler 1932, 1933, 1936; Barton 1979). Pottery types can be sandy (M13A), fine sandy (M13B) and reduced (M13C), but light-firing clays were also used (Streeten 1985). The waster material from the kiln sites shows that a wide number of decorative techniques were employed, such as *sgraffito*, anthropomorphic, applied, stamped and white-slip painted decoration, the latter usually but not exclusively associated with reduced wares (Barton 1979, 191–254). One identifier for this fabric is a band of white slip inside the necks of jugs, regardless of the jug being externally white-slipped or not. This is a tradition found at other East Sussex medieval kiln sites, such as Ringmer (Barton 1979, 181). The dating of the Rye pottery indicates that its manufacture started around 1250, if not earlier, perhaps as early as 1225 and continued until *c.* 1400/1450.

The site produced some 724 sherds of Rye ware (or Rye-type ware) pottery. In the coarse sandy fabric (M13A) it is found in the form of bowls or dishes (Fig. 43.5), a possible cauldron, jars and jugs, including baluster, conical, shouldered, rounded and small rounded examples, as well as pipkins. Roof furniture includes a ventilator and a louver. The finer sandy fabric (M13B) is found only as jugs, while the reduced fabric (M13C) is present in the form of jar and jug sherds. A white firing fabric is found in the form of a single jug sherd. The bowls and dishes are usually glazed on the inside base and decoration is confined to a combed wavy line on a dish rim. On jar-shaped vessels, the rims are mostly flat-topped with a rounded edge and decoration is confined to one vessel, which has an applied notched strip. Decoration of jugs was done while throwing the vessel and comprises cordons on the neck; one vessel has a corrugated surface. More complex decoration techniques include incising and slip-painting, often fitting the highly decorated 13th-century pottery tradition. Applied decoration occurs as vertical strips, often notched with a tool, but also as alternating vertical strips of white and red clay. Two sherds have applied lines of scales, one using white clay, while other sherds have pellets, often with additional types of decoration. Incised decoration is present in the form of horizontal or diagonal lines, sometimes forming rectangular or lozenge-shaped panels, or in wavy or zigzag lines but can occur in combination together with other motifs. The more complex incised designs are found from *c.* 1280 onwards. Combing may be present with horizontal or wavy lines. One sherd has a bossed prunt stamp and dates to after 1287. Barton (1979, 220) places this type

to between 1275 and 1300. One jug sherd is covered in thumbed impressions (this decoration is also found on the M40BR fabric, see below). Here, painted slip decoration can use a red slip, but is more often seen in the form of white-slip lines, the designs are unclear but are probably abstract and some of the white slip lines may be combed. However, many jugs have a plain white slip and green glaze.

?Ashford/Wealden sandy and pasty wares

The Ashford/Wealden wares (M40A, M40B, M40C) are related; they are sandy, slightly pasty with mostly pale brown surfaces and pink, orange, pale brown or blue grey cores, with or without the addition of other inclusions (Cotter 2001, 236). Wasters of the sandy ware with little or no shell (M40B), together with a shelly sandy ware (EM.M5) have been found at Potters corner, Ashford and indicate the presence of a kiln nearby (Grove and Warhurst 1952, Cotter 2006, 168). The characteristics of the sandy with sparse chalk/shell ware (M40A) indicate that it belongs to the Ashford Potters Corner's industry (Cotter 2006, 170). The finer fabric (M40B) occurs on the site in the form of jug and jar sherds, the jugs have a clear-glaze, sometimes splashed, but the only other decoration is a combed wavy line on an uncertain form. The pasty ware with chalk flecks (M40C) is more common and it is found mostly in jug forms with a wide decorative design repertoire. This comprises vertical, horizontal and diagonal incised lines, which are often presented together. Combed wavy lines are also used as well as circular segmented stamps employed together with incised line decoration. The use of white slip is found on one sherd in the form of a narrow, horizontal painted line with green glaze, and another sherd has a white slip coating, while others also have a glaze. Further vessels have a clear, green or an olive brown glaze. They are dated to *c.* 1200/25–1400. Ashford has been tentatively suggested as a source for the pasty ware, because of its similarities to the M40A and M40B pottery types, but the more frequent chalk inclusions suggest a different Wealden production area. Similar medieval tile fabrics from Naccolt, near Wye, 6.5km north east of Ashford and post-medieval tiles from Dover indicate other possible production centres, although a concentration of the pasty ware in the Folkestone area is the most compelling evidence for that location for its kiln sites (Cotter 2006, 173–174).

Ashford/Wealden or Rye sandy ware

The generic fabric (M40BR) has similarities to both the Rye and the Ashford or Wealden pottery industries. The forms recorded from the excavation include bowls or dishes, a lid, jugs in the form of possible balusters, cylindrical, pear-shaped, rounded or shouldered examples, as well as jars. Only one rolled rim of a bowl or dish was present, but there are many bases that could come from such vessels, the majority are internally clear-glazed and frequently sooted. Jars (Fig. 43.6) have a rounded profile with a wide range of rim types and are decorated with vertical or diagonal applied, pinched strips. The decoration of jugs includes many techniques also found in the Rye and the Ashford/Wealden pasty ware (M40C) repertoires, the bodies also being horizontally ribbed and the necks cordoned, vertical applied ribs in a redder clay than the body are used, and incised lines are found horizontally or as zigzags, while combing can be horizontal or in wavy lines. White-slip decoration is present in grid patterns but also as vertical lines and sometimes combed. Thumbed decoration is found on a clear-glazed pear-shaped jug where the vessel was inverted after throwing and bands of thumb impressions were placed around the body, together with horizontal incised lines. Its oval strap handle was attached by pushing a finger through the vessel wall into the handle and is decorated with deep diagonal knife slashes and point stabbing (Fig. 43.7). This vessel's decoration may be closer to a Rye product than an Ashford-Wealden product (J. Cotter, pers. comm.).

?Rye/Wealden pink-buff ware, Wealden white-cream ware

The ?Rye/Wealden pink-buff ware with flint shell or chalk (M45A) ware is present in the form of bowls and dishes, cauldrons, a ventilator and jars. Bowls or dishes usually have flat-topped rims, one with knife stabbing, while another vessel has an internal band of combed arcs below the rim (Fig. 43.8). The bases of these forms

can be internally clear, green or olive-brown glazed and can appear pimply, but the vessels are often externally sooted. However, one base sherd has internal sooting. The cauldrons usually have strap handles with knife cuts running the length of the handle. The jar forms are rounded in shape with squared, rounded rims, bevelled or recessed on the underside. They can be decorated with what appears to be a vertical line of applied scales, or with three incised lines. One body sherd appears to have a lightly burnished or wiped surface, while several vessels have an internal glaze, mostly restricted to the base. The jugs, one with a collared rim, the others externally thickened, are either decorated with incised horizontal lines or with a white slip or green-glaze, while handles have point stabbing. Wealden white-cream ware (M45C). is only found in the form of a probable dripping dish represented by a straight-handle, rectangular in plan, but curved in profile and decorated with point stabbing in an oval pattern. Both wares have a production date of 1250–1450.

Non-local wares

Thames valley wares

There are six sherds of London-type ware (M5), a wheel-thrown sandy redware only present in jug forms, recovered from the site. Four sherds have a white slip and two additionally have a green glaze, while another sherd has applied vertical strips. There is also a large jug

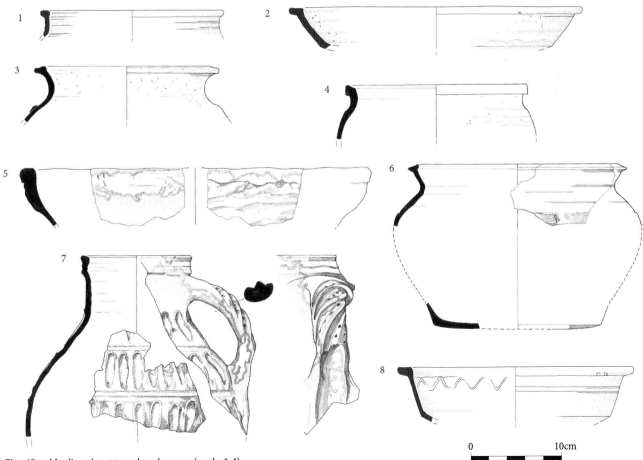

Fig. 43 Medieval pottery, local wares (scale 1:4)

sherd from a Rouen copy, decorated with white-slip in horizontal bands sandwiching lines of white slip dots. London-type ware first appeared in *c.* 1080, but usually in a coarse version, while white-slip jugs are found around *c.* 1140 and continue until 1350 when the industry finished (Pearce *et al.* 1985; Blackmore 1999) or was drastically scaled down in the late 14th century. The London-type wares were heavily influenced by French ceramics from the mid-12th century and were copying Rouen ware between 1180 and 1270. Early 14th-century kilns producing this type of pottery have been found at and adjacent to Woolwich Arsenal in 1999 and 2007 (Mason 2006, 6; Cotter 2008).

Kingston-type ware (M7), a Surrey whiteware, is so named because a number of 14th-century kilns producing this variant have been found in Kingston-upon-Thames, but wasters have also been found in the area around Bankside, Southwark. These may have been ballast from boats plying trade along the Thames rather than representing evidence for pottery production (Vince 1985; Miller and Stephenson 1999; Ayre and Wroe-Brown 2002, 30, 32, 55; Darton *et al.* forthcoming). Kingston-type ware has frequent fine quartz, it is often iron-stained and usually fires to a light buff-colour (Pearce et al.1988). Although it was being made in the late 12th century, it was traded to its main market in London between 1230/40 and 1400. There are 26 sherds present only in the form of jugs and most are green-glazed. There are six sherds in a highly decorated style with vertical applied strips, some of which have a contrasting brown glaze. There is also a sherd with scale decoration. One jug has both a vertical applied strip and a line of scales in a pair, while another sherd has a diamond-rouletted strip (Fig. 44). Highly decorated Kingston-type ware is dated to 1230–1300.

Yorkshire wares

Scarborough ware (M11A; M11 B) is present on the site as 43 sherds, confined to jug forms (Fig. 45). The fabric is soft, friable and pinkish red, usually with a good quality, verdant green glaze. Although its inception date of *c.* 1125 has been questioned, as an export ware it appears *c.* 1200. It first appears at the Southlands School in Phase 3 as two sherds, one of which is decorated with incised diagonal lines below a mid-green quality glaze, but the ware becomes increasingly more frequent in Phases 7 and 8 (see Table 8, Appendix 1). Scarborough jugs (fabric M11A) can have bridge spouts and collared rims, while the rod handles are circular in section with ridged tops, usually attached to the rims with two thumb impressions on the side. Decoration consists of rilling on the neck and body, narrow applied vertical strips, sometimes with applied lines of scale decoration, pellets and incised diagonal and vertical lines. There are two green-glazed jug sherds in a hard, smooth fabric (fabric M11 B), which is dated to *c.* 1225–1350. Scarborough ware has also been identified at Dover and other Kentish coastal sites (Cotter 1997b, 79, Cotter 2006, 194–195).

Fig. 44   Kingston-type ware jug with diamond-rouletted applied strip decoration

Fig. 45   Scarborough ware jug fragments

Fig. 46   Brandsby-type ware jug fragments

There are 38 sherds of Brandsby-type ware (M42), with two fabric types recognised. Three sherds are in a creamy-buff sandy fabric, in the form of light green-glazed jugs. Two sherds from the same vessel have vertically curving, closely spaced ribs and one of these sherds first appears in Phase 5, while another sherd is in Phase 8 from an anthropomorphic jug and comprises a beard with a line of point stabbing (J. Cotter, pers. comm.). There are also 35 sherds in a pinkish red fabric (very similar to that of the Scarborough ware fabric: M11A) with a honey-coloured glaze, decorated either with white-slip vertical lines or diamond-shaped panels made with applied narrow red clay strips, sometimes highlighted in green and occurring with red clay pellets (Fig. 46). This red fabric is present mostly in Phase 8 at the Southlands School excavation. The ridged handles and jug shapes and fabric type indicates that both Brandsby and Scarborough shared technologies and the geology they exploited for the clay. Brandsby-type ware was in production between 1250 and 1400, and thus far it has only been identified on one other site in Kent, in Dover (Cotter 1997b, 79; Cotter 2006, 195–196).

Imported pottery

France

A single sherd of Northern France/Normandy gritty ware (EM15), a white firing fabric with abundant quartz and flint temper is present and is dated to the 11th and 12th century, probably 1050–1200 (Vince and Jenner 1991, 109–110). The body sherd comes from near the base of a possible cresset lamp (J. Cotter, pers. comm.) and has an external green-glaze.

Northern France-type, red-painted ware (EM11A. RP) is represented by a single jug (Fig. 49.1) with a collared and cordoned rim, and a curved strap handle with finger tip decoration along its edges. The handle was attached to the rim by luting and further secured by a finger impression inside the rim, not penetrating the vessel wall. There are two thumb impressions on each side of the handle join. It is decorated with vertical red paint lines starting at the shoulder in discrete groups of up to three lines. It is a hard, buff-coloured fabric, with lighter margins and a grey core and contains moderate to abundant ill-sorted sub-rounded to sub-angular, multi-coloured quartz, sparse, fine red flint and sparse, fine to large black iron ore and black burnt-out organic inclusions. A number of sources for this pottery type are suggested, such as Beauvais, Picardy, the Seine Valley and Upper Normandy (see Cotter 2006, 201–202 for a full discussion of the possible sources and problems of identifying production centres to this pottery type). This ware is dated to *c.* 1050–1200/1250.

Pottery from Rouen (Rouen ware, M19: green-glazed, M19 G; and polychrome M19 P) and the surrounding area of the Seine valley accounts for seven sherds, all probably from jugs. The fabric is a well-fired, fine sandy wheel-thrown whiteware, often buff-coloured (Brown 2002, 23). The five sherds comprise polychrome wares fairly typical for Rouen. One sherd has white slip dots on a brown glazed background, the others have contrasting applied strips of clay and bands or panels of red slip. Rouen ware found in London is dated to between 1170–1300, with a later version continuing to 1350.

Possible 'Orleans'-type ware (M20) was identified in the form of green-glazed tubular handles, one with a D-shaped profile is in a fine sandy fabric and was isolated from the other French medieval whiteware pottery types. The earliest occurrence of this handle is found in a Phase 8 context dated 1287–1350. A Phase 9 residual example has point stabbing and a mottled green glaze (Fig. 47). Tubular handles have been attributed to many of the French whiteware industries: Normandy, Beauvais and Parisian, and the term 'Orleans-type' ware was coined at Exeter for French jugs with incised decoration and idiosyncratic rod handles (Allan 1984, 21). However, although these jugs were marketed to Orleans, their characteristics are not in the repertoire of jugs manufactured from that city and they are still to be provenanced (P. Husi, pers. comm. in McCutcheon 2006, 99). The term 'so-called Orleans-type' is used for this ware found amongst the Miscellaneous French wares in Dublin (McCutcheon 2006, 99).

Saintonge whiteware (M22), green-glazed (M22 G), polychrome (M22 P), *sgraffito* (M22 S) has a fine slightly micaceous fabric with occasional clear or white rounded quartz and rare flecks of iron ore (Brown 2002, 26). Slightly coarser fabric variants were present on this site and have been recorded from other English excavations (Brown 2002, 27–28). It was produced at a number of sites in the Saintonge area of France and was imported to Britain between 1250 and 1650, but evidence in Ireland suggests an earlier, *c.* 1200, introduction and at Southampton an early version of the fabric (coded SOE) appears in the 12th and mid-13th centuries (Brown 2002, 23, 26; McCutcheon forthcoming). At Southlands School it is derived from deposits dated to after 1252/3, based on interpretation of a storm horizon, and is mostly present as jugs. Some sherds show that these vessels were in contact with heat as they were externally sooted, and therefore used possibly to warm water or wine and ale. This pottery type is found here in the form of unglazed or clear-glazed sherds (M22). Some vessels have a buff- or pink-coloured fabric with spalled surfaces. Green-glazed vessels (M22G) are found and decoration is present in the form of applied vertical strips (Fig. 48), often with a triangular cross-section and occasionally in red-slip. Some have a mottled green-glaze and one was decorated with a vertical brown-slip applied strip. One sherd from a post-medieval deposit has an applied face with a hand placed to it (Fig. 49.2) and may be from a 16th-century chafing dish. Polychrome glazed Saintonge ware (M22P) is found in a fragmentary form too small to determine the overall designs on the vessels, but one rim has a green, yellow and brown glazed grid design, while another sherd has an incised line and brown glaze. Saintonge polychrome falls within the category of Archaic Maiolica and is the most westerly, and isolated, production centre for this type of decoration, which centres on Northern Italy, but similar designs and decorative techniques were also used in Spain (Whitehouse 1978; Barton 1980). The production of this ware seems to have occurred over a short period of time and by one or possibly two generations of potters, between the late 13th and early 14th century (Hurst 1974, 221). The excavation at Southlands School indicates that it is present after *c*. 1287. There are four sherds of Saintonge *sgraffito* ware (M22S) including rim sherds with a surviving band of red slip and although no

sgraffito decoration was recovered, the red-slip allowed a design to be incised through it to reveal the white body. *Sgraffito* ware dates to after 1252/3 on this excavaion.

Low Countries

There are three sherds of Flemish/Low Countries highly decorated sandy ware (M14), a high-fired, redware pottery, all in the form of jugs. Two sherds have white-slip decoration, one with a vertical strip of white slip and another with a white slip dot and arcing line, both being clear-glazed. The third sherd has a green-mottled, clear glaze over an externally white-slip with a ring and dot stamp as well as there being evidence for applied decoration. The fabric is dated to 1250–1325/50 but production continued into the late medieval period.

Examples of the reduced northern French/Flanders grey sandy ware (M15) from the continent identified from the excavation vary in their quartz temper from fine to very sandy, possibly representing some of the many production centres in Malines and Ath near Brussels and Sorrus near Boulogne-sur-Mer (Jennings 1981, 27; see also Cotter 2006, 223–225 for a discussion of the problems of attribution of these greywares and other production centres). These imported greywares are higher fired and better made than their English counterparts. The material on the site includes a sooted sherd of a jar with a collared rim whilst the rest are from rounded jugs with one upright and thickened rim and with a cordoned neck, the other rolled or rounded with an incised line below the neck (Fig. 49.3). A handle of rod type was present and some body sherds show pronounced internal throwing lines. This import is mostly confined to late 13th-century dated contexts on the site and has no earlier occurrences. Northern France has a long tradition of producing greywares from the Roman era through the Merovingian to the early post-medieval periods, but this fabric is dated 1250–1500 and is increasingly less common from *c*. 1200.

German wares

The high-fired, light to dark-grey sandy ware with a characteristic blue-grey sheen, Blue-grey/Paffrath-type ware (M36), was represented by one, externally sooted, sherd. The most common form found on English sites comprises small globular cooking vessels with a straight handle, sometimes called ladles, but a spouted form and jars are also known (Vince and Jenner 1991, 103–104). Although Paffrath in the middle Rhine valley is a known production centre, there were other kiln sites in this area. In London the ware may appear as early as 1000, but it is definitely present by 1050 and is at its most common in late 11th and early 12th century contexts. It was probably still being produced in the 13th century (Vince and Jenner 1991, 103–104).

Fig. 47　'Orleans'-type ware tubular jug handle

Fig. 48　Green-glazed Saintonge-type ware jug fragment with applied strip decoration

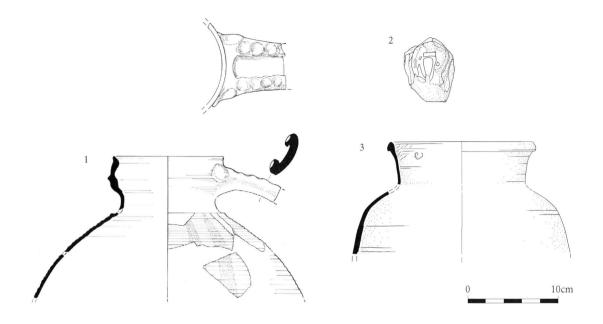

Fig. 49   Medieval pottery, imported wares (scale 1:4)

The Late Medieval and Post-Medieval Pottery

The late medieval and post-medieval pottery types are only considered in summary form here as they are mostly residual or not well stratified and demonstrate little about New Romney as a port after *c.* 1300.

Late medieval pottery

Local wares

The pink-buff fine sandy ware recovered from the excavations (LM14) may represent an import or a Sussex ware and is present in the form of a lid-seated vessel. There are single sherds of both the partially reduced and oxidised Wealden/Hareplain hard fine sandy wares (LM17A, LM17B), dated to 1525–1600 as well as seven sherds of the oxidised ?Wealden/Hareplain hard fine sandy ware (LM32) which may have been made at either Rye or Spilstead and is dated to *c.* 1475–1550. The forms in this ware are difficult to identify, but are probably from thin-walled, closed vessels. There is one example of a rod handle with an oval section, which was mortised to the body through a triangular hole. These vessels are unglazed but one sherd from a probable jug has horizontal white-slip line decoration (LM32R) and is probably a Rye product.

Imports

Single sherds of German stonewares are present comprising the bases of jugs or drinking jugs in iron-washed Langerwehe stoneware (LM9), dated 1350–1500, and Raeren stoneware (LM8), dated 1480–1550. Both bases are frilled in the typical German late medieval and early post-medieval traditions (Gaimster 1997, 186–188). Dutch redware (LM22) is represented by a rim with a pouring lip, which is externally sooted, and another sherd which is an undiagnostic body fragment. This well-made, sandy earthenware was widely exported to the south and east coast of England between the 14th and 17th centuries (Hurst *et al.* 1986, 136). The only Spanish ware identified is present in the form of a curved, strap handle and body sherd of an amphora (LM23A), probably made at Malaga and dated to 1200–1500.

Post-medieval

Local and non-local wares

The post-medieval fabrics recovered comprise: red earthenwares (PM1, LPM1B), ?Wealden buff fine sandy with haematite (PM2), Tin-glazed wares (PM9), Surrey-Hampshire Border wares (PM10), London stoneware (PM25), Staffordshire white salt-glazed stoneware (PM26), Red 'Basalt' ware (PM32), Nottingham or Derbyshire stoneware (PM38, LPM23), Staffordshire-type redware (PM42), Creamware (PM43,

LPM11), Jackfield-type ware (PM54), Staffordshire butter-pot (PM58), Calcareous "Peppered" smooth ware (PM64). South Yorkshire-Midlands redware with internal white slip (LPM3), Yellow ware (LPM5), English porcelain (LPM7), English stoneware (LPM10), Pearl ware (LPM12), Refined whitewares, with or without transfer-printing (LPM14) and Black Basalt ware (LPM18).

The post-medieval redwares from the Southlands School excavation have been divided into two main groups, the red earthenwares (PM1 and LPM1B) and the Wealden-type ware (PM2). The PM1 fabrics come from a number of Kentish sources and from the London area. A jar with a thumbed neck comes from either Deptford or Woolwich (Pryor and Blockley 1978; Jarrett 2004, 96). The ?Wealden wares (fabric PM2) are generally pink-firing and a number of sources are present that include the area of the Weald. There are however also products from the Surrey-Hampshire Border and a slip-trailed dish (in fabric PM2.6S) which may originate in Canterbury (Cotter 1997c, 182-3). The forms in both wares tend to be associated with the kitchen or serving food, but also include storage vessels and flowerpots. Other Kentish earthenwares include Calcareous 'peppered' smooth ware (PM64), a high-fired product dated to *c.* 1550–1650.

Pottery from London is present in the form of Tin-glazed earthenwares (PM9) dating from the mid-17th century through to the 18th century. It is found in a wide range of vessel shapes associated with table or tea drinking wares and chamber pots. London stoneware (PM25), mostly dating to the 18th and 19th century is present in the form of drinking or storage vessels. Non-local pottery comprises late 16th- and 17th- century yellow and green-glazed Surrey-Hampshire Border wares made with white-firing clays. Other non-local pottery consists of the late 18th- and 19th-century industrial finewares made in the Midlands and elsewhere and includes Creamwares, Pearl wares and Refined whitewares, often transfer-printed.

Imports

The imported pottery is commonplace for the post-medieval period and includes Frechen stoneware (PM5) as bartman jugs, dated to 1550–1700. Westerwald stoneware (PM6) dates from 1590 onwards and is found here as a sherd from a chamber pot and rounded mugs with a purple-glaze, dated to 1665–1750 and 19th-century seltzer bottles (PM34). Chinese porcelain (PM40) is present in the form of 18th-century blue and white ware, an Imari-style plate and a *Famille Rose* tea bowl.

Pottery Discussion

Quantification of the pottery types shows that the shelly sandy ware (EM3) was the main fabric present by sherd count in Phases 2 to 8, no matter how small or large a quantity of pottery was present in each period (see Table 8, Appendix 1). This shelly sandy ware may have been produced at the kiln found at the adjacent Southlands School, Dymchurch Road (NCR 02) site, but it is not

certain at present when and for how long that kiln operated. Nevertheless, to date the Southlands School, Dymchurch Road (NCR 02) kiln is important for being one of only three medieval/early post-medieval pottery kilns found in Kent, the other two being Pound Lane, Canterbury, dating to *c.* 1145–1175 (Cotter 1997c) and Hareplain, Biddenden, where a kiln base dating to the second quarter of the 16th-century was recorded (Kelly 1972). Little physical evidence of pottery kiln structures has been noted in Kent, although pottery wasters and kiln furniture from Ashford, Maidstone, and Tyler Hill, near Canterbury indicate other production centres (Grove and Warhurst 1952, Grove 1967, Tatton-Brown and Macpherson-Grant 1983). Pottery from Tyler Hill has been recorded in small quantities in the Romney Marsh area but was absent on the Southlands School site (Cotter 1991). The Romney Marsh area shelly sandy ware is on the whole distinct from the other Kent industries making very similar types of pottery: North and West Kent; fabric EM36 (Cotter 2002; Cotter 2006). During the late 13th century it is the shelly sandy ware (the local source of unglazed pottery) that provides mostly kitchenwares in the form of jar-shaped vessels to the Southlands School site, as well as smaller amounts of bowls or dishes, besides jugs, ventilators and curfews for other functions. In Phase 2 the small quantity of pottery (six sherds) shows that the only other types of pottery present at this time are Kent or Sussex flint-tempered wares (EM28 and EM29) as jar-shapes. In Phase 7 deposits, associated with the *c.* 1287 flood, the shelly sandy ware accounts for 50.2% of the 500 sherds of pottery.

Glazed pottery was supplied from further afield, mainly from Rye (as the M13 fabrics) and as smaller amounts of pottery from Ashford, Rye and the Weald (M40BR). By sherd count the Rye M13 wares are always more frequent in the different phases at the Southland School site, except in Phase 6 when the Ashford, Rye and the Weald glazed sandy ware is more common. Both wares appeared mostly as jugs, although smaller quantities of jars, bowls or dishes and other forms were recovered from the Southlands School site. Both these glazed pottery types occur firstly as low sherd counts in the *c.* 1252 (Phase 3) storm deposits, but Rye wares and the Ashford/Wealden/Rye fabric (M40BR) account for 23.8% and 8.2% respectively in the *c.* 1287 (Phase 7) deposits. The other Kent and Sussex glazed wares tend to be low in number (usually under 10 sherds) in Phases 3 to 7, therefore possibly representing minor wares marketed to New Romney. Non-local English wares are poorly represented in the late 13th century, with Scarborough ware (M11A) present first in Phase 3, but both Thames Valley and Yorkshire wares (particularly from Brandsby), as a group are nominally more common in Phase 5 at 0.22%, than Phase 7 at 1.6%.

Imported wares are on the whole present as jug forms, but occasionally as greyware jars and are first represented minimally in the *c.* 1252 (Phase 3) flood deposits and the subsequent Phase 4 contexts, but only

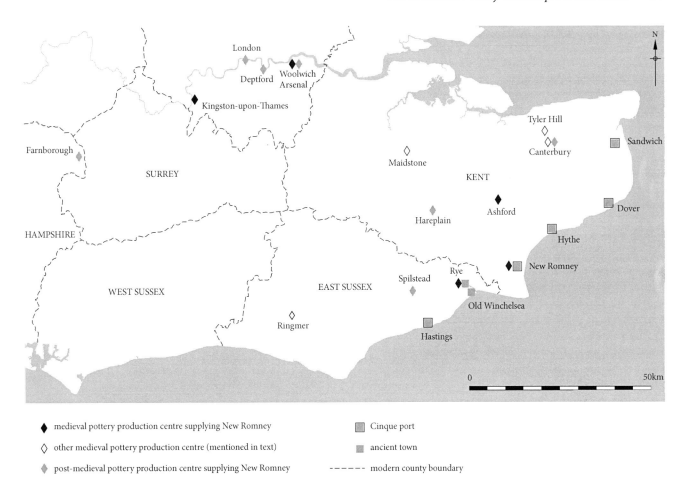

Fig. 50   Medieval and post-medieval pottery production sites in southeast England discussed in the text (scale 1:100 000)

as French Saintonge wares. Imports dating to before 1250, such as Normandy gritty ware (EM15), Northern French red painted pottery (EM11A.RP) and 'Orleans'-type ware are present on the excavation, but appear to be residual. In Phase 5 there is a greater quantity of imported pottery accounting for 3.7% by sherd count. Saintonge wares are the main type in this phase, but German, Low Countries and Flemish/Northern French wares are also represented. The storm deposits attributed to 1287 (Phase 7) produced a larger quantity of continental pottery (27 sherds, 5.4%), but mostly as the same types found in Phase 5. The largest quantity of imported pottery is found in Phase 8 (54 sherds, 3.3 %) and although some of these ceramics may represent activity on the site after the decline of New Romney, following the 1287 storm, many of the sherds are residual.

Excavations at Townwall Street, Dover (Parfitt *et al.* 2006) uncovered evidence of activity between the mid- to late 12th century and the post-medieval period and the site produced a very large assemblage of pottery, indicating the types of ceramics arriving at this Cinque Port (Cotter 2006). Many of the pottery types present at Townwall Street are also found at Southlands School, but in smaller numbers, indicating a similar supply of local pottery and contacts with the English North Sea coast and the continent. However, the Dover excavation did

produce a wider range of imported ceramics, particularly various French fine whiteware pottery types, besides coarser continental sand or shell-tempered wares, Belgian Andenne ware and German Pingsdorf-type ware. The range of non-local English wares at the Townwall Street site is also impressive and contact with the North Sea coast is reflected by the occurrence of Beverly ware, Brandsby-type and Scarborough wares from Yorkshire and Norfolk grey ware and Stamford ware from East Anglia. What is also surprising about the Dover excavation is the recovery of pottery types from the West Country that are outside their normal distribution areas, such as South-East Wiltshire Coarse ware, Laverstock-type ware from Wiltshire and Newbury 'C' ware from Berkshire. Even Kentish pottery types, such as North and West Kent shell and sand (EM36) and greywares (EM4 and M38), are outside their usual distribution pattern, but found their way to Dover, indicating the importance of this port for trade and the movement of ceramics (Cotter 2006).

The historically known bad weather conditions may explain the presence of certain ceramic forms at the Southlands School site. These comprise roof furniture, tiles, louvers and ventilators, as these are often dislodged in high winds. The site produced a total of 23 fragments of medieval ventilators and two probable louver fragments.

Imported ceramics, trade and other contacts

The excavations at New Romney produced quantities of medieval pottery reflecting trade and contact with other parts of England and Northern Europe. Imported and non-local pottery may be present for various reasons; it may have been traded in its own right, or equally ceramic vessels may have found their way to the site as containers for other produce. Alternatively foreign traders may have travelled with their own accoutrements for preparing food according to their own traditions, or carried travellers' and merchants' souvenirs (Davey and Hodges 1983, 10).

Several distinct and distant production centres can be seen to have provided ceramics to New Romney, non-local wares coming from London, Surrey and Yorkshire, while imports come from Germany, the Low Countries, Northern France, and Saintonge. The one sherd of late medieval Langerwehe stoneware may have arrived by indirect means (for instance by being redistributed through London) rather than by direct contact with Germany. There is little evidence for trade with the Mediterranean, except for the presence of a Spanish Malaga amphora.

The Thames Valley wares in the form of London-type and Kingston-type wares could have been traded overland. The principal market for Surrey whitewares was London, the material being transported to the capital using the Thames as a route way (Pearce and Vince 1988). Therefore, it is conceivable that boats plying trade from the entrepôt of London may have been involved in the redistribution of pottery to coastal ports such as New Romney. Certainly at a later date the London port books of 1579/80 and 1585/6 show that the capital was responsible for re-exporting Rhenish stonewares to east and south coastal towns (Allan 1984, 39). Pottery from Yorkshire is represented by Scarborough and Brandsby-type wares. Although Scarborough ware is a high quality product and was being exported in its own right, it is known that Kentish and other east coast fishermen were attending fairs on sand flats off the Norfolk coast at low tide in the 13th century, which might account for the presence of these pottery types and other east coast wares, such as Norfolk ?gritty ware, in Kent (Cotter 1997b).

Davey and Hodges (1983, 3–4) identified the major and minor imported pottery groups found in the British Isles between 1200–1500, and many of these are found at New Romney. Of the major groups, pottery from Saintonge, France is notable while Rouen and North French glazed wares are less so. The Northern French-Normandy gritty ware and Paffrath blue-grey wares are minimally represented and may indicate residual 11th- and 12th-century wares. The relative rarity of Dutch redwares and Langerwehe or Raeren stonewares on the Southlands School site may be due to chronological factors, tied to the decline of Romney as a port, reflecting perhaps the fact that the area was not so intensively used in the late medieval period. Of the minor imported pottery groups, Flemish highly decorated wares, Red painted North French pitchers and a Spanish amphora are present, as are Northern France-Flanders grey sandy wares which are more common than many of the other imports.

In the 14th century New Romney was importing such commodities as timber, building stones and Mediterranean foods such as garlic. Exports from the port included fish, corn and dairy products from the Marsh (Eddison 2000, 20). The pottery from the Southlands School site is indicative of trade between New Romney and the continent. The main imported pottery type, Saintonge wares may indicate a link with the Bordeaux and Gascony wine trade and was being distributed on the back of this. It is known that the Port of Winchelsea was the main haven for importing wine from Bordeaux *en route* to London during the 14th century, although New Romney had some share of this trade. Similarly the import of Rouen and North French glazed ware jugs is also connected with the medieval wine trade, as indicated for example in London where these wares are most concentrated in the Vintry area, a precinct formerly dedicated to the wine trade (Blackmore 1999, 51).

There has been some debate as to whether or not Saintonge pottery was credited as the socially acceptable form from which to serve and consume that area's wine, ie the jugs were an 'integral part of a wine drinking cultural package' and that their presence indicates possibly a higher social status (Courtney 1997, 102). Research by Allan (1984, 67–70) and discussion by Courtney (1997, 102) suggests that although the prices of Saintonge wares are not known, the more decorative wares may have been more expensive, but were still relatively low cost items. Find spots for these wares can occur where different levels of social status can be attributed to the sites, but their presence may be purely due to a factor of easy accessibility. At the Welsh Edwardian Castles, the jugs were probably supplied to the isolated English garrisons from the major importation centre of Chester. When associated with low status sites, such as the urban cob-built houses in Exeter or fishing communities on the Isles of Scilly, then this may be purely due to their coastal location. Turning to the perception of these highly decorated imports, Courtney argues that these wares may be more aesthetically appealing to modern tastes and of less consequence to a medieval world, while their perception may also have contrasted widely between their place of manufacture and their markets, being more mundane in ports, such as New Romney, but exotic, although not necessarily held in high esteem, on sites far from the coast.

The other imported pottery is difficult to link to specific trading activities although obviously a connection between the Low Countries and the wool and cloth trade could be indicated, however this could be potentially misleading. The imports from the Low Countries and the North French or Flemish greywares may simply have come into New Romney as non-trade items, perhaps as containers in the case of the greyware jars. Their tendency to survive in the archaeological record may

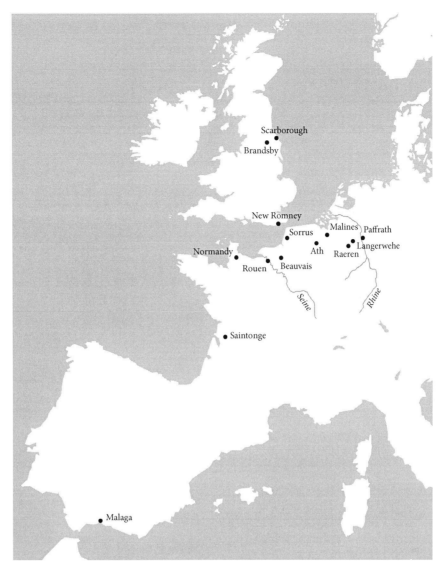

Fig. 51   The sources of Continental and Yorkshire medieval and post-medieval pottery marketed to the Southlands School site, New Romney

overemphasize their actual importance when compared to other categories of material, which do not survive so well. The presence of the Spanish amphora, although difficult to date precisely, does support historical references to the importation of foodstuffs of Mediterranean origin into New Romney.

Other explanations for the presence of imported pottery are possible. One reason may be that foreign traders lived in the town and that some of the vessels reflect their nationality. However, assigning the ethnicity of a localised population by the pottery types present can be unreliable or misleading, although interesting results have been achieved from their study in Southampton (Brown 2002, 163–167). The documentary record for

New Romney indicates the presence of French people in the town by the 13th century, and of close contact and cooperation between traders and mariners of New Romney, Flanders, northern France, Périgord and Bordeaux in the 14th century. This included the hosting of Flemish merchants by New Romney townsmen. Spanish silver coins were acceptable for use in the town in the 14th century (above).

Although New Romney was well served by local pottery industries, it is also probable that the English Channel, weather permitting, made import of pottery products from the continent more cost effective than obtaining ceramics from certain less accessible inland production centres.

Chapter 10 The Metal Finds

Geoff Egan

In addition to recovery by conventional archaeological methods a large part of the non-ceramic finds assemblage from the Southlands School site was retrieved with the aid of metal detectors. This approach massively enhanced the numbers and category range compared with assemblages published from investigations at other sea-side settlements, but it makes specific comparisons difficult and many of the finds are not stratified. Where finds were recorded *in situ* they are mentioned in the description of the archaeological sequence above. Given the large number of unstratified finds and the likely problems of residuality with those finds recovered in context, this discussion presents the finds by material category and concentrates on those of medieval date.

The main focus of the non-ceramic finds assemblage recovered is on lead weights (as discussed in detail by Riddler, see Chapter 11, below), many of which are of forms characteristic of use with fishing nets; some 30 were recovered from the Southlands School site (see Fig. 60). Hooks of appropriate form for line fishing were also found (see Riddler, below) though they are less prominent in this assemblage than in the finds assemblages from King's Lynn (Cowgill 2003) and Great Yarmouth in Norfolk (Rogerson 1976), Meols on the Wirral (Hume 1863, 253 & pl. 26.5), or Townwall Street in the Cinque Port town of Dover (Riddler 2006, 289–290). A variety of iron rivets or rovenails (see Goodburn, Chapter 11) are characteristic of coastal or river craft (see Fig. 59).

The coinage recovered arguably provides a rough economic indicator, both of fluctuations in wealth and of some trade links, through the Norman and later medieval periods into the early-modern era (see coin catalogue, below). A series of 30 of Henry III's Short Cross pennies (which could perhaps include part of a dispersed hoard) are the most prominent component until the routine range of post-Restoration/18th-century small-change copper issues. There are a few pence of Edward I, but no later medieval English issues. The apparent sudden cessation of official issues with those of Edward I could be seen as a reflection of the series of downturns in the fortune of the town in the 13th century as the port became increasingly less usable as the result of the series of storms in 1236, 1250–1252 and 1287–1288, and consequent continuing silting (Eddison 2000, 77–87) and contemporary increases in vessel sizes and draught. The numismatic pattern is only slightly different from the usual archaeological picture of coin loss in the Middle Ages, which sees little later in date than the reign of Edward I, though (in contrast with the present assemblage) that period is usually well represented. All else about the contexts available for investigation being equal, this may be a crucial difference; an accurate measure of the town's changing fortunes, particularly during Edward's reign.

A lead/tin token from the reign of Elizabeth I is not only a rare example of the series from a non-urban context; it also underlines the community's close links with the mainstream economy (many later, crude tokens are present which are routine items). Three Continental medieval coins <3>, <15> and <315> (see coin catalogue below) may be significant, specific indicators of trade links. Like the jettons used for accountancy (which here, unusually, are greatly outnumbered by the contemporary medieval coinage recovered) the few potential commercial weights (restricted as usual to very small units) are not unusual finds. Both these categories fall short of illuminating specifics of trade, whether within the community, looking to the landward side or to coastal and even international links. The vexed question of identifying commercial weights as opposed to ponderous pieces of lead for any other purpose is compounded on a site where fishing as an activity is a virtual certainty (holed weights are most readily explained as being for this purpose).

The only cloth seal is one from the early 17th century assignable to Essex, a plausible indicator of coastal textile trade, though the absence of any recognisable Kent issues suggests the picture provided is a limited one. Among the comparable coastal sites only Meols has produced cloth seals, and, perhaps surprisingly in so few items, its handful does closely reflect the expected medieval and later profile for textile consumption in the Northwest, in terms both of English and Continental seals (Egan 2007).

The domestic objects (security equipment, fragments of cooking vessels, everyday tools etc.) make up a routine assemblage, appropriate for any town in the country.

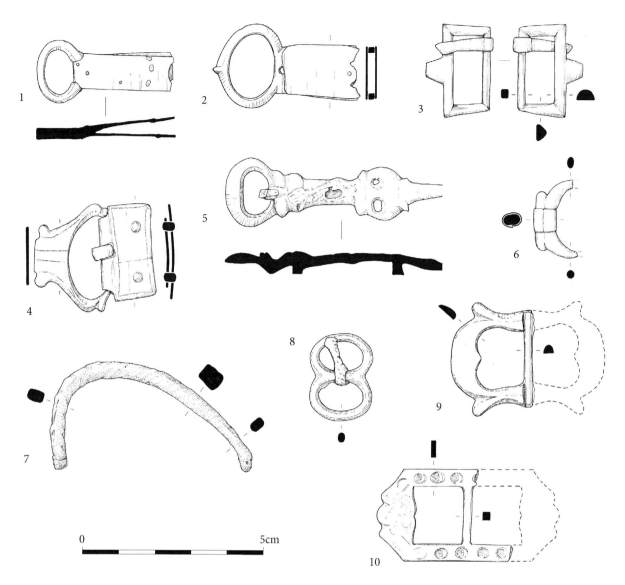

Fig. 52   Dress accessories: medieval and post-medieval buckles (scale 1:1)

Catalogue of illustrated buckles Fig. 52 (1–6 Medieval, 7–10 post-medieval)

1 Copper-alloy buckle (<668> unstratified): oval 16mm x 12mm, with offset bar and notch for missing pin; folded plate 26mm x 110mm with hole for missing pin and remains of two iron rivets, presumably replacements. An unusual form with its plain outside edge.

2 Copper-alloy buckle (<404> unstratified): oval with forked spacer; 39mm x 23mm; angled pin rest; sheets of plate (19mm x 15mm) are doubly nicked on the inside edge; holes for single rivet.

3 Copper-alloy buckle (<56> from Phase 9, post medieval dumping): Slightly trapezoidal; 13mm x 25mm; deep profile at outside edge; prominent lip for sheet pin. (?)12th/early 13th century.

4 Copper-alloy buckle (<37> from the upper floor surface [142] of Phase 6, Building 1) (cf. an example from Meols, Egan 2007)

5 Copper-alloy buckle (<66> from floor [190] in the lean-to, to the rear of Phase 6, Building 1): Corroded, with integral plate

6 Copper-alloy buckle (<504> unstratified): Fragment of oval frame: knops flank roller on outside edge.

7 Lead/tin buckle (<416> unstratified): Fragmentary circular frame (large size), for a shoe, 18th-century.

8 Copper-alloy buckle (<517> unstratified): Double-oval, 21 x 16mm; (?)now-black coating; iron pin.

9 Copper-alloy buckle (<401> unstratified): Incomplete, double frame: ornate, D-shaped survival, 22mm x 29mm, with pair of outward-curving cusps at sides, and biconcave end for aperture; bar is defined by a transverse groove in the sides. This would have been perfectly capable of functioning in this state, given a pin; it was presumably originally symmetrical.

10 Copper-alloy buckle (<476> unstratified): Incomplete: elongated-hexagonal frame with one edge and part of one side broken off; trilobed edge; traces of gilding along perimeter, over a series of circular stamps with separate, (?) squares with irregular grids centrally. (?)Late 17th century, a very elaborate accessory this late.

The series of medieval and later dress accessories, too, presents a broad picture of everyday fashion that has been recognised in many places across England. They include several of the best of the mass-produced buckles and a couple of more individual, earlier ones (see Fig. 52), neither necessarily to be expected at an 'average' sea-side settlement. Absent are any of the most eye-catching styles or the precious-metal high points that occasionally feature in the larger urban assemblages (both a contrast with the remarkable Meols assemblage). Only the brooches (eg Fig. 53.7–Fig. 53.11), which seem relatively numerous and diverse, begin to compare readily with the much larger Meols assemblage. A Restoration commemorative button is so far the only one from any coastal site, in fact it is the first noted outside the capital. Beyond these items, a plaything, in the form of a human figure (Fig. 56.8), perhaps of early 16th-century date, and another rare find outside large urban areas, indicates some level of surplus wealth to cater for non-essentials. A base <50> could be from another toy potentially as early as the 1600s. A pornographic dress hook from the 16th century, although the figurative motif is badly worn, constitutes an item of note (Fig. 53.13).

Overall, the assemblage recovered is large and diverse enough to establish the salient points that mark out Romney as a Cinque Port with good connections in the region, and trade far beyond that, arguably with the foreign coins just perceptibly into mainstream links with Europe. Although its international significance had diminished by the late Middle Ages enough for non-ceramic archaeological indicators to have disappeared from the record, the community's continuation as a regionally significant settlement is attested by the later tokens of the 16th and 17th centuries. Through all this, the basic resource of fishing remained a constant, leaving behind an abundance of equipment from boats and the process of catching fish, even if such material is not generally closely datable.

The assemblages

The range and diversity of the metalwork assemblage is in part the result of the efforts of local detectorists, resulting in more material being recovered than might have been by standard hand-retrieval methods alone. While copper-alloys and lead/tin are generally in good condition, much of the ironwork is very corroded, which has probably prevented the identification of a number of items as definitively medieval or early post-medieval (several of the larger contexts were multi-period). The material is presented below by finds category, with the objects relating to fishing and boat construction and breaking discussed further in separate reports (see Riddler, and Goodburn, Chapter 11).

Dress accessories

A total of 23 copper-alloy buckles were identified, of these two dated to the late 13th to 14th centuries. The first has a cast pin with a length of 43mm, and a transverse ridge at the loop. This form went with circular frames (Egan and Pritchard 1991, 115–116, nos. 540–550). The second <56> is slightly trapezoidal and measures 13mm x 25mm. It has a deep profile with a prominent lip for a sheet pin on the outside (Fig. 52.3). A trapezoidally-shaped buckle of Norman date with a silver coating and niello was also recovered and the decorative materials used on this example are far less common than gold. A fragment of a plate has repoussé trefoil tendrils and foil. This is somewhat reminiscent of the decoration on another lead/tin buckle plate from London assigned to the early 15th century (Egan and Pritchard 1991, 104–105 no. 479).

There are four lead/tin buckles, these include one <416> with a large fragmentary circular frame (Fig. 52.7) and a fragment of a frame side, with a rococo foliate motif, both are for shoes and are of 18th century date. There is one circular type, which is slightly distorted, with a diameter of *c.* 23mm. It has a central bar and beaded rabbet, and the loop of the iron pin survives. This is also for a shoe (cf. Egan and Pritchard 1991, 66–67, figs. 221–259) and dates to the early 15th century.

There are twelve post-medieval copper-alloy buckles, including four that derive from horse harnesses. One double-oval type <517> measuring 21mm x 16mm, with a black coating and an iron pin (Fig. 52.8), and a second double-oval type, with an acorn knop on each edge which is of 16th-century date. A rectangular form measuring 44mm x 52mm with bar offset, and an example with an elongated D-shape measuring 36mm x 31mm are present. The latter has a thickened outside edge, the bar is set back, and rust from the missing pin still adheres.

There is an incomplete, probably originally symmetrical buckle <476>, with an elongated hexagonal frame with one edge and part of the side broken off (Fig. 52.10). It would have measured *c.* 50mm x 24mm when complete, has a trilobed edge and traces of gilding along the perimeter over a series of annular stamps with separate squares and irregular grids over the top. It is of late 17th-century date and very elaborate for this late date. A fragment of a high quality late medieval buckle has an ornate outer edge of an oval frame. Its surviving width is 50mm, and length 27mm. It has open-work with a row of four stylised quatrefoils flanking the frame with cross-hatched recesses flanking the notch for the pin. There is a spur buckle, with an ornate openwork outside

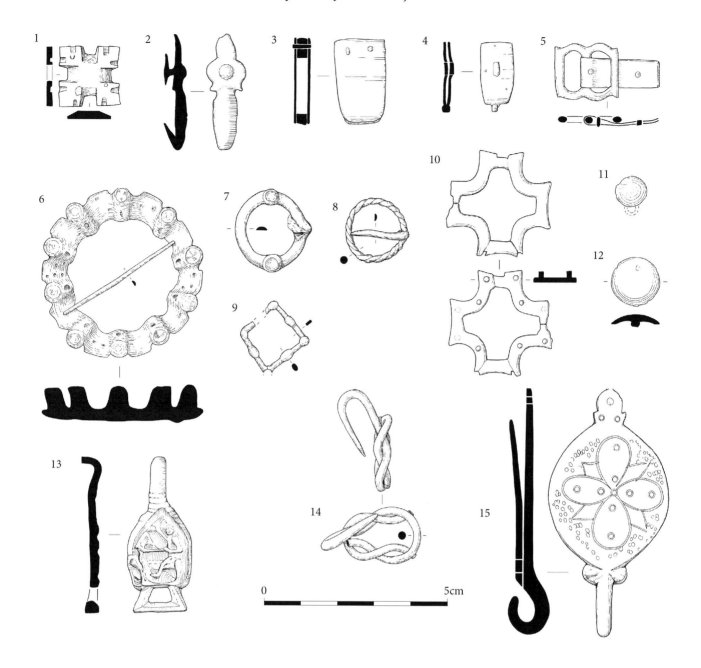

Fig. 53   Medieval and post-medieval dress accessories (scale 1:1)

edge and arched profile. It has elaborately moulded edges, especially around the openwork, and a double trapezoid shape. It has an opposed bird's head terminal motif, and a tin coating. A late 17th-century shoe buckle has a maker's stamp on the plate (HI (or IH)), (Egan 2005). A second shoe buckle probably of 18th-century date comprises a fragment of a probably oblong frame, with a length 42mm, and integral shell and foliate motifs. A copper-alloy clasp was found with a rectangular frame, measuring 15mm x 14mm, with slightly convex sides and ridges near its corners (folding end missing), the plate measures 22mm x 10mm, and has one iron rivet. A second clasp is of iron, comprises a fragment of the frame side, with a rococo foliate motif. It was for a shoe and is of 18th-century date.

There are five copper-alloy mounts and fourteen copper-alloy strap ends (Fig. 53.1–Fig. 53.5). Of the latter,

one <59> has a double-oval frame with straight edges and a folded plate (Fig. 53.5), it measures 17mm x 16mm (20mm x 8mm), and has a white-metal coating on both the frame and plate. A single rivet survives, as does rust from its missing pin (Egan and Pritchard 1991, 88 no. 384). It has been dated to the late 14th century.

Seven brooches were found, of which six are of copper-alloy and one of silver (Fig. 53.6–Fig. 53.10). Of the copper-alloy ones five are circular (eg <4>, <64>, <382> Fig. 53.6–53.8), one lozenge shaped (<63> Fig. 53.9) and one cruciform (<29> Fig. 53.10). The single silver one is also circular in outline.

There is a single medieval button <48>, it is corroded copper-alloy, sub-spherical in shape and has a diameter of 10mm (Fig. 53.11) (Egan and Pritchard 1991, 275–276 nos. 1384–1396). It has been assigned a mid-13th- to late

Catalogue of illustrated dress accessories (Fig. 53)

1 Copper-alloy mount (<8> from post-medieval dumped soil): Cast: square-shaped quatrefoil, 15mm x 16mm; each foil is an angled trifoliate motif; two separate rivets.

2 Copper-alloy mount (<5> from Phase 9 dumping): Cast, damaged bar, surviving dimensions 31mm x 10mm; fleur-de-lis terminal and baluster-like main part, of which 10mm appears to be folded behind. Unclear whether this was originally straight and longer, or curtailed (?possibly once symmetrical); rivet with subrectangular rove survives.

3 Copper-alloy strap end (<25> from Phase 7 sandy fill of the erosion cut which destroyed Building 2): Slightly tapered, subrectangular: two sheets, with incomplete, sheet spacer surviving along two of three sides; 23mm x 14mm; straight end; two rivets and leather from strap survive.

4 Copper-alloy strap end (<535> unstratified): One convex-sided sheet, folded over at terminal/loop; 18mm x 9mm; sheet-iron 'rivet' set through centre of sheets – perhaps a clumsy repair. The form is not readily paralleled.

5 Copper-alloy strap end (<59> from Phase 3 storm-deposited sand): Double-oval frame (straight edges) with folded plate; 17mm x 16mm (20mm x 8mm); white-metal coating on both; single rivet survives; rust from missing pin. Cf. Egan and Pritchard 1991, 88 no. 384, assigned to the late 14th century.

6 Copper-alloy brooch (<4> from dumping associated with tennis court construction, Area A): Corroded; ten collets, some retaining fragments of glass gems. (Cf. an example from Meols, Egan 2007).

7 Copper-alloy brooch (<64> from Phase 3 storm-deposited sand): D 19mm; two collets; rust from missing pin.

8 Copper-alloy brooch (<382> from late post-medieval pit [1098]): Corded border; d 16mm; sheet pin.

9 Copper-alloy brooch (<63> from Phase 2 foreshore deposit [212]): lozenge-shaped: broken.

10 Copper-alloy brooch (<29> from storm/consolidation deposit [102]): cruciform. (Cf. an example from Meols, Egan 2007).

11 Copper-alloy button (<48> from Phase 4 tree-throw hollow [186]): corroded; sub-spherical; 10mm diameter. Medieval form; cf. Egan and Pritchard 1991, 275–276 nos. 1384–1396, assigned to the mid 13th to late 14th centuries.

12 Lead/tin button (unstratified): post-medieval form.

13 Hooked Clasp (<305> unstratified): 40mm x 17mm; angled attachment loop; hook end broken off; inverted-shield shaped palt with rough delineation of couple in flagrante on a couch – the woman reclining, the man straddling her. Several of these are known among detected finds but there seems to be no parallel from an archaeological sequence.

14 Hooked Clasp (<417> unstratified): Incomplete: wire frame in Bourchier knot (cf. Egan 2005, nos. 157–158).

15 Hooked Clasp (<246> unstratified): Cast, overall 31mm x 67mm; main oval plate is engraved with rough, uneven quatrefoil with a central stamped circle, each petal having two stamped circles and there are angled sepals between the petals; a series of smaller stamped circles almost form a surrounding field; hook at one end is defined by a transverse bar, acorn-like terminal (with remains of rusted rivet) defined by transverse tab with pair of stamped circles at other end; on the back a thinner, lozenge-shaped plate (integrally cast) has its free end broken off. From a sword belt; (?)16th century.

14th-century date. Three post-medieval buttons of lead/tin were also recovered, including one comprising an incomplete disc with a diameter of 23mm and a pierced tab on the back. On its face are busts of William and Mary, PRINCE ET PRINCE… around its perimeter. The use of the terms *prince/(?)princess* suggests this is a souvenir of the six-month pre-coronation period between the arrival of William in England at Brixham, on the 5th of November 1688 and the coronation of the couple on the 11th of April 1689. A second button is slightly uneven, has a plano-convex head and a diameter of 16mm, it has a white-metal coating and a copper-alloy wire loop attached to its back.

Three hooked clasps form part of the assemblage. These include a cast fastener <305> measuring 40mm x 17mm with an angled attachment loop. The hook end is broken off, and it has an inverted-shield shaped palt with a rough delineation of a couple in *flagrante delicto* on a couch, the woman reclining with the man straddling her (Fig. 53.13). Several examples of this type of clasp are known among metal detected finds, but there are no parallels from any known archaeological sequence. A further incomplete clasp has a wire frame in a Bourchier knot (<417> Fig. 53.14) (Egan 2005, nos. 157–158). The third is a cast oval example <246> measuring 31 x 67mm. The main oval

plate is engraved with a rough, uneven quatrefoil with a stamped central circle, each petal having two stamped circles with angled sepals between the petals; a series of smaller stamped circles almost form a surrounding field. The hook at one end is defined by a transverse bar, with an acorn-like terminal (it has the remains of a rusted rivet) defined by a transverse tab, with a pair of stamped circles at the other end. On the back is a thinner lozenge-shaped plate (integrally cast). Its free end is broken off (Fig. 53.15). This fastening is from a sword belt of 16th-century date.

A single incomplete lace chape was recovered, with an inward-folded seam; it survives to a length of 28mm. There are also several pins with wound-wire heads; the complete ones have lengths of 24mm and 43mm. One has a length of 47mm; it has an irregular head, which probably lacks its cover.

Two copper-alloy watch keys were found; these can be considered to be high quality accessories. The first is bent and broken in two pieces, it has an openwork oval handle, which measures 15mm x 22mm and has moulded terminals on a pivot. Its overall length is 38mm, and its rod length 17mm. The second is corroded, has a trefoil handle with the remains of an iron chain present. The length of the pivot is 30mm, and the length of key-rod 15mm.

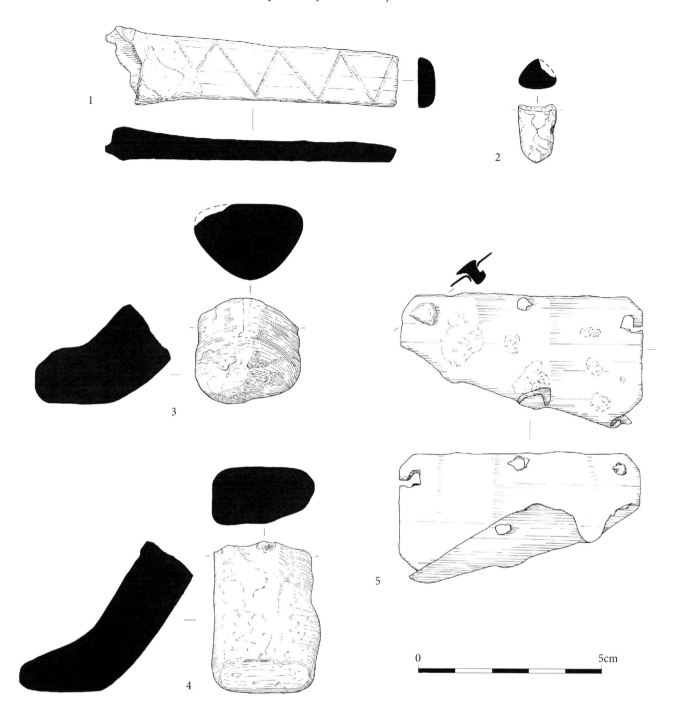

Fig. 54   Household objects (scale 1:1)

Catalogue of illustrated household objects (Fig. 54)

1 Cast copper-alloy vessel (<361> unstratified): Fragment of horizontal, cast handle; surviving l 80mm, D-section 17mm x 14mm; (?)incised zigzag along top; broken off at both ends.

2 Cast copper-alloy vessel (<686> unstratified): Foot: triangular-section; with tenon. Possible repair or ingot.

3 Cast copper-alloy vessel (<11> post-medieval dumped soil): Foot: angled at end; somewhat irregular profile between D-shaped and rectangular 15mm x 28mm, surviving height 40mm.

4 Cast copper-alloy vessel (<630> from Phase 9 post-medieval soil horizon [1032]): Foot: sub-triangular in section, somewhat paw-like; 28mm x 20mm, height *c.* 28mm.

5 Copper-alloy sheeting (<602> sandy fill of Phase 7 erosion cut [148] associated with the storm event which destroyed Building 2):. Incomplete, subrectangular patch, 67mm x 41mm, retaining one of original five spirally rolled rivets survives. (Cf. Egan 2005, fig. 86 & no. 462 for this form of rivet, which is assigned to the late 15th to 17th centuries).

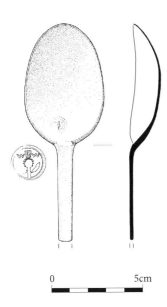

Fig. 55   Copper-alloy spoon (scale 1:2)

Household equipment and fittings

A single structural item, a damaged length of lead window came, made in the medieval (unreeded) tradition was recovered. There is also a fitting, which consists of a copper–alloy curtain ring. It has a diameter of 29mm and has an uneven frame.

Security equipment is represented by two corroded copper-alloy keys, both 37mm in length with circular bows, the first with a diameter of 11mm, the second 10mm and both with symmetrical warding, and a small copper-alloy key of a crude type (Egan 1998, 111–112 fig. 86 nos. 294–298), which has been assigned a late 12th- to late 14th-century date.

Fragments and pieces of cast copper-alloy vessels include a rim fragment with a beaded profile and a diameter of approximately 300mm. The walling is <1mm thick, and it is probably of late medieval or early post-medieval date. There is a second rim fragment as well as a piece of a vessel wall and a fragment of a horizontal cast handle (<361> Fig. 54.1), the surviving length of which is 80mm; D-shaped in section this measures 17mm x 14mm, with an incised zigzag design running along the top, and it is broken at both ends. There are also three foot fragments (<686>, <11>, <630> Fig. 54.2 –Fig. 54.4), as well as a piece of sheeting for repairs with a rivet which can be dated to the late 15th to 17th centuries (<602> Fig. 54.5) (Egan 2005, fig. 86 no. 462).

A copper-alloy spoon with a tin coating, and an oval bowl measuring 62mm x 42mm, and with 50mm of the strap-like handle surviving was found (Fig. 55). A maker's stamp is present in the bowl, comprising a thistle, with W W to the sides above (the mark is not found in Cotterell 1929). The spoon (<454>) is late 17th century in date and was recovered from Phase 9 soil horizon [1072].

Two unstratified copper -alloy thimbles were

recovered (Fig. 56.1–Fig. 56.2) of which one (<304>, Fig. 56.1) is a most unusual decorated medieval example, which is slightly distorted. The sheeting height is 13mm and the diameter at the base is 15mm, where there is a pair of engraved grooves. The (probably drilled) pits are within an engraved (double line) mesh of four large triangles whose apices meet at a pit on the crown. Each triangle is further divided into a chevron, which itself is subdivided into pairs of triangles and lozenges with a six-sided outline above, and embraces a basal triangle.

Two copper-alloy book mounts were recovered (eg Fig. 56.3) as well as a single mason's stylus of lead/tin for inscribing stone. A late 12th- to early 15th-century lead/tin repair plug was identified with a weight of 50g (Egan 1998, fig. 240–242, nos. 733–744). This would have been for the repair of a holed ceramic vessel, it measured 28mm x 22mm and would cater for a hole measuring 14mm x 15mm.

Metalworking

Evidence for metalworking comprises a lead/tin ingot fragment. It is lozenge-shaped in section, and may be part of a tin strake (Egan 1996).

Fishing industry

There are a number of iron fish hooks for line fishing as well as some 30 lead net weights (see Riddler, Chapter 11). These measure between 19mm x 13mm and 50mm x 9mm, and have weights of between 9g and 42g. Over a thousand similar items were found in a shipwreck in London that is assigned to the 15th century.

Commerce

There are two lead seal matrices; the first is a disc of battered appearance <284> with an asterisk with alternate strokes obliquely hatched, and the text +SIGIL+ GVIDI LIE…EL around the periphery in lombardic lettering (Fig. 56.4). The second <380> has a flower motif, and the text +SIGILL CELES(I)RE(FV…)G(…)RI around the periphery also in lombardic style lettering (Fig. 56.5). These add to the relatively large number of lead seal matrices found elsewhere in New Romney (see Chapter 1).

There are six commercial weights, all in lead/tin. Weights of these types and alloys, unless stamped with control marks, are often particularly difficult to identify with certainty, let alone to date accurately. One <402> has a crude squat pyramidal form, measures 42mm x 43mm at the base, has a height of 19mm, and a weight 174g (Fig. 56.6). It has roughly scratched devices on its sides, and is probably post-medieval in date. One, <377> with a crown over rose, GOD SAVE THE QEVE around // double-headed eagle, is one of the few from this series that is well known in London to have been found outside the capital (cf. Mitchiner 1998 1653-4 nos. 4713-37 (including minor varieties) assigned to the 1590s–1603).

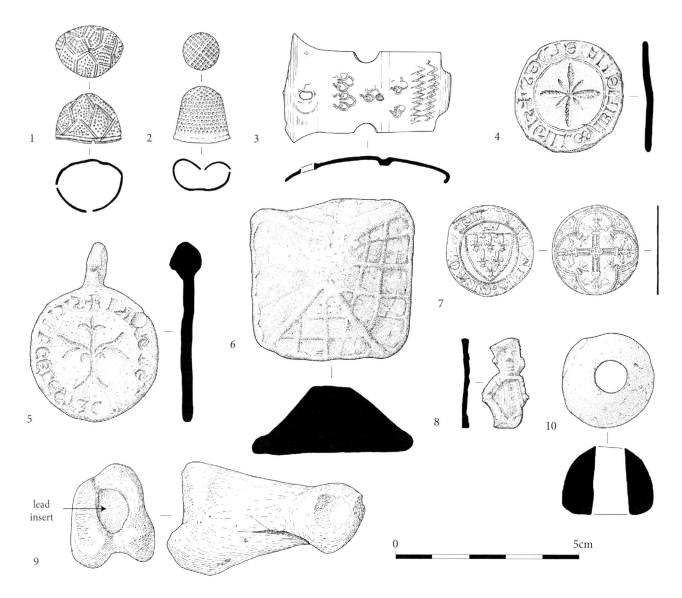

Fig. 56   Household equipment, items of commerce and toys (scale 1:1)

Catalogue of household items, items of commerce and toys (Fig. 56)

1 Copper-alloy thimble (<304> unstratified): Sheeting: height 13mm, diameter at base *c.* 15mm (two grooves here).

2 Copper-alloy thimble (unstratified): height 15mm, diameter at base *c.* 11mm.

3 Copper-alloy book mount (<537> unstratified): ?fleur-de-lis decoration.

4 Seal matrix (<248> unstratified) Disc, diameter 28mm; battered: asterisk with alternate strokes obliquely hatched, +SIGIL+ GVIDI LIE…EL around (lombardic lettering) (?) Guy Li…el.

5 Seal matrix (<380> from Phase 9 road surface): Flower motif, +SIGILL CELES(I)RE(FV…)G(…)RI around (lombardic lettering) (??) Giles Re…g…

6 Lead/tin weight (<402> unstratified): Crude: squat pyramidal form; 42mm x 43mm, height 19mm, wt 174g; roughly scratched devices on sides: 4-like motif, 2 x 4 grid, (?) A-like motif on its side, (no device). Possibly post-medieval. Commercial weights of these alloys, unless stamped with control marks, can be particularly difficult to identify with certainty, let alone to date accurately.

7 Copper-alloy jetton (<312> unstratified): Diameter 25mm: crown over shield semé de lis, AVE MARIA:GRACIA:PLE around (lombardic lettering except for roman-style 'E's) // quatrefoil at centre of triply stranded cross fleur-de-lisée with foliage flanking, all in doubly outlined quatrefoil with collared trefoils inside angles, and pellet, trefoil, trefoil in spandrels.

8 Lead/tin toy (<413> unstratified): Upper part of single-sided flat figure of a man, surviving 23x13mm; tunic with vertical banding, and flat hat; traces of red paint, wearing (?)15th/16th-century dress.

9 Bone toy (<31> from Phase 7 storm deposits) phalange, with lead insert, weighted for playing knucklebones.

10 Lead/tin spindle whorl (<215> unstratified) Plano-convex; height 15mm, diameter at base 26mm; neat, round hole diameter 10mm; wt 54g.

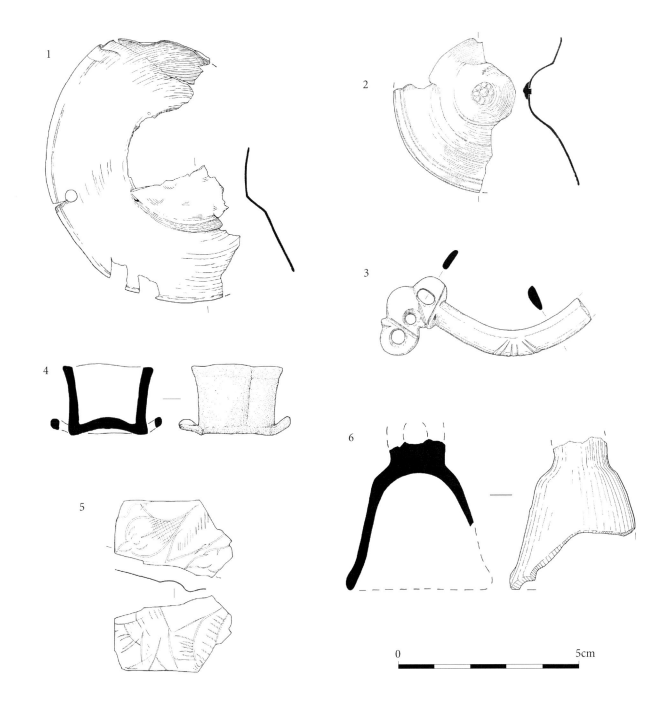

Fig. 57   Horse equipment, militaria and miscellaneous objects (scale 1:1)

Catalogue of horse equipment, militaria and miscellaneous finds (Fig. 57)

1 Copper-alloy bridle boss (<467> unstratified): About half of a damaged boss; diameter *c*. 78mm; engraved line near perimeter presumably 16th-century.

2 Copper-alloy bridle boss (<558> unstratified): About a quarter of a similar item, diameter *c*. 53mm; engraved single and inner paired concentric lines on boss and again at perimeter; octofoil-rosette rivet head survives in centre presumably 16th-century.

3 Copper-alloy spur (<589> unstratified): Terminal fragment: curved arm with engraved motif of radiating lines, and

moulded terminal with pair of large holes flanking smaller one; traces of now-black coating.

4 Lead/tin powder-measure cap (<520> unstratified): Pair of lateral loops at top for attachment to powder holder; height 17mm, diameter at open end 24mm, diameter at top 20mm.

5 Copper-alloy sheet (<516> unstratified): Incomplete: corner fragment of sheet engraved with foliage on both sides. (?)Late 15th/16th century.

6 Copper-alloy open-mouth bell fragment (<234> unstratified): Late medieval (?)sacring bell; cf. Egan 2005.

Surprisingly only one lead/tin cloth seal was recovered; considering the known historical link of the Romney marshes with wool production more could have been expected. This example has diameters of its four superimposed disks of 10mm, 11mm, 13mm, and 14mm respectively. It has a (cast) *fleur-de-lis*//(cast) crown// (ER)/HED, with 'Searched' on fourth disc. This type has parallels in Essex or Colchester stamps, which suggests this is an Essex alnage seal, of early 17th-century date.

Of the English coinage recovered the total face value equals thirteen pence. Of this six pence is in Henry III's Short Cross issue (this does not include one counterfeit penny) and three pennies in the Long Cross issue, with three pence and a farthing of Edward I–II. They derive from mints in London, Northampton, Bury St Edmunds, and Canterbury. There is in addition one continental *Denier tournois* (roughly the equivalent of a farthing), as well as a coin of John the Blind, King of Bohemia and Duke of Luxemburg.

A series of private-issue tokens were recovered including a copper-alloy token (from a Phase 9 post-medieval gravel dump in Area A <67>) with a shield with arms of the Grocers' Company, *RICHARD BAKER // B/RM, IN NEW RVMNEY. This type represents a common find in the area; Richard Baker was the town's mayor during the Commonwealth. From the same context is one from William Sudell (<68>), it has two quatrefoils, and the lettering reads WILLIAM SUDELL // WS, ∴*IN LIDD 1662 and constitutes an issue from Lydd, a little over 4km south-southwest of New Romney. There is also a Macclesfield halfpenny (unstratified, <314>) dated to 1792: it has a hive and bees over an ornate RC ligature, MACCLESFIELD above, and opposed C-shaped incuse stamps on each face. The continental issues comprise one almost smooth worn French *liard* (<367>) of Louis XIV issued 1655–1700 and marked DE / FRANCE // B between *fleurs-de-lis*. Three Continental jettons were recovered. All are copper alloy, all French in origin and post-medieval in date. One, <312> , 25mm diameter has a crown over shield semé de lis, AVE MARIA:GRACIA:PLE around (lombardic lettering except for roman-style 'E's) // quatrefoil at centre of triply stranded cross fleur-de-lisée with foliage flanking, all in doubly outlined quatrefoil with collared trefoils inside angles, and pellet, trefoil, trefoil in spandrels (Fig. 56.7). A second <60> measures 29mm in diameter with a shield with arms of France modern, +MARIE rose STELLA rose V(E[C,L or R]VD) rose // quatrefoil at centre of triply stranded cross fleur-de-lisée, all in quatrefoil, ·§· between each spandrel. A third <554>, 24mm in diameter has fleur de lis in roundel within long cross, sprigged trefoils in quarters, +VIVE* +VIVE* BLAN· PAIN* // three circles with fleurs de lis, three crowns around, wreath *VIVE+VIVE wreath +BLANPAIN (cf. Mitchiner 1988, 191 no. 520). Issuer Jean Blancpain (fl. 11425-54); fine style.

The 21 lead tokens recovered include one waster, presumably locally made, a pair of repeats dated 171(0), one which is dated (?16)67, and one which is a much-

handled blob of waste, these would have been used as tokens or in some cases gaming pieces.

Spindle whorl and toys

An unstratified lead/tin spindle whorl <215> was recovered, plano-convex in form, with a height of 15mm, a diameter at the base of 26mm, and a neat, centrally placed, round hole with a diameter of 10mm and a weight of 54g (Fig. 63.1) further discussed below, see Riddler, Chapter 11).

Two lead/tin toys were recovered; one <413> comprises the upper part of single-sided flat figure of a man. Its surviving dimensions are 23mm x 13mm; the figure wears a tunic with vertical banding, and a flat hat, and it has traces of red paint (Fig. 56.8). The fashion of the clothes on the figure is indicative of a 15th/16th-century date. The second piece consists of an elongated-hexagonal base, measuring 19mm x 24mm, with provision for two feet, probably for a human figure. It is post-medieval in date and the form of base goes back to as early as the late 17th century (Forsyth with Egan 2005), though it continues into the 20th century.

A single bone sheep or goat phalange <31> has a lead insert, and is weighted, perhaps for playing the game of knuckle bones (Fig. 63.5). This is an unusual find for England, as they appear to be more common on the continent (eg Baart *et al.* 1977; Willemsen 1997). An alternatively explanation of this object, that it acted as one of a series of jiggers to attract the attention of fish, is propounded by Riddler Chapter 11, below.

Horse equipment

Two unstratified copper-alloy bridle bosses <467>, <558> were recovered, both probably of 16th-century date (Fig. 57.1, Fig. 57.2) as well as some medieval horseshoe fragments, and a medieval spur terminal fragment (<589> Fig. 57.3).

Militaria

The weaponry uncovered includes eleven pieces of lead shot ranging in diameter from 9mm to 200mm as well as a single fragment of a powder-measure cap (<520> Fig. 57.4) of lead/tin with a pair of lateral loops at the top for attachment to the powder holder. It has a height of 17mm, a diameter at its open end of 24mm, and at the top of 20mm. In addition there is a piece of shrapnel and several copper-alloy cartridge cases likely to date to W W II.

Miscellaneous

An incomplete, corner fragment of sheet engraved with foliage on both sides, which is late 15th/16th century in date (<516> Fig. 57.5) is likely to have been mounted perhaps on a piece of furniture.

Finally there is a copper-alloy open-mouth bell fragment. This constitutes a late-medieval sacring bell.

Coin catalogue

Barry Cook and Richard Kelleher

Short Cross period (1180–1247)

Short Cross penny (fragment) class 1b1 (1180–*c*. 1182)
Moneyer Willelm, mint Northampton Rev: WIL[ ].ON.NOR[ ]
Wt: 0.92g
Deposition: since it seems that this coin was relatively little worn, before it was damaged, it is likely that it was deposited before the partial recoinage of the Short Cross coinage in 1205, although a later deposit is not impossible.
Context [142], floor surface in Phase 6, Building 2, <16>

Short Cross cut halfpenny class 1b1 (1180–*c*. 1182)
Moneyer Iohan, mint London Rev: +IOhAN.O[ ]
Wt: 0.51g
Deposition: before the recoinage of 1247.
Context [1003], unstratified. <498>

Short Cross cut halfpenny class 5b1 (1205)
Moneyer, Fulke, mint Bury St Edmunds Rev: +FVL[ ]DM
Wt: 0.51g
Deposition: the Short Cross coinage was recalled and replaced in 1247, so this coin was deposited in the first half of the 13th century.
Context [1003], unstratified, <425>

Short Cross penny class 5b2 (1205–1207)
Moneyer, Willelm B, mint London Rev: +WILLELM.B.ON.LV
Wt: 0.7g
Deposition: the Short Cross coinage was recalled and replaced in 1247, so this coin was deposited in the first half of the 13th century.
Context [100], unstratified, <202>

Short Cross cut halfpenny class 5b2 (1205–1207)
Moneyer, Roberd T*, mint Northampton Rev: +ROB[ ]N.NO
Wt: 0.51g
Deposition: the Short Cross coinage was recalled and replaced in 1247, so this coin was deposited in the first half of the 13th century.
[*Coins were issued at Northampton by both Roberd and Roberd T, but the reverse legend of the former usually concludes with a longer form of the mint name, typically NORh.]
Context [145], Phase 7 storm deposit, <36>

Short Cross cut halfpenny class 5c (1207–*c*.1210)
Moneyer, Simon, mint Canterbury Rev: [ON.ON.CA[ ]
Wt: 0.61g
Deposition: the Short Cross coinage was recalled and replaced in 1247, so this coin was deposited in the first half of the 13th century.
Context [145] Phase 7 storm deposit, <38>

Short Cross cut halfpenny class 6c3 (*c*. 1217)
Moneyer Roger, mint Canterbury Rev: +ROGER.O[ ]
Wt: 0.59g
Deposition: the Short Cross coinage was recalled and replaced in 1247, so this coin was deposited *c*. 1220–1247.
Context [103], Phase 9 post-medieval deposit, <389>

Short Cross cut halfpenny class 7b2 (*c*. 1229–*c*. 1232)
Moneyer Adam, mint London Rev: +ADAMON[ ]
Wt: 0.59g
Deposition: the Short Cross coinage was recalled and replaced in 1247, so this coin was deposited *c*. 1230–1247.
Context [102], Phase 7 storm deposit, <32>

Short Cross cut halfpenny class 7b2 (*c*. 1229–*c*. 1232)
Moneyer Ledulf, mint London Rev: [ ]VLFONLV[ ]
Wt: 0.49g
Deposition: the Short Cross coinage was recalled and replaced in 1247, so this coin was deposited *c*. 1230–1247.
Context [124], Phase 5 dump, <34>

Imitation Short Cross, cut halfpenny
Obv: [ ] VS Rev: ODO [ ]
Wt: 0.51g
This is an imitation or counterfeit coin, subsequently cut into halfpennies. Very roughly the style resembles that of coins struck after the 1205 reform, so its can be dated to the first half of the 13th century.
Context [145], Phase 7 storm deposit, <35>

Long Cross period (1247–1279)

Long Cross cut halfpenny class 3b (1248–1250)
Moneyer: Nicole, mint Canterbury Rev: [ ]/ OLE/ ONC/ [ ]
Wt: 0.51g
Deposition: The Long Cross coinage was withdrawn and replaced in 1279–1280 and it is virtually certain this coin was deposited before this.
Context [1101], Phase 7 storm deposit, <456>

Long Cross penny (fragment) class 5g (1251–1272)
Moneyer Iohs, mint Canterbury Rev: IOh/ [SON/CAN/] TER
Wt: 0.71g
Deposition: The Long Cross coinage was withdrawn and replaced in 1279–1280 and it is virtually certain this coin was deposited before this.
Context [150], Phase 3 storm deposit, <26>

Long Cross penny Class 5 (1251–1272)
Moneyer Gilbert, mint Canterbury Rev: GIL/ BERT/ONC/ ANT
Wt: 1.05g
Deposition: The Long Cross coinage was withdrawn and replaced in 1279–1280 and it is virtually certain this coin was deposited before this. [NB Crimping and damage to this coin has prevented a more precise identification.]
Context [111], Phase 9 post-medieval soil, <3>

Long Cross cut halfpenny, heavily clipped, details uncertain
Wt: 0.22g
Deposition: The Long Cross coinage was withdrawn and replaced in 1279–1280 and it is virtually certain this coin was deposited before this.
Context [1001], unstratified, <565>

Denier tournois, Louis VIII or IX, King of France, issued *c*. 1223–1250
Ref: Duplessy 187
Deposition: mid to late 13th century. At this time there was a standard relationship between tournois and sterling of 1:4, so the denier was technically equal to an English farthing. Deniers tournois of the 13th century do turn up as English finds, especially in the southeast.
Context [101] Phase 9 post-medieval soil<15>

Edwardian period (1279–)

Coins of Edward I–II were never formally withdrawn and some survive into the late 15th century, although these would be clipped down to the current weight standard. Suggestions on deposition can be made on the basis of weight and wear, although the latter especially is not an objective measure.

Farthing, Edward I Withers class 7 (Fox 2) (c. 1279–1280)
London mint Wt: 0.39g
Deposition: Edwardian coinage was never formally recalled and much remained in currency for centuries; however, the fractional denominations did not survive in this way and this coin shows relatively little wear. It is likely to have been deposited within a couple of decades of issue, at most.
Context [102] Phase 7 storm deposit <1>

Penny, Edward I Class 4a (1282–1289)
London mint Wt: 1.34g
Deposition: given its relatively good weight, this coin was probably deposited within a decade or two of issue, and certainly the weight reduction of 1351, after which older sterlings were usually clipped down to the new standard
Context [1003], unstratified, <315>

Penny, Edward I Class 8b (between 1294 and 1299)
London mint Wt: 1.33g
Deposition: given its relatively good weight and condition, this coin was probably deposited within a decade or two of issue, and certainly the weight reduction of 1351, after which older sterlings were usually clipped down to the new standard.
Context [1003], unstratified, <253>

Penny, Edward I–II Class 10cf3 (*c*. 1305–1210)
Canterbury mint Wt: 1.12g
Deposition: this coin appears to have been clipped down to the level of the new weight standard introduced in 1251, so it may have been deposited in the mid- to late 14th century, although low-weight coins do occur in earlier hoards, so an earlier deposit is not impossible.
Context [1032] Phase 9 post-medieval soil horizon <247>

Sterling of John the Blind, King of Bohemia and duke of Luxemburg (1309–1346)
Arlon mint (ref: Mayhew 286)
Obv: [ ]WANNES.DNSREGYB Rev: MON/ ETA/ ERL/ ONS (square Es, Lombardic Ns)
NB Mayhew describes this as a rare type, of which he only knew of two examples.
Deposition: roughly second quarter of the 14th century.
Context [1003], unstratified, <315>

Chapter 11 Livelihood and Economy: Ship Construction and Breaking, Fishing and Diet

Ship Construction and Breaking

Damian Goodburn

A substantial assemblage of iron nails was recovered at the Southlands School site. This group of material is indicative of ship-building or breaking activities and is therefore considered in detail. These iron nails constitute relatively robust finds and, as many are strongly concreted, it may well be that some are residual in the contexts in which they were found. Therefore for the purposes of this analysis the material is attributed to the whole of the period *c.* 1250–1450 by reference to the pottery dating. The list of the distinctive clear ship nails and fragments provided below takes account of the site's phasing.

Iron nails are often found on late medieval archaeological sites in England and many with square or rectangular section shanks had generalised uses, which are hard to pin down. They were employed in carpentry, engineering in timber (millwrighting), wheelwrights' and farriers' work as well as nautical woodwork. Many sizes and small variations in form can be seen, but such nails cannot be reliably attributed to a nautical use when found in a series of dispersed contexts without associated woodwork. By contrast at the Southlands School site we are concerned with a representative sample of distinctive ship rivets or 'rovenails', which have only been found in a very narrow range of use contexts in later medieval England. By far the most common use was in ship- and boat-building (Milne *et al.* 1998, 62), but they have also been found in some church and other high status doors (Hewett 1982, 78). Occasional documentary references suggest that, even when used in building doors, they were often fitted by shipwrights (eg Salzman 1952, 309).

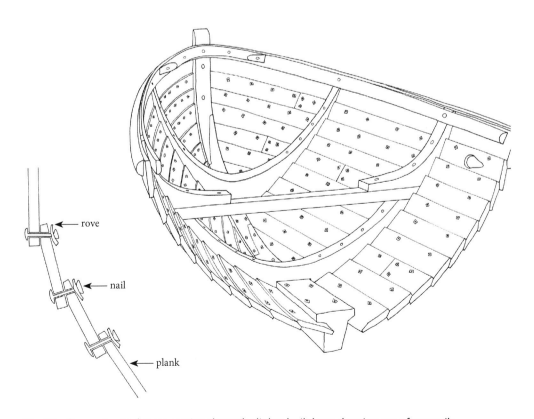

Fig. 58   Reconstructed cross-section through clinker-built boat showing use of rovenails

The origin, use and dating of clinker ship rivets , 'rovenails', in England

The term 'clinker built' ship or boat refers to a craft with a shell of planks (usually called 'boards') which partially overlap, and which are fastened to each other by various means (Fig. 58). The frame timbers were (or are, as the system of building still just survives) inserted afterwards. Current archaeological evidence suggests that this technique of planked boat and ship building developed in South Scandinavia in the 1st millennium BC, where the fastenings were initially lashings and sewing (McGrail 1981, 22). By the 3rd century AD some clinker built vessels had fastenings of iron rivets or 'rovenails' formed of a pointed nail driven through a quadrilateral washer or 'rove' with the tip deformed to make a rivet (Bill 1994, 55). In other cases headed and wedged pegs ('treenails'), or lashings were used.

During the migration period forms of clinker planked boat building were brought to England from a broad area of Northwest Europe and several variants can be documented from finds in southeast England, mainly from London (Goodburn 1994). In 9th- to 11th-century clinker ship and boat materials from southeast England four securely dated forms of lap fastening are known: large iron rovenails with either square, or round, shanks; small irregular iron rovenails driven through wooden plugs; and wedged wooden pegs (treenails) of willow, with the last two types being the most common. By the late 12th century English boat builders and shipwrights appear to have mainly adopted the use of large square-shanked iron rovenails over other techniques. This was also the trend over much of Northwest Europe and Scandinavia (Bill 1994, 60). However, treenails were still used later in a few cases, as seen in some fragmentary material from London. Thus, in a port location, for the period with which we are concerned here we would expect to find square-shanked iron rovenails on sites where clinker built vessels were either being repaired or broken up, or where the timbers were being reused as fuel or for structural purposes either in new vessels or 'land' structures. As many waterfront excavations have shown (Goodburn 1991; Marsden 1996) the reuse of slabs of clinker planking cut from old vessels was common in the medieval period in structures close to navigable water. Most commonly it was used as sheathing to river and dock walls. Obviously if the site was solely used for new construction only unused nails and the associated debris described below would be found, together with other evidence for boat-building such as wood chip layers.

Other uses of rovenails in medieval nautical work, and finds of rove strips

In most cases the same type of fastenings were used for end-to-end joints in the planking ('scarfs') and sometimes the same fastenings were also used to fit repair patches, although smaller plain and turned nails were also used (eg Goodburn 1991, 111). Occasionally small

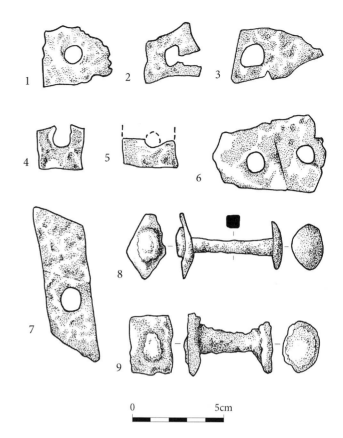

Fig. 59   Medieval roves and rovenails (scale 1:2)

Catalogue of illustrated medieval roves and rovenails (Fig. 59)

1 Rove from post-medieval soil [1002].

2 Broken rove from post-medieval soil [123].

3 End of rove strip from the fill of Phase 4 tree-throw hollow [186].

4 Split rove from post-medieval soil [129].

5 Split rove from post-medieval soil [129].

6 Roves joined as rove strip end from post-medieval soil [118].

7 Large rove from Phase 7 gravel: storm deposited or consolidation dump [102].

8 Used rovenail from post-medieval soil [123].

9 Rovenail from post-medieval soil [118].

framing or other timbers in ships and boats were fastened with rovenails, whilst treenails, large plain nails, and simple iron bolts were more commonly used for larger members. Fastenings used for these other purposes would obviously be of different lengths to those for the laps.

Roves were made for clinker construction in the medieval period by forging flat strips of iron and partially cutting out the shapes of the generally quadrilateral roves, as well as punching holes for the nail tips to pass through (Bill 1994, 56). The shipwrights had simply to snap off the pre-cut rove at the building or repair site. It is likely that loose roves, nails and sometimes the ends of rove strips were lost in the debris layers of the yard and were forgotten about. Such rove strip fragments are known from a number of medieval sites on which boat- or ship-building or repair took place, as well as from various distinct places on the London City waterfront (Milne 2003, 163). Several rove strip ends were found during work at the Southlands School site, which are noted above (Fig. 59). These broken rove strips can be taken as clear evidence of the work of medieval shipwrights where they were found or close by.

Problems of concretion

All the rovenails and related nail and rove fragments from the New Romney site were heavily concreted due to the local soil conditions. Identifications were made based on close examination of the X-rays of selected iron objects from the site and a scan through three boxes of lifted corroded material; lists of the identified material are held with the archive. The material identified comprised *c.* 40 roves, some of which were conjoined (ie parts of rove strips, around sixteen rovenails, some possible cut-off nail tips and several corroded small turned nails possibly from securing 'tingles' (patches on hull boards). Many of the rovenails were retrieved from post-medieval soils and are considered residual in their context. The illustrations (Fig. 59) are based on 1:1 tracings of the X-ray images, except for one example drawn from post-medieval soil horizon [118].

In addition a small number of probable rovenails was found among the non-specific ferrous concretions. No really large rovenails, with a length of over 45mm from the rove to the nail head, were found. The longest clear shanks on used nails were only a little larger than those illustrated (Fig. 59). The largest roves were *c.* 35mm x 30mm x *c.* 3–4m thick. The rove forms varied from irregular through rectangular to diamond shaped, and the round punched holes from *c.* 6mm to 12 mm diameter.

The rovenails; discussion and conclusions

The size of the nails in relation to the possible sizes of the parent vessels

Clearly the thickness of hull boards used tends to increase in general terms with the size of the vessel, although it is likely that functional requirements and local tradition would also have been factors governing the size and type of nails used. This relationship between the proportions of ship and boat elements including nails and the size of the parent vessel from which they came has been much discussed (McGrail 1993, 24). In a preliminary study of the later medieval Smallhythe rovenails, five size categories were identified for the roves according to the maximum dimensions from 40mm to 70mm across (Ayodeji 1998). Milne's thorough study of similarly corroded material to that found at Southlands School, has clearly shown that the type of activities included a range of clinker vessels being broken up, repaired and built, from boats to large ships (Milne 2001). However, detailed examination of slabs of clinker

planking from a large 13th-century galley found reused in London (Goodburn in prep.) have shown that even in the fastenings of a single board the size and form of the roves can vary dramatically. Forms from the 13th-century galley varied between irregular, square, rectangular, and diamond shaped, with sizes varying from 25mm x 30mm and 40mm x 50mm and thickness by 2mm–4mm. As the nails were clearly made quickly, in large quantities and by hand we should expect a fair degree of variation in size and shape. It seems most practical, as far as later medieval rovenails are concerned, to divide them into three probable size categories: from small boats perhaps up to *c.* 10 m long, from large boats or small ships perhaps 11m–20m long and from large ships over that size. However, it must be noted that rovenails used for scarfs in larger vessels have to pass through much less thickness of board and might appear to derive from a much smaller vessel. Despite these provisos we can make some comparisons to get a general idea of the probable size of vessels associated with the New Romney assemblage.

The range of sizes appears smaller than that from the Smallhythe investigations with no roves over *c.* 55mm maximum dimension. The general size of the rovenails and the gaps between the heads and roves in comparison with London medieval clinker vessel finds with intact woodwork suggests that they derive from the building and/or repair of large boats or small ships rather than very large vessels. The space between the heads and roves would rarely, if ever, have accommodated two boards much more than 25mm thick at the mid-point of the lap where the nail would normally be fitted. By contrast, larger vessel planking from the 13th century onwards was often around 35mm–45mm thick. By the 15th century very large clinker ships were sometimes built, with boards laid in more than one layer. The very large mid-15th-century royal vessel the *Grace a Dieu* had lap rovenails of around 200mm long (Friel 1995, 35, 72). Possibly the closest parallels for the bulk of the nails from the New Romney site are those in the Kingston Horse Fair No. 3 boat, tree-ring dated to just before 1300 (Goodburn 1991, 108; Tyers and Hall 1997). The fragmentary remains of this vessel appeared to derive from a cargo vessel of the size of a coastal and estuary trader of *c.* 15m in length. Smaller nails were used in the small coastal trader found in the Severn estuary at Magor Pill (tree-ring dated to 1240) with dimensions of *c.* 13m–14m long by a width ('beam') of *c.* 3.7m and a depth of 1.23m amidships (Nayling 1998, 100–101).

The lack of nails and other iron fittings diagnostic of different styles of medieval ship building such as 'cog' construction

In the medieval period other traditions of planked boat and shipbuilding were known in Northwest Europe, with the most relevant here being the cog building tradition. Shipbuilders from the Low Countries seem to have originated this broad style of construction using edge laid bottom planking and overlapping side planks. They used very distinctive large turned iron nails to fasten the side planks and curious iron staples ('sintels') for holding battens in place over the planking seams (Hutchinson 1994, 15). It is important to note that neither here at New Romney nor at Smallhythe have such distinctive iron fastenings been found, even though contacts with the Low Counties were considerable and the remains of a vessel from that general region were found in the mouth of Rye harbour in the 19th century (Hutchinson 1994, 175). Presumably this means that 'keel' type clinker construction dominated in the Romney Marsh region.

The lack of evidence for a cog-type ship building tradition may be in line with deeper draught vessels being berthed, repaired and constructed in the port or 'Haven' and the difficulties the town was experiencing in maintaining access to larger and deeper draught vessels.

On the fringes of a ship-building region; a site for building, repairing and breaking small and medium sized clinker vessels?

The split, bent and distorted iron roves, nails and complete rovenails found at Southlands School clearly indicate that ship breaking and or dismantling for repair took place on, or very near the site. The abandoned unused rove strips and cut off nail tips also indicate either repair or new building of clinker vessels took place there.

The locality, fringing the marsh and its various tidal waterways on the north and west sides, was clearly a key centre for English clinker ship building in the 13th to 15th centuries, if not before (Friel 1995, 52). Recently archaeological work started to find traces of this at sites like Smallhythe (Milne 2001) and now New Romney and other edge-of-the-marsh sites such as at Playden just northeast of Rye (E. Wetherill, pers. comm.), which may point to other sites where ship building or breaking or repair took place. Such activity in this locality depended on the local resources and topography, abundant timber and iron and wood fuel in the Weald and extensive stretches of sheltered tidal waterways with relatively easy access to the sea. It should be seen in the wider regional context in which the building of small and larger vessels took place in medieval Kent at several locations: along the Thames and Swale from Deptford eastwards (using timber from woodlands on the crest of the North Downs), around the coastline, and along the county's long rivers. Shipbuilding at Smallhythe was a special case since it flourished only in the late Middle Ages under particular conditions and involved the building of large vessels including royal ones (Draper forthcoming).

New Romney was at a distance from the nearest essential heavy resources of large timber and iron, although wool and tallow for waterproofing the hulls would probably have been widely available from marsh-grazed sheep, as would locally produced hemp for rope making (Schofield and Waller 2005). The former may explain the lack of evidence for the use of the largest class of medieval clinker ship nails, which derived from very

large ships. But it is clear that, at the very least, the site was very close to, or part of, a parcel of land on which boat and small ship repairing and probably breaking took place. It is also possible that the building of medium sized vessels such as the 'barge', which appears to have been built as a 'common ship' for the town in 1400 was undertaken in the vicinity. An earlier town barge was repaired in 1381, apparently at New Romney (Friel 1995, 28; and see Chapter 5, above) on or near the same site. As noted, the town barge was used for transporting the jurats to land at New Romney and it may also have been used for transhipping cargoes from large ships to the town waterfront, an essential feature of many Northwest European ports, where the largest ships often had too deep a draught to come alongside the quays. The latter constitutes a further action to mitigate against the silting up of the anchorage and the increasing draught of cargo vessels.

Fishing Implements and Medieval Fishing Practices in East Kent

Ian Riddler

A small collection of fishing implements were recovered from the excavations, including fish hooks, as well as stone and lead net weights and, arguably, a cattle phalange filled with a lead plug. The range of object types is essentially the same as that seen at Townwall Street, Dover, although there are significant differences. The New Romney assemblage, although a small one, widens the range of fishing equipment seen in medieval east Kent. In part, this may reflect the slightly later date of some of the implements, particularly in the case of the cylindrical lead weights. It may also indicate a preference for slightly different fishing practices. The smaller fishing hooks seen at New Romney are scarcely seen at Dover or *Sandtun*, and are not common on other sites. The medium sized and large hooks can be aligned with sources suggesting that they were used to catch eels and in cod fishing, respectively. The smaller hooks may reflect an interest in local line fishing for smaller species of marine fish, including mackerel, gurnards and sea bream.

Fish hooks

Five of the eight fish hooks recovered are fragmentary but measurements of their surviving dimensions allow them to be placed into three size groups, which correspond with those seen elsewhere in east Kent (Fig. 60). Their shapes and methods of attachment to the line also allow them to be set into several types. Rulewicz identified three groups of fish hooks from Polish sites, with a number of sub-types, and these groups have a wider relevance for northern Europe as a whole (Rulewicz 1994, 99–130). Hooks of Group 1 have straight shafts with one end thickened or flattened and a hook that ends in a sharp spike with no barb. Within this group, Type A

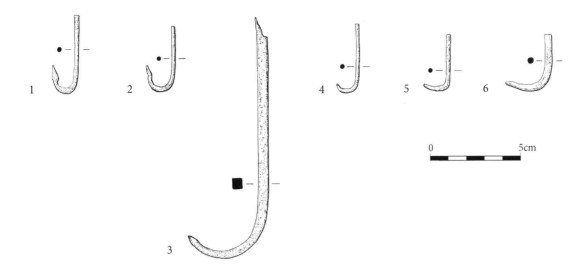

Fig. 60   Examples of fish hooks recovered from the excavations, showing the range of sizes found (scale 1:2)

hooks have shafts of circular section, whilst those of type B are square or rectangular. Hooks of type C are thicker, with looped ends, and those of type D taper to a point at either end, with shafts of square section (Rulewicz 1994, 101–119). Fish hooks of Group 2 were made from a flat strip of iron of rectangular section and they include a curved loop at one end and a barbed hook at the other (Rulewicz 1994, 121). The spiral twisting of the shaft, together with the looped head, defines group 3 hooks, which lack any barbs. Several sub-types were identified within this group (Rulewicz 1994, 123–125).

The New Romney fish hooks all belong to Group 1, with the medium and large sized hooks having shafts of square section, whilst the small hooks are circular in section. One small hook (Fig. 60.1) is barbed, whilst other hooks are not (eg Fig. 60.2 <387>) and, as at Dover, there is no obvious correlation between the size or shape of a hook and the presence of a barb. Another small hook (Fig. 60.2) tapers in size towards the upper end and belongs to type 1D, whilst the large hook (Fig. 60.3) is splayed at that point and may have fractured across a perforation. English examples of fish hooks are generally restricted to the simpler designs of Rulewicz's Groups 1 and 2. Where the shapes of fish hooks could be identified with certainty from Dover, they corresponded largely with Group 1B, although there were also a small number of hooks of type 1D (Riddler 2006a, 289–290).

A more obvious correlation between hooks and fish can be established from their size. The length of a hook relates directly to the type of fish being sought (Steane and Foreman 1991, 92). Four hooks, two of which are complete (Fig. 60.1, Fig. 60.2, Fig. 60.4 and Fig. 60.5), can be placed in the small category, which includes hooks with shafts 20mm–40mm in length. They correspond with the smallest group from Dover, which was poorly represented there and was not seen at all amidst the sample from *Sandtun* (Riddler 2001, 247–248; 2006a, 290 and fig. 197). A second group is represented by two fragmentary hooks, one of which has a shaft length a little in excess of 65mm. These belong

to the most common medieval size group from east Kent, with shafts between 47mm and 70mm in length. A near complete hook (Fig. 60.3) has a shaft length of 125mm, which allows it to be placed in the third group, of large, substantial hooks, alongside a small but equally substantial fragment (Fig. 60.6). Fish hooks from Dover and *Sandtun* follow a similar pattern of size groups, which is reflected also with the assemblage from Fuller's Hill at Great Yarmouth in East Anglia (Riddler 2001, 248; Rogerson 1976, 166 and fig. 53; Steane and Foreman 1991, fig 12.3). Fish hooks from the late medieval fishing settlement at Walraversijde vary from 40 to 140mm in length, whilst medieval examples from York lie between 28 and 79mm (Pieters 2006, 44 and fig. 5.7-11; Ottaway and Rogers 2002, 1747).

Within their overview of medieval English fishing traditions, Steane and Foreman defined zone 5, the southern part of the North Sea, in part by the presence of large fish hooks, and that characteristic is endorsed at New Romney (Steane and Foreman 1991, fig 12.10). There may also be a possible historical correlation to be made with the archaeological evidence, given that the *hokfare* at Rye in east Sussex utilised larger 'herbews' or 'harbour' hooks from Easter onwards for catching eel, whilst smaller hooks are distinguished for use at the Scarborough fair (Dulley 1969, 44). The significance of the New Romney assemblage lies with the establishment of a third, small size group for hooks, which has scarcely been seen elsewhere in east Kent. Smaller hooks would have been used on long lines to catch fish close to shore, and Dulley notes that from the 1280s onwards mackerel became more prominent in fishing at Rye (Dulley 1969, 38).

Lead net weights

Cylindrical net weights are reasonably abundant at New Romney, with sixteen examples occurring in several concentrations within Phases 7 to 9, all in the vicinity of Building 2. Examples in Phase 9 are almost certainly residual and the majority of these weights are likely to

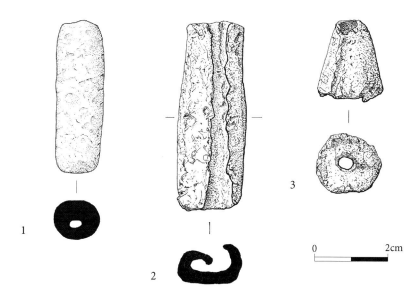

Fig. 61   Examples of rolled and unrolled cylindrical lead weights and conical line weight (scale 1:1)

be of medieval date. They consist of simple rolled sheets of lead, sometimes crimped at either end and whilst some are still rolled, others have been unravelled to a greater or lesser extent (Fig. 61.1, Fig. 61.2). A further series of nine rectangular sections of sheet lead alloy, most of which come from the same contexts as the cylindrical weights, have clearly been rolled at some point and subsequently unravelled and flattened. The range of lengths and weights for the lead alloy sheets is similar to that of the rolled cylinders (Fig. 62) and they were probably unravelled when a net was stripped of its weights. Cylindrical weights and lead sheet were

also found in association in contemporary deposits at Hastings and Walraversijde (Devenish 1979, 129; Van Neer and Ervynck 1993, 80). The rolled cylindrical weights vary in length between 20mm and 66mm, with the majority between 20mm and 50mm, a comparable range to the 20mm–38mm established for similar weights from Walraversijde (Pieters 2006, 44).

Cylindrical lead weights of this type are first found in late Iron Age contexts and occur also in Roman deposits (Steane and Foreman 1991, 97). Within east Kent a group of eighteen late Roman weights of this type were found in a ditch at Ickham and a smaller group was discovered

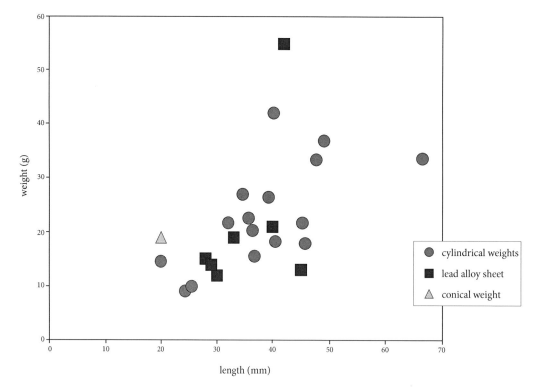

Fig. 62   Lead alloy cylindrical weights and sheet metal

at Worth (Mould forthcoming; Parfitt 2000). Pieters has noted that large collections, extending to several hundred examples, of these weights do not occur before the 13th to 14th centuries, notably at Walraversijde, Whittlesea Mere and Blackfriars (Pieters 2006, 44; Lucas *et al.* 1998; Marsden 1996, 103). The assemblage from New Romney, although substantially smaller than these, fits with his suggestion that the increase in their numbers relates to the spread of the herring gill net at this time. Rolled cylindrical lead weights are absent from Townwall Street at Dover and *Sandtun*, and the widespread use of the herring gill net might therefore be placed closer to the 14th century for east Kent. A conical line weight (Fig. 61.3 <9>) from a Phase 7 context is similar in size and weight

to the rolled cylindrical weights (Fig. 62) but was used with a line, rather than a net. It is similar to lead weights from *Sandtun* and Walraversijde (Riddler 2001, 248–249 and fig. 50.103; Pieters 2006, 47 and fig. 5.5).

Textile manufacturing implements and fishing

A hemispherical lead spindle whorl (Fig. 63.1) is not, at first sight, an obvious candidate as a fishing implement, but it does have an indirect association with fishing practices. It can be placed in Walton Rogers type A1 which, in northern England, was not in use beyond the 11th century (Walton Rogers 1997, 1736). Stone whorls of this shape were, however, still in use in Dover in the 13th

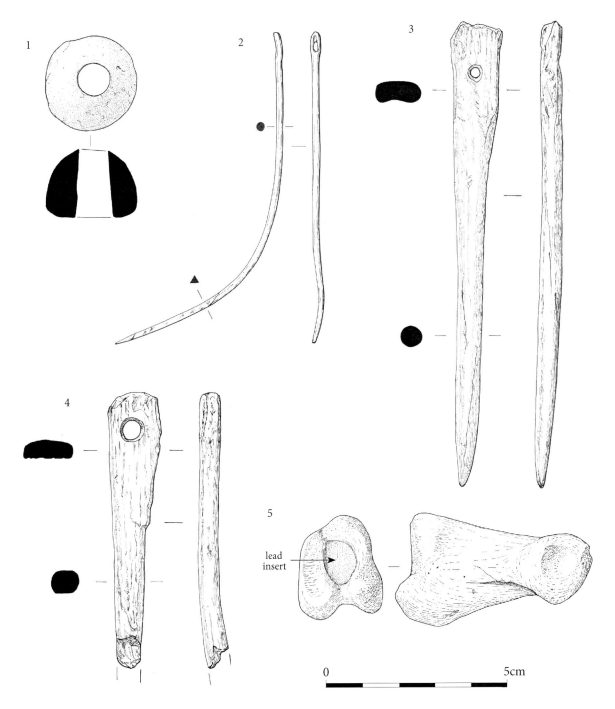

Fig. 63   Lead spindle whorl, netting needle, bone needles and weighted cattle phalange (scale 1:1)

century (Riddler 2006a, 280–282). With a weight of 54g, it is substantially heavier than the lead spindle whorls from York (Walton Rogers 1997, 1839), although it lies within the range of weights for lead whorls from Bergen (Øye 1988, 50). It is comparable also with the large stone whorls from Dover, which were used to ply two or more yarns together in the manufacture of cordage, an important commodity in a fishing community (Riddler 2006a, 282 and fig. 192).

An iron netting needle of Steane and Foreman's Type B came from a late Roman deposit at Ickham. Slender, copper-alloy examples of this object type have been linked with fishing nets, but Walton Rogers has noted that in the late medieval period they were actually used in the production of knotted silk hairnets (Steane and Foreman 1991, fig. 12.7; Walton Rogers 1997, 1790; 2002, 2741–2743). A long, slender copper-alloy needle (Fig. 63.2) recovered from the evaluation at Southlands School Dymchurch Road (NCR 02 <*2000*>) is similar to those seen at York, where they increased in popularity (against iron needles) across the medieval period (Walton Rogers 2002, 2739). It differs from other medieval examples in that it has a lightly curved shaft that tapers to a triangular section across the lower part. The curved shaft would have equipped it for work with looser weaves, and it could also have been used in repairing nets, one of the most common and onerous tasks of fisherman, as noted by Dulley (1969, 50).

Two Bone Needles

A complete bone needle (Fig. 63.3 <*28*>) has a straight shaft of oval section and a rounded point, with a flat head of irregular shape pierced by a splayed, knife-cut circular perforation. A second needle (Fig. 63.4 <*334*>) has a similarly irregular head, with a prominent knife-cut perforation. Both objects are large and relatively stout, with solid shafts, which distinguishes them from pig fibula needles of the Anglo-Saxon period. A transition away from the use of pig fibulae and towards the adoption of these larger bone implements began in the 11th to 12th century. Of the seventeen bone needles from Townwall Street, Dover, recovered from contexts of mid-12th- to late 13th-century date, only four are made from pig fibulae, and it is possible that they are residual (Riddler and Walton Rogers 2006, 294-297). In marked contrast, just seven of 234 needles from Anglo-Saxon Ipswich are made of bone, and eleven further examples are either bone or antler (Riddler *et al.* forthcoming). Amongst them is a large bone needle of precisely the shape seen here, with a flattened and lightly expanded head, and a straight shaft of oval section; it came from a context of 11th- to 12th-century date. Crowfoot described these implements both as pin-beaters and also as 'large bone needles' and the latter interpretation is preferable (Crowfoot 1977). They are widespread in contexts of the 12th to 13th century, both in England and Ireland, and have been found on most urban sites of that date (Pritchard 1991, fig. 3.85.228-9; Margeson

Fig. 64   Naturally perforated flint pebble fishing weights

1993, fig. 137.1449-50; Rogerson and Dallas 1984, fig. 190.39; Hurley 1997a, fig. 17.5.6 and 8; 1997b, fig. 104.5-10). Crowfoot thought that they were used as weaving implements but it is more likely that they were employed in coarser work, to repair nets, or to fasten bags and sacks (Riddler and Walton Rogers 2006, 297).

Perforated cattle phalange

An axially perforated cattle phalange (Fig. 63.5 <31>) from a Phase 7 storm deposited context has been filled with a lead plug. It can be compared with a series of over a hundred weighted phalanges from Schleswig, as well as smaller groups of medieval date from Århus and Rotterdam (Ulbricht 1984, 63 and taf 47.5–12; Riddler 2006b, 174). It has been suggested that a series of weighted phalanges of this type would have been strung together on a line, acting as jiggers to attract the attention of fish (Riddler 2006b, 174).

Stone weights

Barry Bishop and Ian Riddler

Two complete flint pebbles from context [145] are of interest, consisting of large (860g and 645g) rounded and battered 'beach' cobbles, each containing a natural perforation extending right through the cobble. Around the entrances to the perforations is evidence of some smoothing, although a natural origin for this cannot be excluded. Both pebbles would be eminently suitable for tying on to fishing nets to act as weights. A third broken example may have been used in a similar manner. Although there is little evidence of human modification, their context of recovery would suggest that they had been deliberately selected and consciously used. A similar flint weight came from Townwall Street, Dover, and other examples are known from Polish fishing sites (Riddler 2006a, 294 and fig. 201.2852; Rulewicz 1994, 184 and ryc 32.1). A stone weight from Walraversijde had been deliberately perforated and reflects a similar interest in large net weights (Van Neer and Ervynck 1993, 78).

The Mammal, Bird and Fish Bones Recovered from the Excavations

Philip Armitage

The animal bone assemblage from Southlands School comprised a total of 1,351 hand-collected animal bone elements/fragments (NISP). Using standard archaeozoological methodological procedures 1,095 (81% of the total) bones have been identified to species and part of skeleton, and 256 (19%) remain indeterminate. Because of apparent differences in the condition of the bone deriving from two distinct areas of the site the assemblage has been divided into two groups. The first of these is represented by material from Area B and the second by the material from Area A. Because of the considerable degree of mixing and residuality, bone from post-medieval contexts has been largely excluded from this analysis of the assemblage.

Species/taxa present

Sixteen species/taxa were identified:

Mammalian species: horse *Equus* caballus (domestic); cattle *Bos* (domestic); sheep *Ovis* (domestic); pig *Sus* (domestic); dog *Canis* (domestic); cat *Felis* (domestic)

Bird species: grey-lag/domestic goose *Anser anser*/domestic; domestic fowl *Gallus gallus* (domestic); teal *Anas crecca*

Fish species: cod *Gadus morhua*; cod family Gadidae; ling *Molva molva*; gurnard family Triglidae; conger eel *Conger conger*; thornback ray *Raja clavata*; plaice *Pleuronectes platessa*.

Preservation and deposition

While only relatively moderate frequencies of weathered/eroded/abraded bone fragments are noted for the assemblage excavated from Area A deposits (where the incidence of such modified bone contributed 1.8% of the overall total NISP), similar frequencies calculated for the assemblage recovered from the Area B excavation deposits reveal noticeably higher incidences of such bones (32% in the medieval phases, with an overall site frequency of 25%/total NISP). In the Main School excavation area, two associated medieval contexts in particular yielded concentrations of weathered/eroded/abraded bones and all the bones in medieval context [1041] (the fill of a rubbish pit) exhibited evidence of moderate weathering or attritional damage.

All of these relatively poorly preserved bones probably represent refuse material that had been left exposed to sub-aerial weathering, physical attrition or biological degradation prior to burial and possibly also subjected to post-depositional damage, or re-deposited material dug up from elsewhere. For Area A however, it appears the bulk of the bone refuse had been buried in a timely and secure manner after being discarded, and had not been left lying on the ground for any length of time, nor had it been subjected to post-depositional damage.

There is no evidence of the food debris being burnt as a sanitary measure prior to burial. The low numbers of burnt bones present (comprising 1.1%/total NISP in the Area A assemblage and 1.0% in the Main School assemblage) probably represent food scraps casually dropped into cooking fires or accidental burning whilst the meat was being roasted (the most common method of cooking meat throughout the medieval and early-modern period).

Food bones gnawed/chewed by dogs and cats

The incidence of dog-gnawed food bones in the assemblages from both excavation areas is relatively moderate (2.1%/total NISP Area A and 2.5%/total NISP Area B). Evidence for cat chewing is limited to two isolated bird bone elements, a goose coracoid and a domestic fowl ulna, both from post-medieval contexts. Special mention should also be made of an apparent tooth perforation/penetrating mark on the immature cat humerus also of post-medieval date. Perhaps this indicates an injury made by another cat during a fight, shortly after which the wounded animal died.

Descriptions and interpretations of the species represented

In the domestic fowl bones, comparison with modern skeletal material reveals the majority of the Southlands School fowl were comparable in size to bantams, with only a relatively few larger-sized birds analogous to modern laying and boiling fowl. In the cod, the total length (TL) of the fish represented by a cleithrum is estimated at 89.2 cm (method of Rojo 1986) while the fish represented by a precaudal vertebra also medieval in date is comparable in size to those in a modern cod of TL 109 cm in the author's collections. Both fish fall into the larger size-range (88cm to 137cm) documented by Wheeler (1977, 407–408) for the cod from medieval King's Lynn, which he believed represented the 'product of a distant water' rather than an inshore fishery.

Sex

One medieval cattle innominate bone is recognised as female using the criteria of Grigson (1982). Based on the criteria of Armitage (1977) one sheep innominate bone is sexed as castrate.

Age at slaughter in the domestic livestock

Kill-off patterns for the main meat-yielding species (cattle, sheep and pigs) are indicated by the range in ages of these animals at time of death established from their dental eruption and wear stages and from data relating to fusion in their long bones. In cattle, there is evidence of the killing of veal calves and young immature animals as well as older beasts (the latter group probably

Table 1   Fish bone recovered from the Southlands School site: quantification by species (NISP)

Species	Number
Cod	9
Small gadoid	5
Ling	1
Plaice	2
Gurnard	2
Thornback ray	4
Conger eel	1
Unidentified fish	3
Total identified	27

representing culled milk cows and plough oxen). Although a few lambs apparently were being killed for their succulent meat, the diet of the inhabitants of the site seems to mainly comprise meat from sheep kept until 3 to 4 years of age, together with mutton from a few older sheep kept primarily for their wool. Pigs killed at ages between 1 and 3.5 years provided the bulk of the pork eaten by the inhabitants of the Southlands School area in the medieval period.

Discussion of the fish bones

A more detailed appraisal of the fish bones is considered appropriate as it is well documented that New Romney in medieval and early post-medieval times was an important southeast coast fishery. It attracted specialist fish retailer-transporters known as ripiers who paid special tolls to the town's authorities in order to purchase fresh fish supplies direct from the local fishermen as soon as their catches had been landed. This merchandise was then transported speedily to London on packhorses, the fish reportedly reaching the capital in three to four hours (Kowaleski 2000, 31). This appears impossibly fast considering the distance involved and may well represent wishful thinking or exaggeration on the part of the fishmongers, trying to emphasize the freshness of their product.

Table 2   Natural distribution of fish recovered from the Southlands School site and possible methods of capture

Species	Natural distribution around southern English coast and North Sea	Possible methods of capture in medieval/early post-medieval times
Cod	Abundant in both offshore & (seasonally in winter) inshore waters	Hook and line Shore seines in winter Seine net from small boat Permanent shore-line traps (kiddles) in winter
Plaice	Abundant in North Sea in inshore waters and offshore banks; bottom dwelling	Trawl nets Kiddles Seine nets from small boat or on shore
Gurnards	Grey & tub gurnards are frequent in inshore waters/bays	Hook and line Trawl nets
Thornback ray	Abundant in southern North Sea Seasonally (May to July) in shallow coastal waters	Trawl nets Kiddles Hook and line Shore seine nets (occasionally)
Conger eel	Frequents shallow coastal waters, usually living among rocks	Hook and line Kiddles

Although the actual quantities of fish bones (all of them marine species) recovered from the various site phases during the Southlands School excavations are modest, considered as a whole they do complement the historical sources by providing further direct insight into the range of species caught/consumed by the local community (Table 1).

Apart from the ling (which probably is of a quite late date) and possibly also some of the cod, all the fish species represented suggest an inshore, shore-line or coastal fishery rather than a distant, deep-water one. Various methods could have been employed to catch these species (Table 2).

Ling as a species is today uncommon in the southern North Sea and is regarded as a deep-water fish most abundant in depths of 20 to 30 fathoms (Kennedy 1954, 335). The coastal waters off New Romney (Straits of Dover) are relatively shallow with average depths of 7 to 10 fathoms (Edwards 1977, 231), and are therefore a poor habitat for ling. This supports a relatively recent date for this bone element as it would require the fishermen from New Romney to venture further northwards into the North Sea, extending their fishing grounds into deeper waters. More importantly perhaps it must be considered a possibility that the relatively large-sized cod represented in the medieval phases may have been imported in preserved (salted/dried) form to New Romney from distant-water fisheries operating on the north eastern coast.

Fish Remains: Coastal Settlements and Inland Consumer Sites in East Kent

Ian Riddler

Fish remains have been recovered from a number of coastal and inland sites within east Kent. In particular, several sites excavated as a part of recent Channel Tunnel Rail Link (CTRL) work have provided small but intriguing assemblages, which are summarised here from data kindly made available by Helen Glass and Stuart Foreman. As with the other aspects of this study, Dover dominates this category for the sheer quantity of its fish remains, but other sites provide significant insights into the distribution of fish within the region at certain points in time (Table 3). In particular, the relationship between coastal sites like

Dover and *Sandtun* and inland consumer sites, including Mersham, Saltwood and Canterbury can be explored, even if the quantity of fish remains is often very small. Tabulated data for fish remains from the excavations at New Romney is presented below (see Armitage), although quantities here are very small.

Changes in the supply of fish can be considered against recent models for medieval England, France and Belgium (Barrett *et al.* 2004; Clavel 2001; Van Neer and Ervynck 2006). Barrett, Locker and Roberts have argued on the basis of a wide group of fish samples (including those from Canterbury St. Gregorys, Dover Townwall Street and *Sandtun*) that large relative increases in catches of herring and cod occurred in the late tenth to early eleventh century (Barrett *et al.* 2004, 619 and 622–623). They attribute these increases to the development of urbanism and the rise in concomitant trade. Tys (2006, 21) has noted that, aside from a rise in demand for fish from urban centres, the introduction of floating nets at this time would have made it possible to catch herring in coastal waters, and possibly further afield as well. The technology may have developed in response to the demand, but equally it could have helped to further that demand. Within Belgium, it may have been the comital estates that organised the supply of fish during the tenth and eleventh centuries. For east Kent, however, the various ecclesiastical establishments of the city of Canterbury formed a major source of supply and organisation. Most of those establishments held coastal land, which could provide supplies of fish. During the medieval period there was also a demand for fresh fish from London, and a possible indirect reflection of that trade, in the form of ceramics from Rye, has been noted previously (Butler 2006, 77).

Early medieval

Small quantities of fish remains came from the early medieval contexts at Saltwood, which were concentrated largely in the eastern side of the landscape. A single pit from a farmstead produced the majority of the fish remains, as well as the articulated skeleton of a dog. Cod was the most commonly represented fish with 30 identified bones, and other identified species include conger eel, ling, whiting, mackerel and gurnard (Triglidae, including tub gurnard *Trigla lucerna*), as well as flatfish. A

Table 3   Medieval fish remains from southeast Kent sites

Settlement	Quantity of Fish Remains	Date Range
Mersham	1,121	*c.* 1000 – 1600
Sandtun	4,019	*c.* 1100 – 1300
Saltwood	440	*c.* 1100 – 1200
Dover, Townwall Street	88,000	*c.* 1150 – 1300
New Romney	27	*c.* 1150 – 1500
Parsonage Farm	151	*c.* 1175 – 1300
Canterbury, St Gregory's	6,636	*c.* 1375 – 1500

Table 4 Fish remains from selected east Kent sites, 10th to 13th centuries

| | | Mersham | | Saltwood | | Sandtun |
		Late Saxon	Medieval	Early Medieval	Late Medieval	
Fish	Taxon					
Cod	*Gadus morhus*		32	30	2	236
Cod family	Gadidae		29	6	6	49
Haddock					2	7
Ling				1	1	3
Hake						3
3 bearded Rockling	*Gaidropsarus vulgaris*			1		
Eel	*Anguilla anguilla*	1	203		10	15
Conger Eel				2	1	24
Herring	*Clupea harengus*	1	15		234	86
Smelt					69	
Whiting	*Merlangius merlangus*		23	1	4	288
Garfish						43
Gurnard					4	53
Bass						7
Sea Bream						16
Mackerel				1	2	33
Plaice/Flounder/Dab	Pleuronectidae			5	3	
Flatfish	*Pleuronectes platessa*	1	32	2	7	236
Mullet	Murgillidae family		1			1
Wrasse						1
Scad	*Trachurus trachurus*		2		1	85
Thornback	*Raja clavata*		1		1	77
Shark/Ray	*Elasmobranch*	2	2		1	14
Ray	Raja Family		3			
Salmon/Trout						1
Cf Stickleback	*Gasterosteus aculeatus*				3	
Unidentified		56	715	5	4	2,741
Total		61	1,058	54	355	4,019

Table 5   Fish fares in southeast England
(After Parfitt *et al.* 2006, table 79)

Fare	Season	Fishery
Sprotfare	January to March	Sprats
Hokfare	February to May or June	Eel, Flatfish, Rays, Gurnards
?Hokfare	February to May or June	Cod
Shotfare	April and June	Mackerel
Saltfare	August	?Halibut, Ling, Cod
Flewfare and Yarmouth Fare	Late September to December	Herring

Table 6   Fish remains from Parsonage Farm, Westwell
(NB: Medieval 2 = Phase 2, *c.* 1175-1200 – 1250; Medieval 3 = Phase 3, *c.* 1250 – 1300)

Fish	Taxon	Medieval 2	Medieval 3	Total
Cod	*Gadus morhua*		1	1
Cod Family	Gadidae	1		1
Ling	*Molva Molva*		1	1
Eel	*Anguilla anguilla*		1	1
Flatfish	*Pleuronectes platessa*	14	3	17
Herring	*Clupea harengus*	30	6	36
Whiting	*Merlangius merlangus*	22	7	29
Thornback	*Raja clavata*	3		3
Shark/Ray	*Elasmobranch*	1		1
Fish		33	28	61
Total		104	47	151

single vertebra was possibly from three-bearded rockling (*Gaidropsarus vulgaris*). No remains of freshwater fish were recovered. A second pit, of slightly later date, was dominated by the remains of juvenile herring or sprat, alongside smelt. It appeared to be a dumped deposit of these small fish, alongside part of at least one eel and scattered bones of several other fish. As noted above, the quantities of fish remains are small and although cod dominates the assemblage from the earlier pit, those remains stem from a single fish.

The precise dating of the *Sandtun* assemblage is not clear but most of the fishing implements are likely to be of 11th- to 13th-century date. It functioned at that time as a small coastal settlement with additional craft interests, including the manufacture of stone spindle whorls, which were widely distributed across Kent and southeastern England (Riddler 2001, 237–240). Cod, whiting and flatfish were the most common fish species, with herring poorly represented and occurring in the same quantity as scad (Hamilton-Dyer 2001, 258 and table 13). The range of species equates well with Mersham, with the addition of garfish, gurnard, bass and sea bream (Table 4). They are contemporary sites, yet one is coastal and the other is some distance inland. Saltwood is contemporary too and shows a distinct lack of herring in its 10th-to 11th-century phase, albeit from a small sample. The quantity of fish remains for both Mersham and Saltwood are very small, and smaller than those deemed reliable by Barrett, Locker and Roberts (2004, 620–621). Any conclusions must therefore be tentative, but the expected upsurge in herring does not occur and is scarcely in evidence at *Sandtun* either. This raises the possibility that the herring fishery of southeast Kent did not develop fully until the later 11th or 12th century, later than elsewhere in England and later also than the northern littoral of France and Belgium. Aspects of material culture noted above also suggest that east Kent was developing its fishing practices at a later date than other areas. However, larger samples from coastal and inland sites in the region are needed to

confirm this suggestion. Canterbury, in particular, should provide important information concerning the inland supply of marine fish at this time and the development of the herring fishery.

By the late 12th century, herring was being caught in great numbers by Dover fishermen. The overall representation of fish remains from Townwall Street was dominated by herring, sprats and sardines (81%), with a good proportion of cod (13%) and smaller quantities of mackerel (2%) and flatfish (1%). Whiting, conger eel and thornback ray were also numerous. The relative proportions of this large sample confirm well with the models outlined above. The range of fish can also be correlated with the five seasonal *fares* (fairs) mentioned in historical sources, the *fares* themselves reflecting the methods of capture (Dulley 1969, 38; Sweetinburgh 2006, 397). Most of the *fare* names refer to types of nets, namely flew, shot and sprot nets, whilst the *hokfare* relates to the use of hooks, as noted above. The meaning of the term *saltfare* has yet to be determined (Dulley 1969, 38; Sweetinburgh 2006, 397) (Table 5).

The small sample of fish remains from contemporary deposits at Parsonage Farm at Westwell reflects the species range at Dover well and shows the increased significance of herring, as well as whiting. Cod are poorly represented but the sample, once again, is very small (Table 6).

Late medieval: Dover, Folkestone and Canterbury

It is now customary to sieve samples taken from contexts in 1mm or smaller meshes, in order to retrieve the bones of smaller fish. The importance of this procedure was outlined by Smith (2001). Just 1,266 fish bones were retrieved by hand recovery at St Gregory's Priory in Canterbury (794 of which were identifiable) but contexts from the refectory and the kitchen were sieved, providing 5,400 additional identifiable bones from the samples analysed, which themselves represent only a fraction

Table 7   *Fish samples from St Gregory's Priory*

Fish	Taxon	Refectory	Kitchen Floor	Total
Herring	*Clupea harengus*	1,215	1,743	2,958
Cyprinid	Cyprinidae	133	88	221
Eel	*Anguilla anguilla*	171	48	219
Conger Eel	*Conger conger*	11	12	23
Cod Family	Gadidae	34	51	85
Whiting	*Merlangius merlangus*	494	300	794
Cod	*Gadus morhua*	39	30	69
Haddock	*Melanogrammus aeglefinus*	9	15	24
Bass	*Dicentrarchus labrax*	9	3	12
Mackerel	*Scomber scombrus*		4	4
Mullet	Mugilidae	88	22	110
Gurnard	Triglidae	44	78	122
Red Gurnard	*Aspitrigla cuculus*	1		1
Flatfish	Pleuronectidae	464	158	622
Flounder	*Platichthys flesus*	9	3	12
Plaice	*Pleuronectes platessa*	10	9	19
Lemon Sole	*Microstomus kitt*	4	5	9
Sole	*Solea solea*		39	39
Black Sea Bream	*Spondyliosoma cantharus*	4		4
Dace	*Leuciscus leuciscus*	7		7
Pagre	*Pagrus pagrus*	3		3
Pandora	*Pangellus erythrinus*	1		1
Red Sea Bream	*Pagellus bogaraveo*	2		2
Ray	Rajidae		3	3
Pike	*Esox lucius*		4	4
Tench	*Tinca tinca*		1	1
Total:		2,752	2,616	5,368

Table 8   *Fish remains from St Gregory's Priory, species ranked by frequency*

Rank	Hand-Recovered Material	Kitchen	Refectory
1	Herring	Herring	Herring
2	Flatfish	Whiting	Whiting
3	Cod	Flatfish	Flatfish
4	Whiting	Cyprinid	Common Eel
5	Gadid	Gurnard	Cyprinid
6	Conger	Gadid	Mullet

of the total sieved material (Smith 2001, 310). A useful contrast could be drawn between the two areas of the Priory responsible for food production (kitchen) and its consumption (refectory) (Table 7). Samples from both areas can be dated to the late 14th to 15th century (Hicks and Hicks 2001, 110 and 112).

Sixteen species (or broader categories) could be identified within the hand-recovered material. The sieved samples added twelve additional species, albeit all in small quantities. Significantly, the relative presence of the species changed between the hand-recovered and the sieved material (Table 8). The two sieved areas were in general agreement, particularly for the ranking of the three most abundant species in the order Herring – Whiting – Flatfish. That can be compared with the sequence of Herring – Flatfish – Cod for the hand-recovered material. Cod was ranked eighth in the refectory sample and ninth in the kitchen sample.

Herring is dominant in the sieved assemblages and is almost as important in the kitchen samples as it is at Dover. This might suggest that Dover was a main source for fish eaten in Canterbury at this time, although settlement of the eastern suburb at Dover was in decline at this time. Morever, the records for Christ Church Priory in Canterbury suggest that in fact Folkestone was more important as a supplier in the late medieval period, although Dover certainly was a source for the cathedral, providing on one occasion 400 greenfish, *ie* marine fish barrelled in salt and their own pickle. The cathedral purchased both fresh and salted herring from Folkestone, fresh for the monks and salted for the servants (Smith 2001, 313–315). The reference to trade in fresh herring strengthens the argument that the eastern suburb of Dover processed fish caught nearby, in the English Channel.

Marine and freshwater fish

Within a broader perspective, the principal distinction to be made for the medieval period lies between marine fish and freshwater fish. The latter were regarded as 'part of the diet of the aristocracy' (Dyer 1994, 101), their status far exceeding their palatability (Smith 2001, 316), given the effort invested in constructing and managing fish ponds, for example. Freshwater fish are almost entirely absent from this survey. None came from the coastal fishing sites of Dover and *Sandtun*, or from the inland consumer sites of Mersham, Saltwood and Parsonage Farm. They were recovered at St Gregory's Priory, mostly as small cyprinids, with four bones of pike from the kitchen (Table 7). They represented 4% of the identified bone in the kitchen and 4.8% in the refectory (Smith 2001, 316). In effect, this is the expected result; freshwater fish would be reserved for the aristocracy, and for the ecclesiastical hierarchy. Even a small and relatively nondescript establishment like St Gregory's Priory in Canterbury might expect to see freshwater fish consumed on its premises, albeit in small numbers. At first sight, the proportion of freshwater fish is significantly lower than that seen across the English Channel. A direct comparison of rural sites, however, shows the same result. On both sides of the Channel there is a distinct lack of freshwater species, but equally both sides also have very small sample sizes (Clavel 2001, 54–58).

Chapter 12 Discussion and Conclusions

New Romney was always a small town, but it was important at an early period for two main reasons: its coastal location offered the opportunity for a beach market to develop from the original fishing settlement, and the Cinque Ports were an urban focus in this part of the southeast from the 11th century, long before the development of inland towns under the markets-and-commercialisation model which existed elsewhere from *c.* 1200. The basis of the Cinque Ports' early development was different, ie ship service, entailing the provision of vessels for naval and ceremonial purposes and for royal travel. New Romney's period of greatest prosperity was before the end of the 13th century, by which time storm damage to its harbour and to the buildings and streets of the town are often said to have caused its decline. The archaeological remains encountered at the Southlands School site graphically demonstrate the effects of these storms.

References to alluvial and 'storm beach' deposits burying archaeological remains at New Romney abound both in published and unpublished literature (Herdman and Jarman 1996; Thomason and Stafford 2001; Linklater 2001a; Linklater 2001b). The fact that there was a series of particularly serious storms in the 13th century as well as the possibility of other, historically less well-documented storms is undisputed. The archaeological evidence demonstrates that these storms left their mark on the town. However any specific association of deposits with the 1287 storm, which by all accounts was particularly severe and had a major impact on the town, should only be considered likely if there are several independently supportive lines of dating evidence available.

The 13th-century storms pertain to the period immediately preceding the little ice age or to the time the climate was in the process of changing to wetter and cooler conditions. Changes from predominantly more arable to more pastoral land-use for the Romney marshes straddle the start of the little ice age. Catastrophic storms during this period were widespread. The 1287 event at New Romney is thought to have been a tsunami-type occurrence. The latter is said to have caused extensive damage to the town and to have resulted in the laying down of extensive deposits of coarse sandy material over much of the townscape. At the Southlands School site there is evidence not just of widespread occurrence of thick storm deposits but also of the severe truncation of contemporary and earlier surfaces and dumps and the casting up of artefactual material associated with the preceding periods, which reflects the findings from

other excavations in the area. This lends support to the historic records of the seriousness of this and other storm events. It should be noted that the end of the 13th century is archaeologically characterised by much-reduced activity over large parts of the town. The early effects of the onset of the little ice age can be seen to have had a major impact on the economic life of New Romney and its hinterland, triggering a series of changes which contributed to the eventual abandonment of its port and the changes in land-use observed on Romney Marsh proper, from one in which arable agriculture played a significant role to one dominated by sheep pasture.

Engineering works, such as the construction of the Rhee, undertaken to keep New Romney harbour open to trading vessels, clearly had a limited effect and in the long run failed in their intended purpose. The planning for this construction project is likely to have had its basis as much in the increasing draught of merchant vessels as in the silting up of the anchorage. New Romney throughout the 13th century lost trade to deep-water ports with extended quays and harbour facilities such as New Winchelsea and Sandwich. As cogs became the dominant vessels around the North Sea, New Romney's decline in importance as a trading port accelerated. Whilst the beachfront in the vicinity of the Southlands School site might have continued to be used for the beaching, repair and even construction of smaller fishing vessels, larger vessels such as cogs clearly could not use this facility.

Two aspects of the dynamics of the town's topography are of some importance to the distribution and spread of the settlement during medieval times. Along the southern and therefore seaward side of the town the results of four excavations have demonstrated the presence of medieval occupation remains south of the line formed by the old High Street/Church Road. In addition a natural promontory projects southeast from Church Road along Church Lane; the old High Street/Church Road runs along an easily observable shingle ridge, which still stands proud of the land to the southeast. The archaeological evidence for extensive truncation and flooding events from the northeast end of Church Road (Willson and Linklater 2002), and the rear of the old School House along Church Lane (Thomason and Stafford 2001), indicates that medieval New Romney extended beyond the line of the elevated shingle ridge defined by Church Road and that this area was rendered uninhabitable by the 13th century and later storm events.

One of the frequently repeated aspects of the history of the town of New Romney is how the silting up of the harbour, principally as a result of the 13th-century storms, resulted in a marked decline in New Romney's fortunes. This was compounded by subsequent continuation of these silting processes as well as the inability of the town to find a workable response to these. The storms and the dynamics of the sea depositing vast amounts of sand and silts on the seaward side of the town are clear from the historical and archaeological record. Indeed the fact that the medieval beachfront can at present be found between 2.4 and 1.7km from the sea demonstrates the ultimate futility of the town's battle against nature. However another matter is the town's supposed economic decline as a result of these changes, although it appears to have contracted in the 14th century following the impact of the known storm events. This reduction in settlement size is manifest on the Southlands School site and along the northeastern side of the town. It is likely to be related also to the series of plagues and diseases known to have resulted in a dramatic population reduction over much of England from the mid-14th century. Nevertheless documentary and archaeological sources do not suggest that the surviving population was markedly less well off than it was before this reduction. New Romney continued to be involved in activities related to the sea, maintaining an interest in both foreign trade and fishing into the early 16th century. However the trade element particularly appears to have been focussed on smaller-scale coastal ventures with North Sea partners rather than business endeavours farther afield. There was limited access to the hinterland as a result of the comparatively short distance which sea-going vessels could penetrate inland along the Rother river, since the vessels had to be both small and have a shallow draught. The hinterland of New Romney, mainly the Weald of Kent and Sussex, was in any case relatively undeveloped until the 13th century, apart from for the exploitation of timber and iron. As a result the more lucrative long-distance international trade went to other deep-water ports such as London and Southampton, particularly from the 13th century. Locally in the late 13th and early 14th centuries, Sandwich and Dover were much more significant in the export of wool than New Romney, and the building of New Winchelsea further diminished the limited importance of New Romney in the wine trade with Gascony and Bordeaux. The reduced significance of the sea to New Romney's prosperity was accompanied by an increasing dependence on agriculture, in particular sheep management and wool-fells and hide production. The latter is comparatively un-intensive in its labour requirement and would have allowed the reduced post-14th century population to maintain a productive economy. Salt production, tanning, woodland management for the production of firewood, meat and poultry production and arable agriculture were important in the later 14th century, and New Romney tried hard to maintain its position as the local market and fair.

Though the town's access to the sea was gradually disappearing, its commercial maritime interests continued to some extent. Ripiers are known in New Romney by 1340, and in the 15th century a significant element of the population was engaged in transporting fish to the London, Maidstone and Ashford markets. In the 15th century other residents of New Romney were taking advantage of land available to lease locally at low rents and supplying wool to the then-flourishing Wealden cloth industry. The taverns and the activities of the vintners, the town's long-term social elite, contributed to the prosperity of some men in the 15th century and possibly into the early 16th century. By the 17th century, sheep grazing and agrarian activity on Romney Marsh continued to provide occupation and wealth for some inhabitants of New Romney. The lack of evidence for a reduction in the wealth of the town's inhabitants is perhaps explained by the combined elements of population decline and a shifting focus to a wide range of successful alternative economic undertakings.

New Romney was not, as Beresford (1967) suggested, an Anglo-Saxon town planned and planted simultaneously on a grid plan, and in fact such a grid can only be perceived on small-scale or diagrammatic maps of the town such as that of Hasted or of Parkin (1973, fig. 2). In contrast, the analysis of the locations of the early buildings and the documentary record demonstrate how the final street layout of New Romney is based on a much simpler earlier form. The final street layout can be considered in three parts. The rectilinear plan in the centre of the town was laid out in its period of greatest affluence in the late 12th or early 13th centuries. It entailed the extension and creation of streets, not least to fit conveniently around the new burgage plots, as in towns such as Ludlow in other parts of England and Wales (Hindle 2002, 24). The 1840 tithe map in particular demonstrates the very approximate nature of the rectilinear area, and also the centrality of the new wide High Street and market to the development of the town plan. To the west and northeast of the central area there were also some roads, which were approximately straight and some cross streets, giving a false impression of a grid plan. In reality the major thoroughfares linked the commercial foci of New Romney, its market, its haven or port, its beachfront, its fishing industry, and the agricultural hinterland of Romney Marsh. The cross streets ran inland from the waterfront and beach to the commercial and industrial parts of the town. An area of medieval New Romney, now lost, also extended beyond the line of the elevated shingle ridge defined by Church Road until the storm events of the 13th century and later. The modification of New Romney's street layout, which occurred in the period of the town's greatest wealth and local significance, probably contributed to its prosperity. The associated development of more and larger market facilities and ecclesiastical buildings responded to the needs of an enlarged population, the demands of travellers and the development of inland towns in Kent with their requirements for fish, the town's main commodity.

The archival evidence for the 14th century indicates that boat-breaking and repair were carried out along the beach front on the northeastern side of the town, and the archaeological data from Southlands School suggest an even earlier date for this type of operation here. This activity may have intensified at this location as a result of the silting up of the port facility itself. The moderate sizes of vessel indicated by the types of rovenails found at the Southlands School site (see Goodburn, Chapter 11, above) is almost certainly related to the shelving nature of the shoreline here, and the associated limitation in the size of vessel which could be floated on and off the beach. That boat-breaking could turn from the passive dismantling of old boats to a much more proactive wrecking exercise (by tempting innocent ships into the shallows) and outright piracy is demonstrated by records of such actions against the fishermen of Yarmouth, and legally under letters of marque, against the French. Other activities linked with the northeastern sector of New Romney are indicated in the documentary record to have included barrel manufacture, tanning, kiddle fishing, net repair, salt production and the drying and salting of fish. The ceramic assemblages for the 12th and 13th centuries provide evidence of New Romney's widespread interregional and international contacts resulting from its links to the sea, and trading activities during the later medieval period.

Eleven examples of lead shot and a gunpowder measure cap at the Southlands School site (finds uncommon on most archaeological sites) serve to demonstrate that seafaring activities for the late medieval and post-medieval periods involved the arming of the mariners. This could be for the purposes of wrecking and piracy or perhaps for defence. The sea could be a dangerous place, and not just because of the weather.

The small finds assemblage, rovenails and the fish bone from Southlands School, the fish hooks, fishing weights, fish bone and shellfish remains, recovered in excavations by Archaeology South-East along the northeastern side of the Southlands School site, a fish hook from Prospect House and the fishbone and shell from the Old School House site on the south side of Church Lane all serve to confirm the importance of the sea to the operation of New Romney during the Middle Ages and the early post-medieval period. The fishing weights, fish hooks and fish bone fit in with the historically known importance of the New Romney fishery. Documentary sources mention fishing with drift nets and trawling nets at New Romney from probably the late 12th century, and kiddle fishing from the middle of the 13th century. They indicate the continued use of trawling nets in the late 14th century (1392) and of herring, shrimp and kiddle nets during the 15th century (1461) (HMC V, 534, 542). Net fishing is substantiated by the presence of characteristic lead weights, whilst line fishing is attested by the find of fish hooks representative of this activity among the finds from Southlands School (see Riddler, Chapter 11, above). As mentioned above specialist traders known as ripiers from London and inland towns of Kent, perhaps from as early as 1220 and certainly by the 1340s, purchased the catches direct from the fishermen as soon as they were landed (Armitage, Chapter 11; Kowaleski 2000, 31). This may have

ensured that the fish, transported on packhorses, would reach the London fish market within the same day they had been landed.

The fish species recovered in the excavations at the Southlands School site are indicative of inshore, shore-line and coastal fishing and at least access to a more distant deep-water fishery. The size of rovenails present indicates the dismantling, repair and construction of moderate-sized clinker built vessels here; coastal or estuary trading vessels *c.* 15 m in length. The discovery of the 'Warren House' vessel is noteworthy in this respect. Its total reported length of 15.85m fits in well with the projected boat sizes along the beach east of the Southlands School site and its clinker construction technique fits in well with the indicated use of rovenails in ship construction and repair as demonstrated there. This type of vessel reflects limited deep-sea fishing activities with the main techniques of fishing being focussed on inshore, and coastal methods as well as the use of small-sized coastal trading vessels. The use of drift net fishing relatively close to the homeport would be the most effective at this time considering the available fishing technology and methods for preserving and storing fish at sea. It was not until 1397 that long distance deep-sea fishing became economical, when the Dutch invented a greatly improved type of onboard storage involving gutting and salting, giving the catch a much-prolonged 'shelf life' prior to being landed.

Cod, recovered from deposits dated to the later 13th century, reflects the popularity of a commodity which is highly nutritious and when dried and salted could be preserved for significant periods of time, an important factor in times prior to refrigeration. If stored carefully it could keep for up to 2 years (Fagan 2000, 69–70, 76). The comparative difficulties in getting salt in sufficient quantities in England resulted in operations favouring a combined drying and salting method, which used less salt. This was practised at Herring Hang field, close to New Romney's recorded saltern mounds, although in fact large quantities of salt were produced at New Romney and undoubtedly used in the preservation of fish traded through the town. Drying often took place seasonally in winter or far away from home near the distant fishing grounds (Kurlansky 1997, 54–55). Cod was also a food that the Church allowed to be consumed on Fridays and during the 40 days of fasting during Lent (Kurlansky 1997, 69–70).

The presence of ventilators in the ceramic assemblage from the Southlands School site is not unexpected as these form part of the medieval Kentish ceramic repertoire. Here their presence may be indicative of two aspects of the New Romney beachfront. Their quantity and distribution through the archaeological sequence is likely to be related to storm events when they would have been blown off the roofs and broken, and secondly their presence may be indicative of the use of smoke houses for preserving parts of the fish catch.

By the early 13th century the harbour facility for New Romney was almost certainly located near the junction of St John's Rd with Lydd Rd on the southwest side of town, as the street layout indicates. This would have allowed access to larger deep-sea going vessels whilst access to the beach fronting the eastern side of the town further north would have been limited to more shallow draught vessels. Port functions were separated with the managed and controlled operations of the port located in the harbour with its quays. Cargoes landed along the strand could have been transported away from the town without ever actually entering it, perhaps in the direction of Dymchurch, a place notorious for smuggling in the early-modern period. This would be particularly useful to those making a living in the smuggling, wrecking and piracy aspects of New Romney's economy.

New Romney's importance as a Cinque Port stems from the town's geographical position. Though it was, and indeed still is, comparatively small, in the 11th to 13th centuries New Romney occupied a central position organisationally as well as physically in relation to the other towns of the Cinque Port confederation. The confederation's links with the crown throughout this period resulted in its members having a distinct competitive advantage over their rivals. Their privileges meant that they were better able to take rapid and independent commercial and strategic decisions than were other, non-allied towns. Their coastal location and continental contacts also meant that the inhabitants literally had wider horizons and access to a more extensive resource base than was the case for more land-locked communities. One consequence was that a greater degree of literacy prevailed in New Romney than in more isolated contemporary centres of population in England. Notably French continued to be used in the 13th and 14th centuries to mark social status, and until the 15th century in some of the town records such as the custumal and recording of ordinances, and for purposes of communication and record with traders, mariners and pirates from across the Channel.

The absence of formalised defences for the town, particularly of a town wall, appears to stem from New Romney's origin as a non-royal borough on the one hand, and the fact that it never came under attack from the French on the other. The latter is probably partially the result of New Romney's reduced status by the time these raids started and also derives from the intimate contacts which the town's inhabitants maintained at the time with their French counterparts, thus avoiding the need for a defensive posture. The nature and origin of these interactions are likely to have been rooted in the smuggling and piracy interests of the town's business community.

By the 16th century the value of the privileges of the Cinque Ports had been greatly reduced as royal favour shifted elsewhere. While religious conflicts raged on the continent and the confrontation of Catholic and Protestant supporting forces unfolded in England, the inhabitants of New Romney attempted to retain their religious and communal traditions. However, they responded to local political pressure to cease performing the town's passion play and its associated procession under Henry VIII. Traditional religious practices were resumed during the reign of Mary and Philip, but finally succumbed to the pressure to conform to Protestantism after 1568, with the site of the passion play performance well established as a bowling green by 1598. The find of the processional cross of 15th-century date in excavations in the High Street seems likely to represent an act marking these changing circumstances. The chances of the accidental loss of such a prestigious item in one of the principal thoroughfares of the town is so unlikely as to be inconceivable.

There was an early (pre-13th century) guildhall at New Romney. In all probability it was the meeting place of the burgesses or barons who chose the jurats of the town. The jurats governed the town in conjunction with the Archbishop's bailiff and at least on occasion the town mayor. Such an early guildhall was unusual in English towns though paralleled by the burgesses' guildhall in the Cinque Port of Dover, which existed in 1086. The documentary evidence of the early guildhalls of the Cinque Ports of New Romney and Dover make a contribution to understanding such buildings. Dover's burgesses' guildhall was in place by 1086; New Romney's perhaps in the 12th century. They predate most guildhalls, although those of the large towns of York and Northampton, the 'earliest documented examples', date from the 12th and 13th centuries. The early guildhalls of the Cinque Ports reinforce the fact that the Cinque Ports were important early, albeit small, towns. These guildhalls were associated with the freemen of Dover and New Romney rather than, as at large towns a little later, with the 'guild merchant' (Giles 2005, 299). The early guildhall of New Romney appears to have been also called the common house in an early custumal, and to have been the meeting place of the Halimott (hall-moot) of the town, a body whose functions included witnessing town deeds by *c.* 1200. This Halimott had some equivalence also with the hall-moot of Appledore, a nearby then-rural settlement on the River Rother. In the mid-12th century (1152–67) Wibert the Prior of Canterbury Cathedral Priory addressed the hall-moot of Appledore in writing, using terminology which acknowledged the very early literate culture of Romney Marsh, both in English and Latin (Eddison and Draper 1997, 82–83; Draper 2003, 58–59, 68; Draper 2005 B, fig. 5, 30; CCA DCc Reg. C, f. 256). New Romney and Appledore thus reinforce the arguments of Giles (2005, 297) about the connections between moot halls and early guildhalls, and also suggest that an important reason for their existence in the Romney Marsh area was the reading and witnessing of documents.

After the sale of New Romney's early guildhall before 1234, the jurats had no other known meeting place and apparently met in St Nicholas' church. By 1357 the jurats were meeting with the bailiff to conduct legal business in that church. In 1408 they hired a common house, perhaps under pressure not to meet any longer in the church. In 1413 the jurats then made a decision to buy a tenement and build themselves a common house in which to meet. This was kept comfortable, and well-defended at times of threat of invasion. Here the jurats accounted to the townspeople for money raised and spent, with the yearly accounting process open to the inhabitants who were otherwise sometimes excluded from the jurats' meetings, which included a substantial element of drinking at the town's expense. Minor judicial matters, entry to the franchise, and the cleanliness and morals of the town were also regulated by the jurats at the common house in the 15th century. The jurats also socialised at one of the town's taverns, Knobett's. The activities of the Prendergasts, Dame Beatrix and John, the pirate and smuggler, and of certain priests, pilgrims and residents, which were strongly condemned by the jurats in 1412–13, were in contrast concentrated at the Rome tavern.

At the end of the 15th century the jurats' accountability to the commons of the town was being reduced and the town government was beginning to be more closely concentrated in the hands of individual officers, notably the chamberlains. This process also entailed the title Baron being restricted to the membership of the governing body rather than all the freemen (*Rough's Register*, l–li). From this period, meetings in difficult political circumstances or with important outsiders were held in the homes of jurats who had been chosen or elected for roles such as chamberlain. At this time, the common house was apparently pulled down, and the next mention of a communal meeting place is that of the guildhall in 1533. From 1563 the town charter permitted the town to have a mayor, a further concentration of power in the hands of a few rather than in those of the whole assembly of jurats accountable to the townsfolk.

The absence of profitable productive trades of the kind associated with large towns such as London, York and Norwich meant that New Romney had no craft guilds or wealthy merchants in the high and later Middle Ages. There was therefore no craft guildhall, nor prosperous merchants' houses to provide a social base for conspicuous consumption for those who governed the town such as larger towns had (King 2005). New Romney's common house and the homes of one or two of the town's elite provided a meeting place for the political, judicial and financial functions which the jurats exercised. The social pretensions of the town's elite were based not on wealth but on its special relationship with the monarchy, including its ceremonial role at coronations and its parliamentary representation. This relationship continued to have significance at times of heightened political tensions at local and national levels, even though the monarch was decreasingly dependent on the Cinque Ports' ships.

The links between town churches, the Hospital of St John and the jurats were important although difficult to elucidate given the lack of above-ground remains of St Lawrence's and St Martin's Churches, and the few surviving records relating to the church apart from occasional references in wills. However, the following can be established. From at least 1234 until 1407, the jurat body was linked to St Nicholas' Church by meeting in that church. St Nicholas' parish in the late 12th to the late 14th centuries was the location of many fishermen, especially kidelmen, and also ship's masters

and vintners of the town. These men formed the elite of the town by their wealth and their holding of urban offices such as mayor or captain of the town barge. At this period St Nicholas' Church was more prestigious than St Lawrence's, and St Martin's Church seems, from its location opposite 'the Priory' always to have been closely linked to Pontigny Abbey rather than with the townspeople and their governors.

From 1407 the formal link between the jurat body and St Nicholas' made by their meeting in that church was broken. This may have been by the personal decision of the incumbent of St Nicholas (John Hacche) who was apparently keen that the jurats should stop meeting in his church, perhaps because it was unsuitable use of a sacred place. It is clear that in the 1510s that the vicar of St Nicholas supported new religious practices, particularly godly sermons. In contrast the jurats, in conjunction with the townspeople, supported traditional practices such as chantry services, bequests to the saints, religious orders and of course the passion play. By this period the town elite and office-holders was formed by the vintners and to a lesser extent those connected with maritime activity as ripiers, and also traders such as butchers. These people were more closely associated with the town's commercial centre in St Lawrence's parish and with St Lawrence's Church. This also gave them connections with the Hospital of St John since St Lawrence's parishioners were buried in St John's Churchyard, and jurats such as John Bukherst, vintner, supported that hospital by their bequests. St John's Hospital was very firmly under the control of the town via the jurats, and it may be that the jurats worshipped in its chapel in the 15th century, for example by attending memorial prayers for townsmen such as John Ive.

New Romney had two hospitals and this might be taken as a reflection of its size. Schofield and Vince (2003, 206) considered that 'any reasonably vigorous town could expect to maintain three or four hospitals'. In Kent Canterbury, Sandwich, Faversham, Dover and Dartford fell into this category, although all the Cinque Ports and their important limbs had at least one hospital (Sweetinburgh 2004b, 45). The hospital of the Blessed Stephen and Thomas at New Romney provided for up to fifteen lepers or infirm people from *c*. 1180 to *c*. 1300, and also chantry functions for the townsfolk who supported it by their donations. It was moulded to new purposes from the mid-14th century as a chantry for merchant and gentry families, and subsequently as a base for the network of men who supported the fundamental changes in landholding on Romney Marsh between *c*. 1390 and 1440. These changes were brought about by population fall and exploited by Archbishop Chichele for the endowment of his new foundation, All Souls College Oxford. Indeed this hospital itself became part of the general move to endow Oxbridge colleges, in this case Magdalen College Oxford, with the lands of those hospitals which were no longer functioning in the late 15th or early 16th centuries. In contrast, St John's Hospital, New Romney, was a later 13th-century foundation, lying closer to the town centre than the leper hospital. It provided not for lepers but for sick, aged or disabled local inhabitants, especially perhaps those whose families or friends could provide a substantial donation to ensure they were cared for at the hospital. St John's Hospital does not fit the pattern suggested for, presumably, larger towns, that the 'story of the Dissolution' was the same everywhere in relation to hospitals: 'large imposing complexes vanished within a few years' (Schofield and Vince 2003, 207). Instead this old hospital, of appropriate scale for the town of New Romney, was transformed under the impetus of a jurat family into an almshouse, Southlands Hospital, including some new buildings. St John's had close links to the townsfolk, and particularly the jurats, in the medieval period and as Southlands Hospital continued under the control of the jurats in the 16th and 17th centuries. Between the 16th and 19th centuries Southlands Hospital may in addition have provided the location for the schooling also funded by John Southland's will.

The town's other ecclesiastical buildings reflect its history. Two of its three parish churches were demolished in the mid-16th century due to the town's diminished population. Even the site of the town's 13th-century friary is not known, and the inhabitants of the town supported the friars of Rye in the 15th century and those of Canterbury in the early 16th. The buildings of the alien priory were always private, firstly as they belonged to Pontigny Abbey, briefly to the crown and then to All Souls College Oxford. They became a private house when let out by All Souls in the mid-15th century. The moated manor house and chantry chapel of Craythorne were in gentry and knightly hands in 1448–1449, and the advowson of the chapel was still of some value. However, after 1550 the remains of the Craythorne manor house and chapel appear to have been in use as agricultural land and buildings.

New Romney provides an example of the uses of civic and ecclesiastical buildings in a small medieval town, albeit an early one with an unusual history as one of the Cinque Ports. Few historic buildings surveys have been made of the medieval structures of New Romney. There is future potential for such surveys to contribute further to understanding the relationships of the buildings to inhabitants of the town, whose social, economic, cultural and religious characteristics have now been outlined.

It is hoped that this book will play a part in wider study of the Cinque Ports as distinctive and early medieval towns, based on recent and current archaeological, buildings and historical research. Perhaps it may also contribute to understanding the characteristics of early borough and market settlements in southeast England, particularly the urban hierarchy, settlement form, the layout of streets, burgage plots, market places and buildings. These features have recently been re-examined by Slater (2005) for towns in the western part of England but, as he noted, these may be different in the east and south.

Appendix 1

Table 8. NFR 01 Distribution of pottery types by sherd count, Phases 2–8.

Common name	Fabric	Phase 2 SC	%	3 SC	%	4 SC	%	5 SC	%	6 SC	%	7 SC	%	8 SC	%
Shelly	EM2									1	0.3				
Shelly sandy	EM3	6	50.0	17	44.7	36	73.5	281	64.4	200	60.1	251	50.2	595	36.5
Kent/Sussex flint-temper	EM28	4	33.3			1	2.0								
Kent/Sussex flint-temper	EM29	2	16.7	3	7.9					4	1.2	24	4.8	8	0.5
Kent/Sussex flint-temper	EM33							1	0.2			2	0.4	1	0.1
Wealden sandy with flint	M10F			1	2.6			8	1.8	1	0.3	4	0.8	21	1.3
Ashford/Wealden sandy, shell or chalk	M40A							2	0.5			5	1.0	4	0.2
Ashford/Wealden sandy	M40B					2	4.1	3	0.7			2	0.4	3	0.2
Ashford/Wealden sandy	M40BR			3	7.9	2	4.1	46	10.6	55	16.5	41	8.2	216	13.3
Ashford/Wealden pasty	M40C					4	8.2			1	0.3	2	0.4	40	2.5
Wealden white/cream	M45C													1	0.1
Rye/Romney Marsh/Wealden sandy	M10R							1	0.2			1	0.2		
Rye sandy	M13A			6	15.8	1	2.0	49	11.2	35	10.5	115	23.0	373	22.9
Rye fine	M13B							11	2.5			2	0.4	14	0.9
Rye reduced	M13C					1	2.0	1	0.2	4	1.2	2	0.4	18	1.1
Rye whiteware	M13W													1	0.1
Rye/Wealden flint-temper, shell or chalk.	M45A			5	13.2			8	1.8	21	6.3	14	2.8	147	9.0
Non-local															
Fine London-type	M5							2	0.5					4	0.2
Kingston-type	M7							3	0.7	2	0.6	1	0.2	16	1.0
Scarborough Phase I	M11A			2	5.3			2	0.5			7	1.4	46	2.8
Scarborough Phase II	M11B													2	0.1
Brandsby-type	M42							2	0.5					1	0.1
Imports															
N. France type red painted	EM11A.RP													5	0.3
Normandy gritty	EM15							1	0.2						
Rouen-type	M19									2	0.6			1	0.1
Rouen-type polychrome glazed	M19P									1	0.3	1	0.2	4	0.2
'Orlean's'-type	M20													2	0.1
Saintonge	M22					1	2.0	2	0.5	2	0.6	1	0.2	9	0.6
Saintonge green-glazed	M22G			1	2.6			6	1.4	1	0.3	6	1.2	18	1.1
Saintonge polychrome	M22P													6	0.4
Saintonge sgraffito	M22S					1	2.0					2	0.4	1	0.1
German Paffrath	M36							1	0.2					1	0.1
Unidentified Low Countries	M102							1	0.2						
Flemish highly decorated	M14							1	0.2			1	0.2	2	0.1
Med. N. French/Flemish grey	M15							4	0.9			16	3.2	5	0.3
German Langerwehe stoneware	LM8													1	0.1
Dutch redware	LM22									1	0.3			1	0.1
Spanish Amphora	LM23A													2	0.1
Sub-total				*1*	*2.6*	*2*	*4.0*	*16*	*3.7*	*6*	*1.8*	*27*	*5.4*	*54*	*3.3*
Late medieval															
Pink-buff fine sandy	LM14													1	0.1
Wealden/Hareplain hard fine sandy, reduced.	LM17A													2	0.1
Wealden/Hareplain hard fine sandy, oxidised.	LM17B													1	0.1
Rye sandy, sparse flint, shell or chalk.	LM17R													1	0.1
Wealden sandy ware, oxidised	LM32									2	0.6			1	0.1
Post-medieval pottery types														54	3.3
Total		12	100	38	100	49	100	436	100	333	100	500	100	1629	100

Résumé

Cette publication a été inspirée par les recherches archéologiques au site de Southlands School, a New Romney, en avance de la construction d'un nouveau supermarché. Bien que la ville se trouve maintenant à environ deux miles de la côte, la mer était critique à la prospérité et le développement de la ville médiévale de New Romney. Les fouilles ci-décrites, situés dans un secteur qui faisait partie du long front de mer de New Romney dans la période médiévale, ont donne l'occasion d'explorer cette relation. Cette monographie étudie le lien entre ville et mer, en reliant les résultats des fouilles a l'ensemble de l'histoire de New Romney.

Commençant par une analyse des origines de la ville de New Romney son rôle comme Cinque Port est exploré, une question fondamentale pour toute étude de sa croissance. L'examen de documents cartographiques et historiques, l'analyse de bâtiments médiévaux et les résultats des fouilles précédentes ont ensemble permis à former une image de la façon dont le plan des rues a développé, mettant en question la théorie, proposée par Beresford dans les années 1960, que New Romney était une ville planifiée. Dans la période médiévale, New Romney a été pourvu d'un havre ou port protégé, ainsi que d'une longue grève, sur lequel des bateaux ont échoué, ont été déchargé, démoli ou réparé, où la pêche a eu lieu et un marché a développé. Les deux ports et la grève ont été essentielles à la réussite commerciale de la ville médiévale et sa fonction de Cinque Port. La pêche, les relations commerciales, la participation de la ville dans la piraterie, y compris le pillage libre, le gouvernement de ville et le l'assistance publique sont tous considérés grâce à l'étude des sources contemporaines. Toutefois, la mer a aussi contribué au déclin de la ville: une série de tempêtes catastrophiques ont ravagé cette partie de la côte, notamment au cours du 13ème siècle, le port a commencé à s'envaser et, bien que des mesures aient été prises pour maintenir un courant d'eau le long de la grève jusqu'à la mer, la ville est devenue enferme dans les terres et la communauté s'est tourné de plus en plus pour ses revenus vers le marais, où les moutons pouvaient être pâturés. Bien que la ville ait continue à être relativement prospères, les effets des tempêtes, des conditions météorologiques de plus en plus mauvaises et la peste noire ont mené au déclin de la population.

Les fouilles situées sur ce qui avait été la laisse de mer médiévale, ont révélé de puissantes preuves de la force de ces tempêtes, qui ont abouti à la destruction d'un bâtiment au bord de l'eau. L'assemblage de poterie récupérée démontre la production locale et les réseaux d'échange ainsi que les relations commerciales plus éloignées, tandis que des ventilateurs et louvres céramiques manifestent les traditions locales du bâtiment médiéval. Les résultats archéologiques démontrent le mouvement et le déplacement d'objets arrachés par les hautes marées et puis redéployés. Néanmoins, un assemblage remarquable de vestiges métalliques a été découvert, certainement un résultat des efforts des groupes de détecteurs de la région, ce qui élucide la vie quotidienne des habitants de cette zone de la ville. Parmi les objets en métaux récupérés étaient des rivets, indicative de la casse ou de la réparation de navires ainsi que des hameçons et des poids, qui témoignent de la gamme de méthodes de pêche employées, cette variété étant affirmé par les arêtes de poisson récupéré lors des fouilles. Cette information a été rassemblée afin de pouvoir fournir une comparaison des navires de pêche, des techniques et des prises des environs de la côte sud-est.

Les auteurs concluent en exprimant l'espoir que ce livre aura un rôle à jouer dans les recherches plus générales des Cinque Ports comme anciennes villes médiévales distinctives et aussi contribuera à la compréhension des caractéristiques des villes marchandes en Sud-Angleterre. Bien que la ville soit riche en structures médiévales survivantes, peu d'analyses de bâtiments historiques des ont été faites à New Romney et cette publication dénote une étude plus approfondie de ces éléments dans le futur et met en évidence l'importance de la poursuite de fouilles dans la ville.

Zusammenfassung

Diese Ausgabe wurde angeregt von archäologischen Untersuchungen an der Stätte der Southlands School, New Romney, die in Vorbereitung des Baus eines neuen Großmarktes durchgeführt wurden. Obwohl die Stadt mittlerweile etwa zwei Meilen von der Küste entfernt liegt, war das Meer ausschlaggebend für New Romneys mittelalterliche Entwicklung und ihr Gedeihen, und diese Ausgrabungen, die in einem Gebiet durchgeführt wurden, das in der mittelalterlichen Periode einen Teil der langen Strandfront von New Romney ausmachte, bereiteten eine Gelegenheit diese Verbindung zu untersuchen. Dieser Monograph behandelt die Verbindung zwischen Stadt und Meer, indem er die Funde der Ausgrabung mit der breiteren Geschichte von New Romney in seiner Gesamtheit verbindet.

New Romneys Rolle als Cinque Port wird beginnend mit der Betrachtung der Erstehungsgeschichte der Stadt untersucht. Diese Untersuchung ist fundamental für die Anschauung ihres folgenden Wachstums. Durch die Auswertung von kartografischen und geschichtlichen Aufzeichnungen, überlebenden, mittelalterlichen Gebäuden und den Ergebnissen früherer Ausgrabungen, konnte man sich ein Bild machen, wie sich der Straßenverlauf entwickelt hat. Diese Funde lassen die Theorie anzweifeln, die von Beresford in den 60er Jahren aufgestellt wurde, dass New Romney eine geplante Stadt war. In der mittelalterlichen Periode war New Romney im Besitz eines geschützten Hafens oder Ports sowie eines langen Strandes, an welchem Boote anlegten, entladen wurden, abgebrochen oder repariert wurden, wo gefischt wurde und sich ein Markt entwickelte. Sowohl der Port als auch der Strand waren entscheidend für den kommerziellen Erfolg der mittelalterlichen Stadt und ihrer Funktion als Cinque Port. Fischerei, Handelsverbindungen, die Teilnahme der Stadt an Seeräuberei einschließlich lizenzierter Freibeuterei, Stadtregierung und soziale Fürsorge werden alle anhand der Studie von zeitgenössischen Quellen behandelt. Jedoch trug das Meer auch letztendlich zu dem Verfall der Stadt bei: eine Reihe von katastrophalen Stürmen verwüsteten, insbesondere während des 13. Jahrhunderts, diesen Teil der Küste. Der Hafen begann sich mit Schlick zu füllen und, obwohl Maßnahmen ergriffen wurden den Fluss von Wasser am Strand vorbei in das Meer beizubehalten, wurde die Siedlung von Land umschlossen und die

Gemeinde wendete sich zunehmend aufgrund seiner Erträge zum Marsch hin, wo Schafe geweidet werden konnten. Obwohl die Stadt weiterhin relativ wohlhabend war, führte der Effekt der Stürme, zunehmend schlechtes Wetter und die Pest zu einer Verringerung in der Population.

Die Ausgrabungen, durchgeführt auf einstmals mittelalterlichem Uferland, deckten schlagkräftiges Beweismaterial der Mächtigkeit dieser Stürme auf, welche in der Zerstörung eines Gebäudes am Wasserrand gipfelten. Die geborgene Keramik-Ansammlung liefert Beweise von einheimischer Produktion und Tauschnetzwerken sowie auch weiter entfernten Handels, während Keramik-Ventilatoren und Lüftungsschlitze eine einheimische, mittelalterliche Bautraditionen erkennen lassen. Die archäologischen Funde zeigen eine Bewegung und Verschiebung von Artefakten an, als Ablagerungen von Sturmfluten aufgerissen wurden und sich dann wieder absetzten. Jedoch wurde, nicht zuletzt als Ergebnis der Bemühungen von ortsansässigen Metalldetektor Anwendern, eine bemerkenswerte Metallfund-Ansammlung geborgen, welche ein neues Licht auf das alltägliche Leben der Bewohner dieses Bereiches der Stadt wirft. Unter den Metallfunden waren Spiekernägel, welche auf Schiffabbruch oder Reparatur hinwiesen. Ebenso entdeckt wurden Fischereihaken und Gewichte, die Zeugnis tragen über das Angebot der angewendeten Fischereimethoden und deren Vielfalt von den Fischgräten offenbart wurde, die bei den Ausgrabungen gefunden wurden. Diese Information wurde zusammengestellt, um einen Vergleich der Boote, Techniken und Fänge der Fischerei um die südöstliche Küste herum zu ermöglichen.

Die Autoren schließen ab, indem sie ihre Hoffnung zum Ausdruck bringen, dass dieses Buch eine Rolle spielen wird in der weiträumigeren Studie von Cinque Ports in ihrer Rolle als unverkennbare, früh-mittelalterliche Städte und ebenso dazu beitragen wird die Charakteristiken der frühen Gemeinden und Marktansiedlungen im Südosten Englands zu verstehen. Obwohl reich in überlebenden, mittelalterlichen, strukturellen Überresten, nur wenige Untersuchungen von historischen Gebäuden wurden für New Romney angefertigt und diese Publikation weist den Weg zu ihrer weiteren, zukünftigen Studie und hebt die Wichtigkeit von weiteren Ausgrabungen in der Stadt hervor.

Bibliography

Allan, J.P. 1984. *Medieval and Post-Medieval Finds from Exeter, 1971–1980.* Exeter Archaeological Reports 3. Exeter City Council and the University of Exeter.

Allen, J. 2002. The Rumensea Wall, Romney and Walland Marshes: a commentary. In: A. Long, S. Hipkin and H. Clarke (eds.), *Romney Marsh: coastal and landscape change through the ages.* Oxford University School of Archaeology Monograph 56, 121–26.

Armitage, P.L. 1977. The Mammalian Remains from the Tudor Site of Baynard's Castle London: a biometrical and historical analysis. Ph.D. Thesis: Royal Holloway College & British Museum (Natural History).

Ayodeji, K. 1998. Smallhythe nail types. Preliminary unpublished report.

Ayre, J. and Wroe-Brown, R. 2002. *The London Millennium Bridge: excavations of the medieval and later waterfronts at Peter's Hill, City of London, and Bankside, Southwark.* Museum of London Archaeology Service Archaeology Studies Series 6.

Baart, J., Krook, W., Lagerweij, A., Ockers, N., van Regteren Altena, H., Stam, T., Stoepker, H., Stouthart, G., and van der Zwan, M. 1977. *Opgravingen in Amsterdam.* Twintig jaar stadskernonderzoek, Amsterdam-Haarlem. Amsterdams Historisch Museum-Fibula-Van Dishoeck.

Banyard, G. 2004. Duke William's Conquest of Kent 1066. In: T. Lawson and D. Killingray (eds.), *An Historical Atlas of Kent*, 34–35. Phillimore. Chichester.

Barber, L. 1998. Medieval rural settlement and economy at Lydd: preliminary results from the excavations at Lydd Quarry. In: J. Eddison, M. Gardiner and A. Long (eds.), *Environmental change and human occupation in a coastal lowland.* OUCA Monograph 46, 89–108. Oxford University Committee for Archaeology. Oxford.

Barber, L. 2005. The Pottery. In: J. Stevenson and S. Hunter. Dymchurch Road, New Romney, Kent: Archaeological Excavations 2003. A Post-Excavation Assessment Report & Proposals for Publication, Project No. 1694, Unpublished report for Archaeology South-East. 36.

Barrett, J.H., Locker, A.M. and Roberts, C.M. 2004. 'Dark Age Economics' revisited: the English Fish Bone Evidence AD 600–1600. *Antiquity* 78, 618–636.

Barton, K.J. 1979. *Medieval Sussex pottery.* Philimore & Co. Ltd, Chichester.

Barton, K.J., 1980. A further note on the origins of Saintonge polychrome jugs. *Medieval Ceramics* 4, 45–46.

Beresford, M. 1967. *New Towns of the Middle Ages: town plantation in England, Wales and Gascony.* London.

Bill, J. 1994. Iron Nails in Iron Age and Medieval Shipbuilding. In: C. Westerdahl (ed), Crossroads in Ancient Shipbuilding. Oxbow Monograph 40, 55–63. Oxbow. Oxford.

Blackmore, L. 1999, Aspects of trade and exchange evidenced by recent work on Saxon and medieval pottery from London. *Transactions of the London and Middlesex Archaeology Society*, 50, 38–54.

Bleach, J. and Gardiner, M. 1999. 'Medieval markets and ports'. In: K. Leslie, B. Short, and S. Rowland 1999. *An Historical Atlas of Sussex*, 42–43. Chichester. Phillimore.

Boden, D. 2006. New Romney Sewer Scheme In: *Canterbury's Archaeology 2004–2005, Annual Report 34.* Canterbury Archaeological Trust.

Bowdon, L. 2003. 'Politics of Value', a paper given at the Leeds International Medieval Congress 16.7.2003, with a revised version given and discussed at the Culture and Society Seminar of the Canterbury Centre for Medieval Studies, University of Kent, 21 November 2003 (unpublished).

Boys, W. 1792. *Collections for an History of Sandwich in Kent with Notices of the Other Cinque Ports, etc.* Canterbury.

Brooks, N. 1988. Romney Marsh in the Early Middle Ages. In: J. Eddison and C. Green (eds.), *Romney Marsh: Evolution, Occupation, Reclamation.* OUCA Monograph 24, 90–104. Oxford University Committee for Archaeology. Oxford.

Brown, D. 2002. *Pottery in Medieval Southampton, c.1066–1510.* Council for British Archaeology Research Report 133.

Burke, T. 2004. The Tithe Map and the search for a small port at Appledore. *The Romney Marsh Irregular* 23 [newsletter of Romney Marsh Research Trust], 3–11.

Butcher, A. 1980. The Hospital of St. Stephen and St. Thomas, New Romney: the documentary evidence. *Archaeologia Cantiana* 96, 17–26.

Butcher, A. 1992. Citizens and Farmers in the Romney Marshes c.1350–1540. Paper given at the Second Romney Marsh Conference, 26 September 1992.

Butcher, A. 2001. 'At the death of Emma Gobilonde'. *The Romney Marsh Irregular* 17 [newsletter of Romney Marsh Research Trust], 17–20.

Butcher, A. 2003. The functions of script in a speech community of a late medieval town, *c*.1300–1550. In: A. Walsham, and J. Crick, (eds.), *Script And Print*, 157–170. Cambridge University Press. Cambridge.

Butler, J., 2006. Reclaiming the Marsh. *Archaeological Excavations at Moor House, City of London*. PCA Monograph 6. Pre-Construct Archaeology. London.

Canterbury Archaeological Trust 2005. Melaine, Fairfield Road, New Romney (TR 9899 2508). *Archaeologia Cantiana* 125, 271–272.

Challinor, D. 2001. Environmental Assessment. In: D. Thomason and E. Stafford, Land to the rear of the Old School House, Church Lane, New Romney, Kent. Oxford Archaeological Unit, unpublished Evaluation Report, 21–22.

Clarke, H. 2005. Sandwich before the Cinque Port: initial finds of the Sandwich project. *Kent Archaeological Society newsletter* 65, 13–15.

Clarke, H. and Carter, A. (eds.) 1977. *Excavations at Kings Lynn*. Society for Medieval Archaeology Monograph 7.

Clavel, B., 2001. *L'animal dans l'alimentation médiévale et moderne en France du Nord (XIIe – XVIIe siècles)*. Revue Archéologique de Picardie, Nº Spécial 19, Amiens.

Coatts, B. 2005. Some Thoughts on the Harbour(s) of Lydd. *Romney Marsh Irregular* 26, 15–20.

Cotter, J. 1991. The medieval pottery and tile industry at Tyler Hill. *Canterbury's Archaeology 1990–1991*, 49–56.

Cotter, J. 1997a. Medieval and later pottery. In: K., Blockley, M. Sparks and T. Tatton-Brown, *Canterbury Cathedral Nave Archaeology, History and Architecture*. The Archaeology of Canterbury, New Series 1, 179–194. Dean and Chapter of Canterbury Cathedral and Canterbury Archaeological Trust.

Cotter, J. 1997b. *Ports, pots and packed lunches? An overview of the medieval pottery from Townwall Street, Dover*. Canterbury's Archaeology 1995–1996, 74–81.

Cotter, J. 1997c. *A Twelfth-Century Pottery Kiln at Pound Lane, Canterbury: Evidence for an Immigrant Potter in the Late Norman Period*. Canterbury Archaeological Trust Occasional Paper No. 1.

Cotter, J. 2001. The Pottery. In: M. Hicks and A. Hicks, *St Gregory's Priory, Northgate, Canterbury Excavations 1988–1991*. The Archaeology of Canterbury, New Series, 2, 231–266. Canterbury Archaeological Trust Ltd.

Cotter, J. 2002, Pottery studies; medieval shelly wares in Kent: a summary of recent research. Canterbury's Archaeology, 1999–2000, 56–60. Canterbury Archaeological Trust Ltd.

Cotter, J. 2006. The pottery. In: K. Parfitt, B. Corke & J. Cotter, *Townwall Street, Dover Excavations 1996*. The Archaeology of Canterbury New Series Volume 3. Canterbury Archaeological Trust. 121–254.

Cotter, J. 2008. Medieval London-type Ware Kilns Discovered at Woolwich. *Medieval Pottery Research Group Newsletter*, 61, 3–5.

Cotterell, H.H. 1929. *Old Pewter, its Makers and Marks*. London (reprinted 1963).

Courtney, P. 1997. Ceramics and the history of consumption: pitfalls and prospects. *Medieval Ceramics* 21, 95–108.

Cowgill, J. 2003. Fish hook production in 13th-14th century Kings Lynn. *Historical Metallurgy Society Newsletter* 53, 4–5.

Crowfoot, E., 1977. Pin beaters. In: H. Clarke and A. Carter, *Excavations in King's Lynn 1963-1970*. Society for Medieval Archaeology Monograph 7, 311–312.

Crumlin-Perdersen, O. 1972. The Vikings and the Hanseatic merchants: 900–1450. In: G.F. Bass (ed.) *A History of Seafaring, Based on Underwater Archaeology*, 181–204. Thames and Hudson. London.

Darton L., Jarrett, C. Leary, J. and Mayo. C. forthcoming. *Evidence for medieval pottery and tile production in Kingston-upon-Thames: Excavations at four multi-period sites on London Road*. PCA monograph.

Davey, P. and Hodges, R. 1983. Ceramics and trade: a critique of the archaeological evidence. In: P. Davey and R. Hodges (eds.), *Ceramics and Trade. The production and distribution of later medieval pottery in north-west Europe*. Department of Prehistory & Archaeology, University of Sheffield, 1-14.

Devenish, D.C. 1979. Excavations in Winding Street, Hastings, 1974, *Sussex Archaeological Collections* 117, 125–134.

Diack, M. and Boden, D.C. 2004. New Romney Sewer Scheme, Shepway, Kent, Preliminary results of the evaluation trenching and sample excavation in advance of the First Time Sewerage Scheme, CAT site code: SSNR/EV-04. Canterbury Archaeological Trust, unpublished report.

Dobson, M. 1998. Death and Disease on Romney Marsh in the 17th to 19th centuries. In: J. Eddison, M. Gardiner and A. Long 1998. *Romney Marsh: Environmental Change and Human Occupation in a Coastal Lowland.* OUCA Monograph 24. 46, 165–182. Oxford University Committee for Archaeology. Oxford.

Draper, G. 1998, The Farmers of Canterbury Cathedral; Priory and All Souls College on Romney Marsh *c.* 1443–1545. In: J. Eddison, M. Gardiner and A. Long 1998. *Romney Marsh: Environmental Change and Human Occupation in a Coastal Lowland,* OUCA Monograph 46, 109–128. Oxford University Committee for Archaeology. Oxford.

Draper, G. 2000. Church, Chapel and Clergy on Romney Marsh after the Black Death. *The Romney Marsh Irregular* 16, [newsletter of Romney Marsh Research Trust], 6–8.

Draper, G. 2003. Literacy and its transmission in the Romney Marsh area *c.*1150–1550. Unpublished Ph.D. thesis, University of Kent at Canterbury.

Draper, G. 2004a. Cockreed Land and Craythorne manor, New Romney, in the Middle Ages: the historical and topographical evidence. *The Romney Marsh Irregular* 23, [newsletter of Romney Marsh Research Trust], 12–18.

Draper, G. 2004b. Romney Marsh and its Towns and Villages *c.*800–1500. In: T. Lawson and D. Killingray (eds.), *An Historical Atlas of Kent,* 56–57. Phillimore. Chichester.

Draper, G. 2005. Small Fields and Wet Land: inheritance practices and the transmission of real property in the Romney Marshes *c.*1150–1390. *Landscapes* 6, no. 1, 18–45.

Draper, G. M. 2007a. Writing English, French and Latin in the fifteenth century: a regional perspective. In: *The Fifteenth Century,* 7. Boydell press.

Draper G. 2007b. 'There hath not bene any gramar scole kepte, preacher maytened or pore people releved, other then… by the same chauntreye:' educational provision and piety in Kent *c.*1400 to 1640. In: R. Lutton and E. Salter (eds.), *Pieties in Transition: Religious Practices and Experiences, c. 1400–1640.* Ashgate Press.

Draper, G. 2008. The education of children in Kent and Sussex: interpreting the medieval and Tudor ways. *Nottingham Medieval Studies* 52, 213–42.

Draper, G. forthcoming. 'Timber and iron: natural resources for the late medieval shipbuilding industry in Kent'. In: S. Sweetinburgh (ed.), *Late Medieval Kent.* Kent History Project/ Boydell Press.

Draper G. with contributions by Martin D., Martin B. and Tyler A. forthcoming. *Rye: a History of a Sussex Cinque Port to 1660.*

Du Boulay, F. 1966. *The Lordship of Canterbury.* Nelson. London.

Dulley, A. J. F. 1969. The Early History of the Rye Fishing Industry. *Sussex Archaeological Collections* 107, 36–64.

Dunkin, D. 2005. Marine Molluscs. In: J. Stevenson, and S. Hunter, Dymchurch Road, New Romney, Kent: Archaeological Excavations 2003, A Post-Excavation Assessment Report & Proposals for Publication, Project No. 1694. Unpublished report for Archaeology South-East, 43–45.

Dunning, G. 1961. Medieval Chimney pots. In: E. M. Jope (ed), *Studies in Building History.* 78–93.London.

Dyer, C., 1994. *Everyday Life in Medieval England.* Hambledon Press. London and Rio Grande.

Eales, J. 2000. The rise of ideological politics in Kent, 1580–1640. In: M. Zell (ed.), *Early Modern Kent 1540–1640,* 279–314. Woodbridge. Kent County Council and the Boydell Press.

Eddison, J. 2000. *Romney Marsh, Survival on a Frontier.* Tempus. Stroud

Eddison, J. 2002. The purpose, construction and operation of a 13th-century watercourse: the Rhee, Romney Marsh, Kent. In: A., Long, S. Hipkin and H. Clarke (eds.), *Romney Marsh: coastal and landscape change through the ages.* Oxford University School of Archaeology Monograph 56, 127–139.

Eddison, J. and Draper, G. 1997. A landscape of medieval reclamation: Walland Marsh, Kent. *Landscape History* 19, 75–88.

Eddison, J. and Green, C. (eds.) 1988. *Romney Marsh: Evolution, Occupation, Reclamation.* OUCA Monograph 24. Oxford University Committee for Archaeology. Oxford.

Edwards, R. 1977. *Where to fish: Kent and the coast, The Marshall Cavendish Fisherman's Handbook,* Part 9, 228–235.

Egan, G. and Pritchard, F. 1991. *Dress Accessories (Medieval Finds from Excavations in London 3)*. Boydell and Brewer/Museum of London. London.

Egan, G. 1996. Some archaeological evidence for metalworking in London, *c*. 1050AD–1700AD. *Historical Metallurgy* 30.2, 8–9.

Egan, G. 1998. *The Medieval Household (Medieval Finds from Excavations in London 6)*. Museum of London/Stationery Office. London.

Egan, M. 2003. The Church in medieval Greenwich. *Archaeologia Cantiana* 123, 233–254.

Egan, G. 2005. *Material culture in London in an age of transition: Tudor and Stuart period finds c 1450–c 1700 from excavations at riverside sites in Southwark*, MoLAS Monograph Series 19. Museum of London Archaeology Service. London.

Egan, G. 2007. Cloth seals from Meols. In: D.W. Griffiths, R.A. Philpott and G. Egan, *Meols: The Archaeology of the North Wirral Coast, Discoveries and observations in the 19th and 20th centuries, with a catalogue of collections,* Oxford University School of Archaeology Monograph 68. Institute of Archaeology, University of Oxford. Oxford.

Forsyth, H. with Egan, G. 2005. *Toys, trifles and trinkets: base metal miniatures from London 1200–1800.* Unicorn/Museum of London. London.

Fagan, B. 2000. *The Little Ice Age: How Climate Made History 1300–1850.* Basic Books. New York.

Fenwick, V. 1978. The Barge from the River Rother, Kent. In: V. Fenwick (ed), *The Graveney Boat.* BAR British Series 53, 258–260.

Friel, I. 1995. *The Good Ship. Ships, Shipbuilding and Technology in England 1200–1520.* British Museum. London.

Gaimster, D. 1997. *German stoneware, 1200–1900.* Trustees of the British Museum. London.

Gardiner, M. 1989. Some lost Anglo-Saxon charters and the endowment of Hastings College. *Sussex Archaeological Collections* 127, 39–48.

Gardiner, M. 1994. Old Romney: an examination of the evidence for a lost Saxo-Norman port. *Archaeologia Cantiana,* CXIV, 339–345.

Gardiner, M. 2000. Shipping and trade between England and the Continent during the eleventh century. *Anglo-Norman Studies 22 Proceedings of the Battle Conference 1999.* Boydell Press.

Gibson, J. and Harvey, I. 2000. A Sociological study of the New Romney Passion Play. In: *Research Opportunities in Renaissance Drama* 39, 203–221.

Giles, K. 2005. Public Space in Town and Village 1110 1500. In: K. Giles and C. Dyer, *Town and Country in the Middle Ages: contrasts, contacts and interconnections, 1100–1500.* Society for Medieval Archaeology Monograph 22. Maney. Leeds.

Goodburn, D. 1991. New Light on early ship and boatbuilding in the London Area, In: G. Good, R. Jones and M. Ponsford (eds.), *Waterfront Archaeology, Proceedings of the third international conference, Bristol, 1988.* CBA Research Report No.74, 105–111.

Goodburn, D, 1994, Anglo-Saxon Boat Finds From London are they English? In: C. Westerdahl, (ed), *Crossroads in Ancient Shipbuilding.* Oxbow Monograph 40. 97–104. Oxbow. Oxford.

Green, C. 1988. Palaeogeography of the marine inlets of the Romney Marsh area. In: J. Eddison and C. Green (eds.), 1988. *Romney Marsh: Evolution, Occupation, Reclamation.* OUCA Monograph 24. Oxford University Committee for Archaeology. Oxford 167-174.

Grenville, J. 1997. *Medieval Housing.* Leicester University Press. Leicester.

Grigson, C. 1982. Sex and age determination of some bones and teeth of domestic cattle: a review of the literature. In: B. Wilson, C. Grigson and S. Payne (eds.), *Ageing and Sexing Animal Bones from Archaeological Sites.* BAR British Series 109, 7–23.

Grove, L.R.A. 1967 Researches and discoveries in Kent: New Romney. *Archaeologia Cantiana* 82, 296.

Grove, L.R.A. and Warhurst, A. 1952. A thirteenth-century kiln site at Ashford. *Archaeologia Cantiana*, 82, 294–296.

Haigh, C. 1987. *The English Reformation Revised.* Cambridge University Press. Cambridge.

Hamilton-Dyer, S., 2001. Bird and Fish Remains. In: M. Gardiner, R. Cross, N. Macpherson-Grant and I. Riddler, Continental Trade and Non-Urban Ports in Mid-Anglo-Saxon England: Excavations at *Sandtun*, West Hythe, Kent. *Archaeological Journal* 158, 255–261.

Harris, R. 1990. The Rubble Stonework of St Nicholas, New Romney. *The Romney Marsh Irregular* 5, [newsletter of Romney Marsh Research Trust] April 1990.

Harris, R. 1992. 3–4 West Street. New Romney. *The Romney Marsh Irregular* 7, [newsletter of Romney Marsh Research Trust], January 1992.

Hasted E. 1797–1801. *The History and Topographical Survey of the County of Kent,* (2nd ed.). W. Bristow. Canterbury.

Hawkins, D. 2000. Archaeological Desk Based Assessment of Proposed Sainsbury's Community Store Site, Derville Site, Southlands School, New Romney Kent. CGMS Consulting unpublished report.

Hawkins, D. 2001. Specification for an Archaeological Investigation at Proposed Sainsbury's Community Store Site, Derville Site, Southlands School, New Romney Kent. CGMS Consulting unpublished report.

Herdman, M.L. and Jarman C., 1996 An Archaeological Watching Brief on a new gas main, New Romney, Kent. Canterbury Archaeological Trust unpublished report, Project number 95/61.

Hewett, C. 1982. *Church Carpentry*. Phillimore. Chichester.

Hicks, M. and Hicks, A., 2001. *St. Gregory's Priory, Northgate, Canterbury. Excavations 1988–1991*. The Archaeology of Canterbury, New Series II, Canterbury.

Hindle, B. 2002. *Medieval town plans*. Shire. Princes Risborough.

Hipkin, S. 1995a. The impact of marshland drainage on Rye harbour, 1550–1650. In: J. Eddison (ed.), *Romney Marsh: the Debatable Ground* . OUCA Monograph **41**, 138–147. Oxford University Committee for Archaeology. Oxford.

Hipkin, S. 1995b. Closing ranks: oligarchy and government at Rye, 1570–1640. *Urban History* 22, part 3, 319–340.

Hipkin, S. 2002. The Worlds of Daniel Langdon: public office and private enterprise in the Romney Marsh region in the early-18th century. In: A. Long, S. Hipkin and H. Clarke (eds.), *Romney Marsh: coastal and landscape change through the ages*, 173–189. Oxford University School of Archaeology monograph 56.

Homan, W. 1949. The Founding of New Winchelsea. *Sussex Archaeological Collections* 88, 22–41.

Hughes, M. and Stamper, P. 1981. The alien priory of St Andrew, Hamble, Hampshire. *Proceedings of the Hampshire Field Club Archaeological* Society 37, 23–39.

Hume, A. 1863. *Ancient Meols*. London.

Hunt, E. and Murray, J. 1999. *A History of Business in Medieval Europe 1200–1550*. Cambridge University Press. Cambridge.

Hurley, M. F. 1997a. Artefacts of Skeletal Material. In: M.H. Hurley, O.M.B. Scully and S.W.J. McCutcheon. *Late Viking Age and Medieval Waterford: Excavations 1986–1992*, 650–699. Waterford corporation. Waterford.

Hurley, M. F. 1997b. Artefacts of Skeletal Material. In: R. M. Cleary, M. F. Hurley and E. Shee Twohig, *Skiddy's Castle and Christ Church Cork. Excavations 1974–1977 by D. C. Twohig*, 239–273. Cork.

Hurst, J.G. 1974. Sixteenth- and Seventeenth-centur imported pottery from the Saintonge. In: V. I. Evison, H. Hodges & J.G. Hurst, *Medieval pottery from excavations: studies presented to Gerald Clough Dunning*, with a bibliography of his works. London, 221–262.

Hurst, J. G., Neal, D. S. and van Beuningen, H. J. E. 1986. Pottery produced and traded in north-west Europe, 1350–1650. *Rotterdam Papers* IV.

Hutchinson, G. 1994. *Medieval Ships and Shipping*. Leicester University Press. Leicester.

Hutton, R. 1987. The local impact of the Tudor Reformation. In: C. Haigh (ed.), *The English Reformation Revised*, 114–38. Cambridge University Press. Cambridge.

James, R., Draper, G., Martin, D. 2005, Archaeological and Historic Landscape Survey, Smallhythe Place Kent, commissioned by the National Trust, Project No. 1967. Unpublished report for Archaeology South-East, 47–50.

Jaques, D. 2005. Fish and Bird remains. In J. Stevenson, and S. Hunter, Dymchurch Road, New Romney, Kent: Archaeological Excavations 2003, A Post-Excavation Assessment Report & Proposals for Publication, Project No. 1694, Unpublished report for Archaeology South-East, 47–50.

Jarrett, C. with Sabel, K. 2004. The Post-medieval red earthenware and Peninsular House Earthenware Pottery. In D. Divers, Excavations at Deptford on the site of the East India Company dockyards and the Trinity House almshouses, London. *Post-Medieval Archaeology* 38:1, 89–120.

Jeake, S. 1728, *Charters of the Cinque Ports, two ancient towns and their members*.

Jennings S. 1981. *Eighteen Centuries of pottery from Norwich*. East Anglian Archaeology No 13.

Jones. E. 2001. Illicit business: accounting for smuggling in mid-sixteenth-century Bristol. *Economic History Review* 54, no. 1, 138.

Jope E. M. (ed), 1961. *Studies in Building History*. London.

Kelly, D. B. 1972. An early Tudor kiln at Hareplain, Biddenden. *Archaeologia Cantiana* 97, 159–76.

Kennedy, M. 1954. *The Sea Angler's Fishes*. Hutchinson. London.

Keynes, S. 1990. The Æthelings in Normandy. In: M. Chibnall (ed.), *Anglo-Norman Studies, Proceedings of the Battle Conference* 13, 173–205.

Killock, D. and Meddens, F. 2005. Pottery as Plunder, A 17th Century Maritime Site in Limehouse, London. *Post-Medieval Archaeology* 39, part 1, 1–91.

King, C. 2005. Private lives and public power: the merchants of Norwich and their houses 1450–1660, paper given at Culture and Society seminar of Canterbury Centre for Medieval and Tudor studies, University of Kent, 4/11/05.

Kowaleski, M. 2000, Fish production, trade and consumption, *c*.1300–1530. In: D.J. Starkey, C. Reid and N. Ashcroft (eds.), *England's Sea Fisheries. The Commercial Sea Fisheries of England and Wales since 1300.* 29–32. Chatham Publishing. London.

Kurlansky, M. 1997. *Cod: a biography of the fish that changed the world.* Walker Publishing Company.

Lawson. T. 2004. The Cinque Ports. In: T. Lawson and D. Killingray (eds.), *An Historical Atlas of Kent*, 52–53. Phillimore. Chichester.

Linklater, A. 2001a. An Archaeological Evaluation on a Plot of Land to the rear of Prospect House, Fairfield Rd, New Romney, Kent, Canterbury Archaeological Trust, Unpublished report, Project number 1520.

Linklater, A. 2001b. An Archaeological Watching Brief on a Plot of Land to the rear of Prospect House, Fairfield Rd, New Romney, Kent, Canterbury Archaeological Trust, Unpublished report, Project number 1520.

Linklater, A. 2003. An Archaeological Watching Brief During the Excavation of Foundation Trenches to the Rear of 'Melaine', Fairfield Road, New Romney, Shepway, Kent. Unpublished archive report for Canterbury Archaeological Trust.

Little, A.G. 1939. The Franciscan Friary at Romney. *Archaeologia Cantiana*, 50, 151–152.

Long, A., Waller, M. and Stupples, P. 2006. Driving mechanisms of coastal change: peat compaction and the destruction of late Holocene coastal wetlands. *Marine Geology* 225, 63–84.

Lucas, G., Hall, D., Fryer, V., Irving, B. and French, C. 1998. A Medieval Fishery on Whittlesea Mere, Cambridgeshire. *Medieval Archaeology* 42, 19–44.

Margeson, S., 1993. *Norwich Households. Medieval and Post-Medieval Finds from Norwich Survey Excavations 1971–8*, East Anglian Archaeology 58, Gressenhall.

Marsden, P., 1996, Ships of the Port of London twelfth to seventeenth centuries AD, English Heritage, London.

Martin, D. 1993. The development of Old Hastings. In: D. Rudling, L. Barber, D. Martin 1993. Excavations at the Phoenix Brewery Site, Hastings, 1988. 73–80. *Sussex Archaeological Collections* 131, 73–113.

Martin, D. 1999. 'Winchelsea- a new medieval town. In: K. Leslie, B. Short and S. Rowland, *An Historical Atlas of Sussex*, 44–45. Chichester: Phillimore.

Martin, D. and Martin B. with contributions by Eddison, J. Rudling, D. and Sylvester, D. 2004. *New Winchelsea Sussex: A Medieval Port Town*. Field Archaeology Unit monograph 2. Institute of Archaeology, University College London. London.

Mason, R. (ed.) 2000. Excavations at the Royal Arsenal, Woolwich. *Greater London Industrial Archaeology Society Newsletter*, 191, 5-6.

Mate, M. 1999. *Women in Medieval English Society*. Cambridge University Press. Cambridge.

Mate, M. 2006. *Trade and Economic Developments, 1450–1550: the experience of Kent, Surrey and Sussex*. The Boydell Press. Woodbridge.

Mayhew, G. 1987. *Tudor Rye*. Falmer Centre for Continuing Education, University of Sussex.

McCutcheon, C., 2006. *Medieval Pottery from Wood Quay, Dublin: The 1974–6 Waterfront excavations*. Royal Irish Academy Dublin.

McCutcheon, C., forthcoming . Medieval pottery in Ireland: a tale of three cities and some towns. *Medieval Ceramics* 28.

McGrail, S. 1981. *The Ship, Rafts, Boats and Ships From Prehistoric Times to the Medieval Era*. HMSO. London.

McGrail, S. 1993. Medieval boat and ship timbers from *Dublin*. National Museum of Ireland. Dublin.

McLain, B.1997. Factors in market establishment in Medieval England: the evidence from Kent 1086–1350. *Archaeologia Cantiana* 107, 83–104.

Meddens, F. and Wooldridge, K. 2002. An Assessment of Archaeological Excavation on the site of Southlands School, Fairfield Road, New Romney, Kent. Unpublished archive report for PCA.

Mercer, M. 2005. The administration of the Cinque Ports in the early Lancastrian period. In: K. Dockray and P. Fleming (eds), *People, Places and Perspectives: essays on later Medieval and early Tudor England in honour of Ralph A. Griffiths*, 47–67. Nonsuch Publishing. Stroud.

Miller, P. and Stephenson, R. 1999. *A 14th century pottery site in Kingston upon Thames Surrey: Excavations at 70–76 Eden Street*. Archaeological Studies 1. Museum of London Archaeological Service. London.

Milne, G, McKewan, C & Goodburn, D, 1998. *Nautical Archaeology on the Foreshore; hulk recording on the Medway*. RCHME.

Milne, G. 2001. Joining The Medieval Fleet. *British Archaeology*, 61.

Milne, G. 2003. *The Port of Medieval London*. Tempus. Stroud.

Mould, Q. forthcoming. The Small Finds. In: P. Bennett, C. Sparey Green and C. Young, *The Roman Watermills at Ickham, Kent*. The Archaeology of Canterbury. New Series, Canterbury.

Morris, J. (ed.) 1976, from a translation by J. Mothersill. *Domesday Book: Sussex*. Phillimore. Chichester.

Murray, K. 1935a. Excavations on the site of the Leper Hospital New Romney. *Archaeologia Cantiana*, 47, 198–204.

Murray, K. 1935b. *The Constitutional History of the Cinque Ports*. Manchester University Press. Manchester.

Murray, K. 1945. *The Register of Daniel Rough*. KAS Records 16.

Nayling, N, 1998. *The Magor Pill medieval wreck*. CBA Research Report, 115.

Ottaway, P. and Rogers, N. S. H. 2002. *Craft, Industry and Everyday Life: Finds from Medieval York*. The Archaeology of York. The Small Finds 17/15, York.

Øye, I. 1988. *Textile Equipment and its Working Environment, Bryggen in Bergen c1150—1500*. The Bryggen Papers, Main Series 2. Oslo.

Palliser, D. 1987. Popular reactions to the Reformation during the years of uncertainty, 1530–70. In: C. Haigh (ed.) *The English Reformation Revised*, 94–113. Cambridge University Press. Cambridge.

Parfitt, K. Corke B. and Cotter. J. 2006. *Townwall Street, Dover Excavations 1996. The archaeology of Canterbury New Series Volume III*. Canterbury Archaeological Trust.

Parfitt, K.P. 2000. A Roman occupation site at Dixon's Corner, Worth. *Archaeologia Cantiana* 120, 107–148.

Parkin E. W. 1973. The Ancient Buildings of New Romney. *Archaeologia Cantiana* 88, 117–128.

Pearce, J. and Vince, A. 1988. *A dated type-series of London medieval pottery Part 4: Surrey Whitewares*. London and Middlesex Archaeology Society Special Paper 10. London.

Pearce, J., Vince, A. G. and Jenner, A. 1985. *A dated type-series of London medieval pottery Part 2: London-type ware*. London and Middlesex Archaeology Society, Special Paper No. 6. London.

Pelham, R. 1932. Some aspects of the East Kent wool trade in the thirteenth century. *Archaeologia Cantiana* 44, 218–228.

Pieters, M. 2006. The Archaeology of Fishery, Trade and Piracy. The material environment of Walraversijde and other late medieval and early modern fishing communities along the southern North Sea. In: M. Pieters, F. Verhaege and G. Gevaert, *Fishing, Trade and Piracy. Fishermen and Fishermen's Settlements in and around the North Sea Area in the Middle Ages and Later*. Archeologie in Vlaanderen 6, Brussels, 41–61.

Priestley-Bell, G. 1999. An Archaeological Evaluation of Land at Church Road, New Romney, Kent, Project No. 1057. Unpublished report for Archaeology South-East.

Pritchard, F., 1991. Small Finds, in A. G. Vince, *Finds and Environmental Evidence, Aspects of Saxo-Norman London: II*. London. 120–278.

Pryor, S. and Blockley, K. 1978. A seventeenth century Kiln site at Woolwich. *Post-Medieval Archaeology* 12, 30–85.

Purefoy, P.B. 2005. The Denge Marsh Hoard and the Dungeness Coastline. *Romney Marsh Irregular* [newsletter of Romney Marsh Research Trust], 26.

Reeves, A. 1995. Romney Marsh : the field-walking evidence. In: J. Eddison, (ed.), *Romney Marsh: the Debatable Ground*. OUCA Monograph 41. Oxford University Committee for Archaeology. Oxford 78-91.

Reeves, A. and Eve, D. 1998. Sheep-keeping and Lookers' huts on Romney Marsh. In: J. Eddison, M. Gardiner and A. Long 1998. *Romney Marsh: Environmental Change and Human Occupation in a Coastal Lowland*. OUCA Monograph 46, 191–208. Oxford University Committee for Archaeology. Oxford.

Reynolds, M. 2004. Reformation and Reaction, 1534–69. In: T. Lawson and D. Killingray (eds.), *An Historical Atlas of Kent*, 42–43. Phillimore. Chichester.

Riddler, I.D., Trzaska-Nartowski, N.T.N. and Hatton, S. forthcoming. *An Early Medieval Craft. Antler and Boneworking from Ipswich Excavations 1974–1994*. East Anglian Archaeology, Gressenhall.

Riddler, I. 2006. Part 5: the coins, small finds and building material. In: *Townwall Street, Dover Excavations 1996. The archaeology of Canterbury New Series 3*, 255–318. Canterbury Archaeological Trust. Canterbury.

Riddler, I.D., 2001. The Small Finds. In: M. Gardiner, R. Cross, N. Macpherson-Grant and I. Riddler, Continental Trade and Non-Urban Ports in Mid-Anglo-Saxon England: Excavations at *Sandtun*, West Hythe, Kent. *Archaeological Journal* 158, 228–252.

Riddler, I. D. 2006a. The Coins, Small Finds and Building Materials. In: K. Parfitt, B. Corke and J. Cotter, *Townwall Street, Dover. Excavations 1996.* The Archaeology of Canterbury New Series 3, 255–318. Canterbury.

Riddler, I. D. 2006b. Early Medieval Fishing Implements of Bone and Antler. In: M. Pieters, F. Verhaege and G. Gevaert, *Fishing, Trade and Piracy. Fishermen and Fishermen's Settlements in and around the North Sea Area in the Middle Ages and Later.* Archeologie in Vlaanderen 6, Brussels, 171–180.

Rigold S. E. 1964. Two Kentish Hospitals Re-examined. *Archaeologia Cantiana* 79, 47–69.

Rippon, S. 2002. Romney Marsh: evolution of the historical landscape and its wider setting. In: A. Long, S. Hipkin and H. Clarke (eds.) *Romney Marsh: coastal and landscape change through the ages.* Oxford University School of Archaeology monograph 56, 84–100.

Robertson, S. 1880. Destroyed Churches of New Romney. *Archaeologia Cantiana* 13, 237–249.

Rogerson, A., 1976. *Excavations on Fuller's Hill, Great Yarmouth.* East Anglian Archaeology Report No. 2. Norfolk, Gressenhall, 131–245.

Rogerson, A and Dallas, C., 1984. *Excavations in Thetford 1948–59 and 1973–80.* East Anglian Archaeology 22, Gressenhall.

Rojo, A. 1986. Live length and weight of cod (*Gadus morhua*) estimated from various skeletal elements. *North American Archaeologist* 7 (4), 329–351.

Rudling, D., Barber, L. and Martin, D. 1993. Excavations at the Phoenix Brewery Site, Hastings, 1988. *Sussex Archaeological Collections* 131, 73–113.

Rulewicz, M., 1994. *Rybolowstwo Gdanska na tle Osrodkow Miejskich Pomorza od IX do XIII Wieku.* Gdansk Wczesnosredniowieczny 10, Gdansk.

Salisbury, E. 1887. Mr Edward Salisbury's report of the records of New Romney. *Archaeologia Cantiana* 17, 12–33.

Salzman, L, 1952. Building in England down to 1540. Oxford.

Schofield, J. and Vince, A. 2003. *Medieval towns: the archaeology of British towns in their European setting.* 2nd ed. Continuum. London.

Schofield, J.E. and Waller, M., 2005. A Pollen Analytical Record for Hemp Retting from Dungeness Foreland, UK. *Journal of Archaeological Science* 32, 715–726.

Scott, N. 2001. Animal Bone. In: D. Thomason and E. Stafford, Land to the Rear of Old School House, Church Lane, New Romney, Kent. Oxford Archaeological Unit, unpublished document number F7234.

Scott Robertson, W. 1880. Destroyed Churches of New Romney. *Archaeologia Cantiana* 13, 237–49.

Sinclair Williams, C. 1973. Maritime East Malling. *Archaeologia Cantiana* 88, 51–55.

Slater, T. 2005. Plan Characteristics and market settlements: evidence from the Midlands. In: K. Giles and C. Dyer, *Town and Country in the Middle Ages: contrasts, contacts and interconnections, 1100–1500.* Society for Medieval Archaeology Monograph 22. Maney, Leeds 23–42.

Smith, P., 2001. The Fish Bones. In: M. Hicks and A. Hicks, *St. Gregory's Priory, Northgate, Canterbury, Excavations 1988–1991.* The Archaeology of Canterbury, New Series 2, 308–317. Canterbury Archaeological Trust. Canterbury.

Stacey, R. 1995, Jewish lending and the medieval English economy. In: R. Britnell and B. Campbell, *A commercialising economy: England 1086 to c.1300.* Manchester University Press, 78–101.

Steane, J. M. and Foreman, M., 1991. The Archaeology of Medieval Fishing Tackle. In: G. L. Good, R. H. Jones and M. W. Ponsford, *Waterfront Archaeology.* CBA Research Report 74, London, 88–101.

Stevenson, J. and Hunter, S.W. 2005, Dymchurch Road, New Romney, Kent: Archaeological Excavations, A Post-excavation Assessment Report & Proposals for Publication, Project No. 1694, Unpublished report for Archaeology South-East.

Streeten, A. D. F. 1985. The pottery. In: J. N. Hare, *Battle Abbey: the eastern range and the excavations of 1978–80.* HBMCE Archaeological Report 2, 103–126.

Sweetinburgh, S., 2006. Documentary Evidence. In: K. Parfitt, B. Corke and J. Cotter, *Townwall Street, Dover. Excavations 1996,* The Archaeology of Canterbury. New Series 3, 396–402. Canterbury Archaeological Trust. Canterbury.

Sweetinburgh, S. 2004a. Monastic Houses. In: T. Lawson and D. Killingray (eds.), *An Historical Atlas of Kent,* 42–43. Phillimore. Chichester.

Sweetinburgh, S. 2004b. Medieval Hospitals and Almshouses. In: T. Lawson and D. Killingray (eds.), *An Historical Atlas of Kent*, 44–45. Phillimore. Chichester.

Sweetinburgh, S. 2008. Eternal town servants: civic elections and the Stuppeny tombs of New Romney and Lydd. In: M.B.Bruun and S. Glasser (eds), *Negotiating Heritage: Memories of the Middle Ages, Ritus et Artes: Traditions and Transformations.* Turnhout, Brepols.

Tatton-Brown, T. and Macpherson-Grant, N. 1983. Medieval kilns in the Tyler Hill area. In: T. Tatton Brown, P. Bennett, J. Bowen and N. Macpherson-Grant, Recent fieldwork around Canterbury. *Archaeologia Cantiana*, 99, 127–131.

Tatton-Brown T. 1987. St Nicholas Church New Romney. *Archaeologia Cantiana*, 104, 344–346.

Tatton-Brown T. 1989. Church Building on Romney Marsh in the later Middle Ages. *Archaeologia Cantiana*, 107, 253–265.

Tatton-Brown, T. 1988. The topography of the Walland Marsh area between the eleventh and the thirteenth centuries. In: J. Eddison and C. Green, (eds.), *Romney Marsh : Evolution, Occupation, Reclamation.* OUCA Monograph 24. Oxford University Committee for Archaeology. Oxford 105-111.

Teichman-Derville, M. 1936 Bronze Fifteenth Century Crucifix from New Romney. *Archaeologia Cantiana* 48, 248–249.

Teichman-Derville M. 1929. The annals of the town and port of New Romney. *Archaeologia Cantiana* 41,153–174.

Thomason, D. and Stafford E. 2001 Land to the Rear of Old School House, Church Lane, New Romney, Kent. Oxford Archaeological Unit, unpublished document number F7234.

Thomson, J. 1983. *The Transformation of Medieval England, 1370–1579.* Longman. London and New York.

Toulmin Smith, L. ed. 1964. *The itinerary of John Leland in or about the years 1535–1543.* Centaur Press. London.

Tyers, I. and Hall, C. 1997. Dendrochronological Spot Date Report 302, Unpublished report for ARCUS, Sheffield University.

Tyler, A. 2004. Ships of the Marsh. *The Romney Marsh Irregular* 24, [newsletter of Romney Marsh Research Trust], 8–13.

Tyler, A. 2007. Romney Marsh and the Western River Valleys: An Archaeological Gazetteer. http://www.arac50.dsl.pipex.com/gazetteer.pdf [accessed 12 March 2009].

Tys, D., 2006. Walraversijde, another kettle of fish ? Dynamics and identity of a late medieval coastal settlement in a proto-capitalistic landscape. In: M. Pieters, F. Verhaege and G. Gevaert, *Fishing, Trade and Piracy. Fishermen and Fishermen's Settlements in and around the North Sea Area in the Middle Ages and Later*, Archeologie in Vlaanderen 6, Brussels, 19–40.

Ulbricht, I., 1984. *Die Verarbeitung von Knochen, Geweih und Horn im mittelalterlichen Schleswig*, Ausgrabungen in Schleswig. Berichte und Studien 3, Neumünster.

Urban, S. 1834 Ancient vessel found at Romney. *Gentlemen's Magazine* 104 (1), 94–95.

Van Neer, W. and Ervynck, A., 1993. *Archeologie en Vis*, Herlevend Verleden 1, Zellik.

Van Neer, W. and Ervynck, A. 2006. The Zooarchaeological Reconstruction of the Development of the Exploitation of the Sea: a *status quaestionis* for Flanders. In: M. Pieters, F. Verhaege and G. Gevaert, *Fishing, Trade and Piracy. Fishermen and Fishermen's Settlements in and around the North Sea Area in the Middle Ages and Later.* Archeologie in Vlaanderen 6, Brussels, 95–104.

Vidler, L. 1932. Floor tiles and kilns near the site of St. Bartholomew's Hospital, Rye. *Sussex Archaeological Collections* 73, 83–102.

Vidler, L. 1933. Medieval pottery and kilns found at Rye Sussex Archaeological Collections, 74, 45-64.

Vidler, L. 1936. Medieval pottery, tiles and kilns found at Rye. Final Report. Sussex Archaeological Collections, 77, 106-18.

Vince, A. 1985. Kingston-type ware. *Popular Archaeology*, 6:12, 34–39.

Vince, A. G. and Jenner, A. 1991. The Saxon and early medieval pottery of London. In: A.Vince (ed.), Aspects of Saxo-Norman London: Finds and Environmental work.

Vollans, E. 1988. New Romney and the 'River of Newenden' in the later Middle Ages'. In: J. Eddison and C. Green, (eds.), *Romney Marsh: Evolution, Occupation, Reclamation.* OUCA Monograph 24, 128–141. Oxford University Committee for Archaeology, Oxford.

Walton Rogers, P. 1997. *Textile Production at 16-22 Coppergate.* The Archaeology of York. The Small Finds 17/11, York.

Walton Rogers, P. 2002. Textile Production. In: P. Ottaway and N.S.H. Rogers, *Craft, Industry and Everyday Life: Finds from Medieval York.* The Archaeology of York. The Small Finds 17/15, York, 2732–45.

Ward, G. 1933. The lists of Saxon churches in the Domesday Monachorum and white book of St. Augustine. *Archaeologia Cantiana* 45, 60–89. in de Nederlanden. *Nijmeegse Kunsthistorische Studie 6.* Katholiek Universiteit Nijmegen, Nijmegen

Ward, G. 1952 The Saxon History of the Town and Port of Romney. *Archaeologia Cantiana* 65, 12–25.

Webb, D. 2004. Pilgrimage. In: Eds. T. Lawson and D. Killingray, An *Historical Atlas of Kent,* 46–47. Phillimore. Chichester.

Webster, B. 1984. The Community of Kent in the Reign of Richard II. In *Archaeologia Cantiana* 100, 217–30.

Wessex Archaeology 2000: Proposed Sainsbury's Community Store Site, Derville Site, Southlfands School, New Romney Kent. Unpublished archaeological evaluation report ref: 47707.1.

Wheeler, A. 1977. Fish bone. In: H. Clarke and A. Carter Excavations in King's Lynn 1963 – 1970 Society for Medieval Archaeology Monograph Series No. 7. 403–408.

Whitehouse, D. 1978. Polychrome ware and Italy. Medieval *Ceramics* 2, 51–52.

Willemsen, A 1998. Kinder Delijt: Middeleeuws Speelgoed

Willson J. and Linklater A. 2002. An Archaeological Watching Brief on a Plot of Land at Church Road, New Romney , Kent, Canterbury Archaeological Trust, Unpublished report number 1642.

Willson, J and Linklater, A. 2003. Church Road, New Romney. In: *Canterbury's Archaeology 2001–2002, Annual Report* 41–43. Canterbury Archaeological Trust. Canterbury.

Willson, J. 2003. Fairfield Road, New Romney. In: *Canterbury's Archaeology 2000–2001, Annual Report* 38–40. Canterbury Archaeological Trust. Canterbury.

Wragg E. 2002. An Archaeological evaluation at Southlands School, New Romney, Kent, Pre-Construct Archaeology Unpublished Report.

Zell, M. (ed.), 2000. *Early Modern Kent 1540–1640.* Kent County Council and the Boydell Press. Woodbridge.

Primary sources, printed:

Cal. Feet of Fines [H. III]: Churchill, I., Griffin, R. and Hardman, F., with introduction by Jessup, F. 1956. *Calendar of Kent Feet of Fines to the end of Henry III's Reign,* Ashford: Kent Archaeological Society Records Branch [Kent Records XV].*Cal. Chancery Warrants:* Public Record Office, *Calendar of chancery warrants preserved in the Public Record Office; 1244– 1326.* London: HMSO, 1927.

CClR: *Calendar of the Close Rolls ... : Henry III, 1242–1247,* vol. V,. London : H.M.S.O., 1916.

CPR: *Calendar of the Patent Rolls ... : Henry III, 1232–1247,* vol. III,. London : H.M.S.O., 1906.

DB: Kent: Morgan, P., ed., 1983, from a draft translation prepared by V. Sankaran, *Domesday Book: Kent,* Chichester: Phillimore.

HMC V: Riley, H. 1876, Manuscripts of the Corporation of New Romney, Second Notice. *Historic Manuscripts Commission, 5th report, part 1,* 533–554.

Lay Subsidy: Hanley, H. and Chalklin, C. 1964. 'The Kent Lay Subsidy Roll of 1334/5', in Du Boulay, F., ed. 1964. *Documents Illustrative of Medieval Kentish Society* [Kent Records 18], Ashford: Kent Archaeological Society Records Publication Committee.

Sede Vacante institutions: Calendar of institutions by the chapter of Canterbury sede vacante, edited by C. Eveleigh Woodruff [Kent Records 8], Canterbury: Gibbs and Sons, 1924.

Pecham's Survey: Witney, K., ed., 2000. *The Survey of Archbishop Pecham's manors, 1283–85,* Maidstone: Kent Archaeological Society.

Reg. Chich.: Jacob, E. 1943. *The Register of Archbishop Chichele Archbishop of Canterbury 1414–1443,* 4 vols, Clarendon Press, Oxford.

Rough's Register: Murray K. (ed.) 1945. *The Register of Daniel Rough,* Kent Archaeological Society, Records Branch [Kent Records 16].

Custumals of Battle Abbey: Scargill-Bird, S. (ed.) 1887. *Custumals of Battle Abbey in the Reigns of Edward I and Edward II (1283–1312)* Camden society new series, 41.

Fourth Report of the Historical Manuscripts Commission, part 1 (1874).

Index

Page numbers in *italics* denote illustrations. Street names, buildings and locations are in New Romney.